Density projects

projects

36 nuevos conceptos de vivienda colectiva **36 new concepts on collective housing**

AURORA FERNÁNDEZ PER

JAVIER ARPA

Título **Title**
Density projects

Subtítulo **Subtitle**
36 nuevos conceptos de vivienda colectiva
36 new concepts on collective housing

a+t Density series

Autores **Authors**
Aurora Fernández Per
Javier Arpa

Asesor editorial **Editorial Advisor**
Javier Mozas

Maquetación y producción **Layout and production**
Ricardo Unquera
Delia Argote

Coordinación **Coordination**
Idoia Esteban

Publicado por **Edited by**
a+t ediciones

ISBN 978-84-612-1335-1

Impresion **Printing**
Gráficas Santamaría
VI-581/07
Vitoria-Gasteiz, 2007

a+t ediciones. General Álava 15, 2º A. E-01005.
Vitoria-Gasteiz. Spain
www.aplust.net

Agradecimientos **Acknowledgments**
a+t ediciones agradece a todos los autores y
colaboradores de las obras que se incluyen en esta
publicación, su esfuerzo en la comprobación de datos y
en la recopilación de la información.
a+t ediciones thanks the authors of the works featured
in this publication as well as their collaborators
including for their efforts in collecting information and
verifying data.

ÍNDICE DE ARQUITECTOS **ARCHITECTS INDEX** 11

SOBRE LA DENSIDAD Y OTRAS PREOCUPACIONES 12

ON DENSITY AND OTHER CONCERNS.. 28

MANUAL DE USO **USER'S MANUAL** 42

ANÁLISIS TEMÁTICO **THEMATIC ANALYSIS** 44

PROYECTOS **PROJECTS** 70

CRÉDITOS **CREDITS** 394

Density projects contiene 36 ideas sobre vivienda colectiva que apuestan por el aumento de la densidad.

Son proyectos que proponen un ahorro en la ocupación del territorio y, como consecuencia, un entorno más sostenible.

La estrategia de diseño de los autores, la implantación en el contexto y el desarrollo de las tipologías de vivienda son analizadas y comparadas por temas, siguiendo el camino iniciado por la serie de *a+t* dedicada a la *Densidad*.

Los proyectos –en fase de desarrollo o de ejecución a lo largo de 2007– se caracterizan por favorecer la densificación a través de la buena arquitectura. Muchos de ellos incluyen en su programa otros usos distintos del residencial, que contribuyen a dotar, no sólo de densidad, sino también de intensidad, el entorno en que se sitúan.

Creemos que la mezcla de distintas funciones dentro de un mismo proyecto es la clave para la regeneración de la ciudad consolidada y para la creación de nuevos núcleos urbanos y que la vivienda colectiva, situada en ese contexto variado de usos y generando un entorno construido denso, es la única solución frente al consumo de recursos.

LOS AUTORES

Density projects contains 36 ideas on collective housing that are committed to increasing density.

They are projects that propose savings in land use and, consequently, a more sustainable environment.

The design strategy of the authors, the implementation in the context and the development of the housing typologies are analysed and compared by themes, following the path begun by the *a+t* series dedicated to *Density*.

The projects, in phase of development or execution throughout 2007, are characterised for favouring densification through good architecture. Many of them include other uses besides residential uses in their programmes. This contributes not only density, but also intensity to their respective environments.

We believe that the combination of different functions inside the same project is the key to the regeneration of the consolidated city and for the creation of new urban nuclei and that collective housing in this context of mixed-use, generating a dense built environment, is the only solution to the consumption of resources.

THE AUTHORS

ÍNDICE DE ARQUITECTOS **ARCHITECTS INDEX**

Número de proyecto
Project number

Página **Page**

3XN Architects 28 306-317

3XN Architects/UN Studio 31 344-353

AOC 03 84-89

Atelier Thomas Pucher & Bramberger 22 272-277

BIG .... 07 116-127 .... 17 210-219 ...... 29 318-335

Brenac & Gonzalez 24 284-289

Cino Zucchi Architetti .... 09 138-143 ..... 23 278-283

ECDM Architectes 12 168-173

Eric Lapierre Architecture 08 128-137

Estudio FAM 16 206-209

Flexo Arquitectura 27 302-305

FÜNDC 05 100-107

Jean Nouvel 35 378-385

Kohn Pedersen Fox 25 290-293

MAB Arquitectura 02 76-83

MBM Arquitectes/MAB Arquitectura 04 90-99

MGM Morales, Giles 21 264-271

NO.MAD, Eduardo Arroyo 33 360-371

Oppenheim Architecture+Design 26 294-301

Peter L. Gluck and Partners 20 252-263

PLOT=BIG+JDS 15 196-205

Rex Architecture 19 238-251

Riches Hawley Mikhail Architects .... 01 72-75 ..... 06 108-115

Rojkind Arquitectos 34 372-377

Selgascano 11 152-167

Steven Holl Architects 18 220-237

Studio Gang Architects .... 30 336-343 ...... 32 354-359

Tatiana Bilbao/mx.a 13 174-183

VMX Architects 14 184-195

Witherford Watson Mann Architects 10 144-151

X-TU Architects 36 386-393

Sobre la densidad

On density

y otras preocupaciones

Datos, opiniones, quejas y deseos sobre la ocupación del territorio 14

and other concerns

Data, views, complaints and desires on land occupation 28

recogidos por collected by
AURORA FERNÁNDEZ PER

Monique Ruzicka-Rossier. 2007

La cuestión no es lo densos que deberían ser nuestros barrios, sino lo diversos que tendrían que ser.

Ecole Polytechnique Fédérale de Lausanne. www.geos.ed.ac.uk/geography/DensityInsideOut.html

El estado de la población mundial. 2007
Formulemos algunas preguntas definitorias. Si la población mundial estuviera más dispersa, ¿ocuparía más o menos superficie de tierras valiosas? La dispersión, ¿liberaría tierras agrícolas de primera calidad? ¿ayudaría a evitar la invasión de ecosistemas frágiles?". En la mayoría de los países las respuestas serían "¡no!". La mayor densidad es potencialmente útil. Dado que la población mundial es en 2007 de 6.700 millones de personas, y que va aumentando a razón de más de 75 millones por año, la concentración demográfica da lugar a una mayor sostenibilidad. En última instancia, la protección de los ecosistemas rurales requiere que la población esté concentrada en actividades distintas del sector primario y en zonas densamente pobladas.

Informe de Fondo de Población de Naciones Unidas. Capítulo IV: Crecimiento urbano y uso sostenible del espacio
www.unfpa.org/swp/2007/

Rectificar es de sabios. Cuando engañe a un primo forofo de las escaleras nos volvemos a Madrid y dejamos de gastarnos los dos sueldos en gasolina y coches (van 3 en 9 años) y en el mantenimiento de un "adobadito" enorme del que nos sobra la mitad. Aah, y no nos olvidemos del magnífico *glamour* de los centros comerciales un sábado por la tarde. Eso sí, cuando lo compré parecia bonito y tenía 24 años.

(el suburbial)
www.idealista.com/pagina/boletin.comentarios

Edward Soja. 2002

Ustedes [los arquitectos] tienden generalmente a decir que la ciudad consiste en calles, carreteras y un entorno edificado ubicado en una "nebulosa urbana" un tanto indefinida. Según esta tesis, la ciudad sería un conjunto de células independientes, con entornos edificados agregados hasta dar lugar a la masa urbana. Esta visión es radicalmente diferente de otra con un enfoque a escala regional, para la que la ciudad es un sistema urbano de flujos y movimiento, de generación de bienestar donde la gente no habita entornos edificados sino geografías construidas que se caracterizan por tener diferentes ingresos, tasa de desempleo, nivel educativo, composición racial, identidad cultural, tipos de vivienda y mercado laboral. Dichos aspectos se obvian a menudo por la obsesión –perdón por mi vehemente preocupación– de los arquitectos por el diseño. Estas geografías construidas desaparecen cuando la ciudad es reducida por completo a una colección de formas edificadas.

Transurbanism. Edward Soja in conversation with Arjen Mulder: Restructuring the industrial Capitalist City. Nai Publishers. Rotterdam, 2002, p. 90.

Madrid es una ciudad estupenda para tener ocio y disfrute de ella, pero para vivir nos tenemos que ir fuera porque no podemos pagar los precios.

(agregena)
www.idealista.com/pagina/
boletin.comentarios

The Washington Post. 14 de octubre, 2007

Los estudios sobre ciudades de todo el mundo –Pekín, Roma, Londres, Tokio, Los Ángeles...– demuestran que las concentraciones de hormigón, asfalto, acero y vidrio, pueden desencadenar el fenómeno de "islas de calor" con mucha más virulencia que los parajes suburbanos de baja densidad poblados de árboles. Tal y como destacaba un artículo de *New Scientist*, "la temperatura en las ciudades puede ser unos 2° C mayor durante el día y hasta 6° C mayor durante la noche".

Wally Siembab define como "dispersión inteligente" a un tipo de desarrollo urbano que debe cumplir los siguientes requisitos: reducción del consumo de combustible mediante la utilización de automóviles más eficientes, dispersión suburbana de los centros de trabajo y la promoción del trabajo desde casa.

Desde el año 2000 más del 90% del crecimiento metropolitano ha tenido lugar en los suburbios. Forzar a los estadounidenses a vivir en un entorno denso, que sólo le resulta atractivo a una pequeña minoría, no es la mejor manera de enfrentarse a la escasez de los recursos energéticos y al calentamiento global. Por el contrario, debemos tomar medidas graduales, sensatas y realistas encaminadas a mejorar la dispersión suburbana donde la mayoría de nosotros ha elegido vivir y trabajar.

Joel kotkin, Ali Modarres: *Hot world? Blame cities.*
www.washingtonpost.com

Le Corbusier. 1946

La ciudad jardín es como un fuego fatuo. La naturaleza se difumina bajo la irrupción de infraestructuras y edificación, y el aislamiento que nos prometían deja paso a un lugar abarrotado. Me refiero a la "ciudad jardín horizontal" de viviendas unifamiliares. Por el contrario, la solución se halla en la "ciudad jardín vertical", fruto de la tecnología moderna adaptada a los nuevos modos de vida.

Concerning town planning. Translated by Clive Entwistle from the French *Propos D'Urbanisme.* Yale University Press, New Haven, 1948 p 68.

Yo lo que quiero es vivir en un lugar tranquilo y seguro; quiero disfrutar de la vida en una buena casa (de 400 m² en adelante no estaría mal), de 2 plantas por lo menos (aunque 3 o 4 estaría todavía mejor) y un sótano. Con 4000 m² de parcela, aunque me puedo conformar con algo menos si la casa está muy bien. Necesito un montón de espacio para mis cosas y para mi familia y los amigos que vendrán a verme. ¡No hay quién invite a nadie en un piso de un dormitorio!

(wpb, fl. Dreaming of oil city, pa) www.citydata.com/forum/general-u-s

Vuestros exurbios no sólo han destruido el campo, sino que también han destruido nuestros suburbios, convirtiéndolos en una pesadilla permanentemente llena de automovilistas.

(hkv)
http://app.businessweek.com/usercomments/get_reviews

Liberation. 16 de octubre, 2007
La Comisión para la consecución del crecimiento en Francia (CLCF), presidida por Jacques Attali, se propone como objetivo la construcción de 500.000 nuevas viviendas cada año hasta 2010, principalmente densificando el tejido urbano existente.

www.liberation.fr

Los exurbios encarnan una vida de derroche, excesos y voracidad.

(cesc)
(concerned-envirofriendly american)
http://app.businessweek.com/usercomments/get_reviews

No es que a la gente no le guste vivir en las ciudades; lo que no le gusta son los problemas que la ciudad acarrea: inseguridad y peor educación. Creo que si a la gente no le gustase las grandes ciudades, se marcharía a vivir a poblaciones de medio o pequeño tamaño; y no lo hace: prefiere quedarse en el extrarradio, no por cómo es (infraestructuras, centros comerciales, casas grandes), sino porque el mejor nivel de la educación, la seguridad y los precios más bajos, lo hacen más atractivo.

(minnehahapolitan)
www.city-data.com/forum/general-u-s

Richard Simmons, CABE. 2007

Los nuevos desarrollos urbanos consisten en un sistema viario supervisado por ingenieros, donde las viviendas se encajan entre el asfalto. Un urbanismo tan aleatorio como ése tiene además otra consecuencia: incentiva el uso del automóvil y contribuye por ende a un aumento del tráfico y la contaminación. Cabe destacar cómo, en los últimos tiempos, al hablar con promotores sobre desarrollos urbanos densos, que requieren un complejo sistema de gestión, surgen cuestiones como el empleo de materiales más duraderos o la necesidad de economizar la cantidad de viario que se construye y que alguien tendrá que mantener. Y cabe destacar cómo estos promotores se muestran cada vez más preocupados por el tipo de vida que implica un urbanismo u otro. De modo que algo está cambiando.

Commission for Architecture and the Built Environment (CABE), www.guardian.co.uk/society

Meta Berghauser Pont y Per Haupt. 2007

A menudo, el enfoque que se da a la densidad carece de precisión espacial y no describe correctamente la forma urbana. Sólo cuando la densidad es entendida en tanto que combinación de factores como intensidad, compacidad, altura y espacialidad podemos emplearla correctamente para diferenciar tejidos urbanos, comprender sus características y establecer orientaciones para el planeamiento futuro. Preferimos definir la densidad como un fenómeno dependiente de múltiples variables. Para ello, empleamos unas variables que denominamos "fsi", "gsi", "n", "osr" y "l", que significan, respectivamente, intensidad de la edificación, ocupación, densidad de infraestructuras, presión sobre el espacio libre (o espacialidad) y altura media de la edificación en una zona. Estas variables se interrelacionan y pueden presentarse en un solo diagrama, el *spacemate*.

TU Delft School of Design. www.geos.ed.ac.uk/geography/DensityInsideOut.html

The Guardian. 31 de julio, 2007

La vida en adosados es responsable de que Gran Bretaña tenga el mayor índice de robos en viviendas de Europa. Por su parte, la vivienda en altura permite mejoras en la seguridad gracias a los ascensores privados y la presencia de porteros. Los lados negativos de este modo de vida, como no poder tener un perro o un gato, son positivos para el medio ambiente. Los residentes no tendrían por qué depender del automóvil, ya que las líneas de autobús y el carril-bici llegarían hasta las torres. La torre se podría levantar sobre un área inundable, sin necesidad de alterar la hidrología natural del terreno. Dentro, los usuarios dispondrían de un amplio abanico de servicios: gimnasio, salón de belleza, restaurante, cine, discoteca y asistencia a ancianos, minusválidos o madres solteras. Piénselo. Siéntese y dibuje un rascacielos hoy.

Germaine Creer: Forget the high-rise slums of the past.
Building upwards not outwards is the way ahead.
arts.guardian.co.uk

Jane Jacobs. 1961

Cuatro condiciones son indispensables para generar diversidad en las calles y barrios de una ciudad:

1. El barrio debe alojar más de una función primaria y preferiblemente más de dos. Con ello se garantiza la presencia de gente en las calles a horas diferentes y por motivos distintos, pero haciendo uso de las mismas instalaciones.
2. Las manzanas no deben ser muy largas, esto es, debe haber un gran número de calles trasversales y posibilidades de girar en otra dirección.
3. El barrio debe tener edificios de época y condición distintas, incluyendo en este sentido a una buena proporción de edificios antiguos, de manera que el rendimiento económico de cada uno sea variable.
4. Ha de darse una densidad de población suficientemente alta para cualquier actividad que se quiera realizar, lo que implica una alta densidad de residentes en el área.

La necesidad de estas cuatro condiciones es el mensaje principal que este libro quiere trasmitir.

The Death and life of Great American Cities. Modern Library Edition. New York, 1993. pp 196-197.

Julie Campoli and Alex S. MacLean. 2007

La dispersión es mala. La densidad es buena. Los estadounidenses deben detener la dispersión urbana y vivir más cerca unos de otros. En fín..., eso es la teoría. Sin embargo, tal como cualquiera que intente desarrollar formas urbanas más compactas puede confirmar, si hay algo que los estadounidenses detestan más que la dispersión, es precisamente la densidad. Esto se hace evidente durante la elaboración de los planes urbanísticos públicos. En todo el país, cualquier esfuerzo por aumentar la densidad se topa con una fuerte oposición. Uno de los motivos por los que la opinión pública se resiste a la alta densidad es que no sabe bien qué aspecto tiene, cómo se materializa, o si se puede vivir en ella. Disponemos de métodos razonados para calcular la densidad, pero nuestra percepción es todo menos racional.

Visualizing Density. www.lincolninst.edu/subcenters/VD/

¿Que no hacen ejercicio los de los adosados? ¡Pero si se pasa uno el día subiendo y bajando escaleras! El próximo, en una sola planta.

(harta de las escaleritas)
www.idealista.com/pagina
/boletin.comentarios

Yo lo que hice fue irme de París a provincias y no me arrepiento en absoluto. Ahora tengo cerca el centro de la ciudad y además es más seguro. Antes vivía en un ruinoso bloque de protección oficial (con mi familia) y ahora estoy muy contenta de no tener a locos gritando debajo de mi ventana. Esto está limpio y no me aburro para nada.

(vilain bisounours)
http://qc.answers.yahoo.com/question/

Alain Dinin, Nexity. 2007

Hay que plantearse la cuestión de la densificación urbana, por mucho que se aproximen las elecciones municipales. Los franceses comprenderán que es más sencillo y económico añadir un piso más que construir un edificio nuevo al lado. La diversidad de la sociedad francesa pasa por la diversidad urbana. Hay que acabar con la disociación entre público y privado para abrir la construcción de vivienda social a la intervención de los promotores privados, exigiéndoles compromisos precisos en cuanto a precios. Debemos acabar con la segregación espacial que separa la vivienda pública de la privada. Es necesario mezclar viviendas para familias con ingresos diferentes.

www.liberation.fr

Periodista Digital. 9 de octubre, 2007

El 91,5% de los edificios que comenzaron a construirse en la Comunidad entre 1994 y 2005 no superaron las tres alturas, según un estudio elaborado por la Comunidad de Madrid, basado en datos del Ministerio de Fomento, que refleja que el urbanismo madrileño de la última década ha estado basado en inmuebles de baja altura.

blogs.periodistadigital.com

Michael Manville. 2006

Debemos preguntarnos cuál es el objetivo de la revitalización de los centros consolidados. Revitalizar el centro no tiene por qué implicar la revitalización de toda la ciudad, ni tratarse de una medida progresista. Un centro renovado puede contribuir al progreso de la ciudad, pero también podría tener el efecto contrario. Si bien los centros revitalizados podrían beneficiar más a pobres que a ricos, parece, por el contrario, que estas políticas lo que pretenden es atraer a los más favorecidos a edificios comerciales abandonados y a nuevas promociones residenciales. La validez de semejantes estrategias queda pues, en entredicho, especialmente en aquellos lugares donde no hay crecimiento o disponen de mercados inmobiliarios reducidos.

Downtown revitalization: What, How and Why. planningresearch.blogspot.com

Los únicos, aquí, que ahora no están interesados en que vivamos en casas, son los ayuntamientos, que se han dado cuenta de que les costamos menos dinero apilados en bloques de pisos.

(cesc)
www.idealista.com/pagina/
boletin.comentarios

II Informe Vivienda en España 2006,
Casi un 70% del total de los encuestados se decantan por vivir en los grandes núcleos urbanos, aunque sacrifiquen metros cuadrados y se vean obligados a convivir en espacios más pequeños.
Más del 90% reside en pisos en altura, frente a un 10% que lo hace en un chalet o vivienda horizontal. Por eso, España se considera un país vertical.

Elaborado por Demoscopia. www.elmundo.es

No tengo el mínimo interés en tener una casa y prefiero mil veces vivir en un piso minúsculo en el centro, que en una casa enorme en las afueras (y no porque no me la pueda permitir). Prefiero vivir en el centro por su actividad, poder caminar a la tienda de al lado, ver vida en la calle y relacionarme con los demás, poder ir a todas partes sin necesidad de coger el coche, ir a pie o en transporte público a ver a mis amigos, o asistir a eventos culturales.

(in exile, plotting my coup)
www.citydata.com/forum/
general-u-s

Victor Gruen. 1954

El tan manido conflicto entre centro y periferia es una falacia. Ambos son partes complementarias de un todo.

Dynamic Planning for Retail Areas, Harvard Business Review, Nov.-Dec. 1954, pp 53-54.

Los Angeles Times. 11 de agosto, 2007

Para afrontar las cuestiones derivadas de la densificación que implica la vivienda colectiva (aumento de la matriculación en las escuelas, sobrecarga de los sistemas de abastecimiento de agua y energía, alcantarillado y el aumento del tráfico), se pueden aplicar soluciones sencillas y muy en boga: el urbanismo verde se basa en densidades apropiadas para hacer rentable el transporte público, sistemas descentralizados de alcantarillado que reciclan el agua para volverla a hacer potable, la reducción radical del consumo de agua, la transformación de algunas calles en auténticas granjas comunitarias y la penalización del tráfico entre otras medidas.

Sharon Bernstein: *Our changing neighborhoods.* www.latimes.com

Paul Jenkins. 2007

En el África subsahariana está apareciendo un tipo de asentamiento que no es ni urbano ni rural. Este fenómeno, que está planteando retos desconocidos para el desarrollo urbano, es consecuencia del declive de las áreas rurales y de la saturación de las áreas urbanas con una población muy pobre. Los nuevos pobladores optan por el método más adecuado para la supervivencia, que consiste en establecer pueblos lineales, a caballo entre lo urbano y lo rural, según complejos patrones migratorios multidireccionales que ponen en entredicho los conceptos geográficos, demográficos y socioeconómicos tradicionales de lo urbano.

School of the Built Environment, Heriot-watt university and Edinburgh College of Art. www.geos.ed.ac.uk/geography/DensityInsideOut.html

Respecto a la cuestión medioambiental, el centro es peor que los suburbios en cuanto que hay más contaminación procedente de los automóviles. Pero se concentra más gente y por tanto hay más oportunidades.

(mike t)
http://answers.yahoo.com/question/index

Los hombres son como las manzanas: cuanto más los acercamos, más rápido se pudren.

Dr. Bernard Auriol
www.lespetites-toulousaines.com

Hennie Reynders. 2007

Los asentamientos espontáneos en los límites de las ciudades surafricanas, surgidos después del *apartheid,* se han convertido en las salas de espera de la tierra prometida. En la mayoría de los casos, estas poblaciones han sido legalizadas y contrastan con otras entidades irregulares que se confunden en la trama urbana, como inmigrantes ilegales, redes criminales y barrios cerrados, amparados por el mal funcionamiento pasado y presente de la burocracia.

School of the Art Institute of Chicago and University of Edinburgh. www.geos.ed.ac.uk/geography/DensityInsideOut.html

The Guardian. 5 de septiembre, 2007

Los más ricos están abandonando las periferias hacia pueblos y aldeas más lejanas y dependientes del automóvil.

Peter Hetherington: *No joke - suburbia is ripe for renaissance.*
www.guardian.co.uk/society

Richard Burdett, Miguel Kanai. 2006

Las ciudades del siglo XXI deberían asumir un papel como centros de tolerancia y justicia en vez de ser lugares de conflicto y exclusión. Además, deberían reducir su impacto medioambiental, adoptando un crecimiento compacto, en vez de permitir el derroche de la dispersión.

City-building in an age of global urban transformation. Cities. Architecture and Society. 10 Mostra Internazionale di Architettura. Venecia, 2006

Gunawan Tjahjono. 2007

La promociones residenciales de alta densidad, con más de 3.000 habitantes por hectárea, es en la actualidad el objetivo principal de los promotores en Yakarta, empujados por el aumento vertiginoso de los precios del suelo en las zonas estratégicas. Dado que la legislación local obliga a que cualquier promoción inmobiliaria incorpore equipamientos públicos (incluyendo escuelas), los arquitectos introducen el programa escolar en alturas impensables, en el sexto o decimotercer piso, por ejemplo, para evitar la presencia de una escuela en la parcela.

Department of Architecture. Faculty of engineering. Universitas Indonesia
www.geos.ed.ac.uk/geography/DensityInsideOut.html

¿Y qué son unos adosados, mas que una torre tumbada que ocupa más espacio, gasta más agua, combustible, asfalto y deja menos espacio libre común para relaciones?

(trujillo)
www.idealista.com/pagina/boletin.comentarios

Cuando todo el mundo
quiere un pedacito de
vida en el campo, esa
vida deja de existir.

(drl)
app.businessweek.com/
usercomments/get_reviews

Serge Chermayeff, Christopher Alexander. 1963

Puede que no esté lejos el día en que planificadores,
diseñadores, promotores del desarrollo y otros profesionales,
reconozcan el simple hecho de que el espacio entre los
edificios es tan importante para la vida del hombre urbano
como los edificios mismos, y actúen en consecuencia.
Si la totalidad del uso del terreno se planeara
escrupulosamente para obtener una utilización óptima a
cualquier nivel, la ciudad interior podría alojar tanto edificios
verticales de múltiples funciones y ocupación a corto plazo,
como viviendas en planta baja para familias con niños.
Funcionando como partes activas del contexto tecnológico
urbano, estas viviendas en planta baja podrían tener éxito allí
donde los suburbios fracasaron.

Comunidad y Privacidad. Ediciones Nueva Visión, Buenos Aires, 1984. p. 68

Monique Ruzicka-Rossier. 2007

The appropriate question is not how dense city districts should be, but how diverse it should be?

Ecole Polytechnique Fédérale de Lausanne. www.geos.ed.ac.uk/geography/DensityInsideOut.html

State of world population. 2007

Asked the defining questions–'If the world's population were more dispersed, would it take up more valuable land or less? Would dispersion release prime agricultural land? Would it help avoid the invasion of fragile ecosystems?'–the answer, in most countries, would be 'No!' Density is potentially useful. With world population at 6.7 billion people in 2007 and growing at over 75 million a year, demographic concentration gives sustainability a better chance. The protection of rural ecosystems ultimately requires that population be concentrated in non-primary sector activities and densely populated areas.

United Nations Population Fund Report. Chapter IV: Urban Growth and Sustainable Use of Space
www.unfpa.org/swp/2007/

Correcting oneself is wise. When I finally trick some great fan of stairs, we're moving back to Madrid and will stop spending our two salaries on petrol and cars (3 in 9 years) and on the maintenance of a huge terrace house that we only need half of. Ah, and don't forget the magnificent glamour of shopping malls on a Saturday afternoon. It is true, though, that when I bought it, it looked nice and I was 24 years old.

(el suburbial)
www.idealista.com/pagina/
boletin.comentarios

Edward Soja. 2002

You [architects] describe in many ways the core architectural view when you say that a city consists of streets, roads and a built environment located within a vaguely defines "urban cloud". In this vision, the city becomes a collection of separates cells with built environments compacted together to form an urban mass. This view is radically different from the larger-scale spatial or regional vision of the city as an expansive urban system of movements and flows, of good being produced and people living not just in built environments but in constructed geographies characterized by different patterns of income, unemplyoyment, education levels, ethnic and racial cultures, housing and job densities, etc. All these things are often push aside in the obsession –sorry the passionate concern– architects have for desing. These constructed geographies get lost when the city is reduced enterely to a collection of built forms.

Transurbanism. Edward Soja in conversation with Arjen Mulder:
Restructuring the industrial Capitalist City. Nai Publishers. Rotterdam, 2002, p. 90.

Madrid is a great city to have free time to enjoy, but to live, we have to leave the city because we can't pay the prices.

(agregena)
www.idealista.com/pagina/
boletin.comentarios

The Washington Post. 14 October, 2007
Studies in cities around the world –Beijing, Rome, London, Tokyo, Los Angeles and more– have found that packed concentrations of concrete, asphalt, steel and glass can contribute to a phenomenon known as 'heat islands' far more than typically low-density, tree-shaded suburban landscapes. As an October 2006 article in the *New Scientist* highlighted, 'cities can be a couple of degrees warmer during the day and up to 6°C (11°F) warmer at night'.

Wally Siembab, has dubbed 'smart sprawl'. Encouraging this sort of development will require a series of steps: reducing commuters' gas consumption with more fuel-efficient cars, dispersing work to centers close to where workers live and promoting continued growth in homebased work.

And since 2000, more than 90 per cent of all metropolitan growth –even in a legendary new planners' paradise such as Portland, Ore.– has taken place in the suburbs. Dragooning americans into a dense urban lifestyle that's attractive to only a relatively small minority isn't the best way to address concerns about energy and resource depletion or global warming. Instead, we need to take gradual, sensible, realistic steps to improve the increasingly dispersed places where most of us choose to live and work.

Joel kotkin, Ali Modarres: *Hot world? Blame cities.*
www.washingtonpost.com

> I want a quiet, laid back place with low or no crime, I want to enjoy living in a nice big house (4000+square feet would be nice) with at least 2 stories (3 or even 4 is better) and basement. I prefer at least an acre but will settle for less if the house is amazing. I need lots of space for my collections and stuff as well as for family and friends that will come to visit. You cant invite anyone in a 1 bedroom condo!
>
> (wpb, fl. Dreaming of oil city, pa) www.citydata.com/forum/general-u-s

> Not only has your exurbia destroyed the countryside, but you have destroyed our suburbs as well, turning them into a nightmare full of commuters who never go away.
>
> (hkv)
> http://app.businessweek.com/usercomments/get_reviews

> Exurbia is a life of misuse, overuse and gluttony.
>
> (cesc)
> (concerned-envirofriendly american)
> http://app.businessweek.com/usercomments/get_reviews

Le Corbusier. 1946

The garden city is a will-o'-the-wisp. Nature melts under the invasion of roads and houses and the promised seclusion becomes a crowed settlement. I spoke above the 'horizontal garden-city' (so-called family houses). But the solution will be found in the 'vertical garden-city' the fruit of modern techniques adapted to the conditions of modern life.

Concerning town planning. Translated by Clive Entwistle from the French *Propos D'Urbanisme.* Yale University Press, New Haven, 1948 p 68.

> **Liberation.** 16 October, 2007
> The Commission for achievement of economical growth in France (CLCF), chaired by Jacques Attali, plans the construction of 500,000 new housing units per year until 2010 by increasing the current density of the existing urban fabric.
>
> www.liberation.fr

The Star. 20 October, 2007
A growing number of commuter-based communities in the Toronto region are experimenting with free or discounted transit in the hope that residents just might like the bus if they try it.

Tess Kalinowski: *Suburbanites taken for a free (bus) ride*
http://www.thestar.com

The Washington Post. 11 August, 2007
The average family may be smaller than it was 10 years ago, but the average single-family house is larger –and more luxurious. It has more bathrooms, higher ceilings, more elaborate master bedrooms, and bigger kitchens and outdoor space.

Nancy Trejos. *For 2015, it's what's inside that counts.*
www.washingtonpost.com

Richard Simmons, CABE. 2007

New developments are determined by a road system overseen by highway engineers –with the houses having somehow to fit in between the tarmac. Such random planning, of course, has another side-effect: encouraging more car use, and hence congestion and pollution, 'it's interesting now that when you talk to developers building high density developments, which require a management company, they are thinking much harder about the use of robust materials, not wasting so much money on building large amounts of street that won't be needed, which someone has to maintain. And they're looking much harder at the lifestyle that will be lived in certain places. So there is a bit of a change happening'.

Commission for Architecture and the Built Environment (CABE), www.guardian.co.uk/society

Meta Berghauser Pont and Per Haupt. 2007

Many of the established uses of density lack spatial precision and are unsatisfactorily for describing and prescribing urban form. Only when density is seen as a composite of aspects, such as intensity, compactness, height, and spaciousness can it be satisfactorily used to differentiate between urban fabrics, understand their characteristics, and design guidelines for future developments. We choose to define density as a multi-variable phenomenon. The variables used are 'fsi', 'gsi', 'n', 'osr' and 'l'. These express respectively built intensity, land coverage, network density, pressure on the non-built ground (or spaciousness) and the average building height of an area. These variables are closely related to each other and can therefore be integrated into one diagram, the spacemate.

TU Delft School of Design. www.geos.ed.ac.uk/geography/DensityInsideOut.html

Jane Jacobs. 1961

To generate exhuberant diversity in a city's streets and districts, four conditions are indispensable:

1. The district, and indeed as many of its internal parts as possible, must serve more than one primary function; preferably more than two. These must insure the presence of people who go outdoors on different schedules and are in the place for different purposes, but who are able to use many facilities in common.
2. Most of the blocks must be short; that is, streets and opportunities to turn corners must be frequent.
3. The district must mingle buildings that vary in age and condition, including a good proportion of old ones so that they can vary in the economic yield they must produce. This mingling must be fairly closegrained.
4. There must be sufficiently dense concentration of people, for whatever purpose they may be there. This include dense concentration in the case of people who are there because of residence.

The necessity of these four condition in the most important point this book has to make.

The Death and life of Great American Cities. Modern Library Edition. New York, 1993. pp 196-197.

Julie Campoli and Alex S. MacLean. 2007

Sprawl is bad. Density is good. Americans need to stop spreading out and live closer together. Well… that's the theory, anyway. But, as anyone who has tried to build compact development recently will tell you, if there's one thing Americans hate more than sprawl, it's density. This is evident in the public planning process as regulations are written and projects are reviewed. Across the country, efforts to increase density have met with stiff resistance. One reason people reject density is that they don't know much about it-what it looks like, how to build it, or whether it's something they can call home. We have very rational ways of measuring density, but our perception of it is anything but rational.

Visualizing Density. www.lincolninst.edu/subcenters/VD/

What do you mean that people who live in houses don't exercise? You spend all day going up and down stairs! The next one will be on one floor.

(harta de las escaleritas)
www.idealista.com/pagina
/boletin.comentarios

Alain Dinin, Nexity. 2007

Increasing urban density is an issue that must faced, even if local elections approach. The French people will understand that it is easier and cheaper to add a storey on top than building a new construction aside.
The diversity of the French society is tied to urban mixture. We must end the dissociation between public and private developments and let private developers enter the social housing market, after demanding from them precise commitments on pricing policies. We must end the spatial segregation that divides public from private housing. It is necessary to reunite families with different income.

www.liberation.fr

Periodista Digital. 9 October, 2007
91.5% of the buildings that they started building in the autonomous community of Madrid between 1994 and 2005 were no higher than three storeys, according to a study carried out by the Community of Madrid, based on data from the Ministry of Public Works, which reveals that urban planning in Madrid over the last decade has been based on low-rise buildings.

blogs.periodistadigital.com

Michael Manville. 2006

We should ask what the goal of downtown revitalization is. Revitalizing the downtown is not necessarily the same as revitalizing the center city, nor is it necessarily progressive. A revitalized downtown might help revitalize a center city, but the causality could just as easily run the other way. And a revitalized downtown might help the poor more than the affluent, but the goal of many revitalization efforts seems to be luring affluent people into empty commercial buildings and/or new residential buildings. The equity effects of such a policy seem ambiguous, especially in regions that aren't growing and don't have tight housing markets.

Downtown revitalization: What, How and Why. planningresearch.blogspot.com

The only ones here who now have no interest in our living in detatched houses are the city halls, who have figured out that we cost them less money when we are piled up in blocks of flats.

(cesc)
www.idealista.com/pagina/
boletin.comentarios

II Spanish Housing Report 2006,
by Demoscopia
Almost 70% of those surveyed decided to live in large urban nucleuses, even though they give up square metres and have to live in smaller spaces. Over 90% live in high-rise buildings where as 10% live in a detached or horizontal home. For this reason, Spain is considered to be a vertical country.

www.elmundo.es

I have absolutely no desire to own a home and would much rather live in a tiny cramped apartment in the city than an expansive house in the suburbs (not that I could afford one). I prefer being in the center of the action, enjoy being able to walk to the store, seeing street life and having day-to-day human interaction, being able to get around without my car if need be, and being in close proximity and walking (or public transit) distance to friends and various cultural events.

(in exile, plotting my coup)
www.citydata.com/forum/
general-u-s

Victor Gruen. 1954
This conflict between downtown and the suburbs is a phony. The two are complementary parts of a whole.

Dynamic Planning for Retail Areas, Harvard Business Review, Nov.-Dec. 1954, pp 53-54.

Los Angeles Times. 11 August, 2007
Regarding our increasing density of multi-family housing in relation to potentially over-crowded schools, burdened water supplies, sewer and power systems and traffic –the solutions are simple, even trendy and fashionable: Green building means appropriate density to support high-quality public trans-portation, decentralized sewage systems that biologically clean waste water to potable quality, radically reduced water use, transfor-mation of many residential streets into organic community farms, and serious congestion pricing, among other measures.

Sharon Bernstein: *Our changing neighborhoods.* www.latimes.com

Ponte City

From high fashion to low life, berea's land-mark Ponte City has seen it all and lived to see another day.

When it was built in 1976, it was the most fashionable address in town. With its 70s-style decor of brown, shag carpet-lined walls and orange tiles, and endless views, the 54-storey building offered the ultimate in sophisticated, modern living.

Today, Africa's highest apartment building is slowly recovering from an effective state of war. The bullet-proof glass has been removed from the reception area, and the security guards disarmed.

en.wikipedia.org/wiki/ponte_city_apartments

Paul Jenkins. 2007

New forms of 'not urban, not rural' areas are emerging in Sub-saharan Africa, as rural areas stagnate and urban areas become saturated with the poor, creating unprecedented challenges for urban development. In this context the majority seem to be opting for best survival opportunities through 'straddling' urban and rural, creating 'linear villages' and complex multi-directional migrancy patterns that undermine 'traditional' geographical, demographic and socio-economic concepts of 'urban'.

School of the built environment, Heriot-watt university and Edinburgh College of Art. www.geos.ed.ac.uk/geography/DensityInsideOut.html

Environmentally, downtown is worse than the suburbs since there's more emissions from cars. More people are concentrated there so there's more opportunity.

(mike t)
http://answers.yahoo.com/question/index

Global cities Exhibition. August, 2007

In Mumbai with 34,000 people per km^2, urban housing is cramped and expensive, and open public space is limited —only 1% of the city's area— and often poorly-maintained. More affluent classes live in a corridor stretching along the city's north-south axis. Taller residential structures are surrounded by densely-packed, low rise slum buildings. As the city diversifies from its core industries, former mill areas and docklands offer the potential to produce affordable housing and accessible public spaces, but given current development trends, are likely to become exclusive office and residential zones.

www.tate.org.uk/modern/exhibitions/globalcities/density.shtm

Men are like apples:
the closer they are, the
faster they rot.

Dr. Bernard Auriol
www.lespetites-toulousaines.
com

Hennie Reynders. 2007

Informal settlements on the fringes of postapartheid South African cities have become the waiting rooms of a promised land. In most cases these communities are now rendered legal and stand in contrast to an emerging other defined as those extralegal communities existing underneath the surface of the visible urban fabric. Including illegal immigrants, criminal networks, and gated communities privileged by past and current bureaucratic malfunction.

School of the Art Institute of Chicago and University of Edinburgh. www.geos.ed.ac.uk/geography/DensityInsideOut.html

Urban and demographical scenarios of the Mexico City metropolitan area

The achievement of the densification of the centre, considered to be the optimum situation by the governmental bodies of the federated entities involved in the ZMVM, rests in the future flexibility of the real estate market. This is because a significant part of the new inhabitable park will continue to be used by families with scarce resources and who cannot economically acquire expensive prices in the central area of the city. It is thus necessary to design mechanisms that allow the accessibility to these new inhabitable spaces, formerly industrial and presently unused, to all or almost all levels of the population. Two challenges are, perhaps, even more complicated than ensuring a decent home to the entire population of the city. These are the generation of formal, well-paid employment and the eradication of public insecurity and crime. Solving both problems is urgent as delaying only causes, as we have seen over the past twenty years, growth in emigration to other parts of the country and probably even to the U.S., increasing the decentralisation of the metropolis and reducing the considered optimum of densification of the centre.

Virgilio Partida y Carlos Anzaldo
www.conapo.gob.mx/publicaciones/2003/04.pdf

Richard Burdett, Miguel Kanai. 2006

Cities in the 21st century should increasingly recognize their role as centres of tolerance and justice for people rather than sites of conflict and exclusion. They should reduce their impact on the global environment by embracing dense and compact development rather than allowing profligate sprawl.

City-building in an age of global urban transformation. Cities. Architecture and Society. 10 Mostra Internazionale de Architettura. Venecia, 2006

Gunawan Tjahjono. 2007

The promotion of over 3,000 person per hectare of high density living is now the prime target of developers in Jakarta as a result of rocketing land price in strategic areas. As the law requires any housing development provide public facilities including school, architects insert school at unthinkable level, at the sixth or even thirteenth floor of the apartment to kill the existence of school in the complex.

Department of Architecture. Faculty of Engineering. Universitas Indonesia
www.geos.ed.ac.uk/geography/DensityInsideOut.html

And what are semidetatched houses, other than just a tower on its back, taking up more space, using more water and asphalt, and taking away common space for social relations?

(trujillo)
www.idealista.com/pagina/boletin.comentarios

When everyone wants a little piece of the country life, that life itself ceases to exist.

(drl)
app.businessweek.com/
usercomments/get_reviews

Globe and mail. 23 October, 2007
Since 1990, an estimated eight million new homes have been built in the western U.S. States, chiefly in areas described as 'the urban-wild land interface,' code for uprooted city dwellers, many retired, who live in big houses or near pristine forests and deserts.

Timothy Appleby: *Two crucial factors fuelling California blazes.* http://www.theglobeandmail.com

Serge Chermayeff, Christopher Alexander. 1963

Maybe the day is not far off when planners, designers, development promoters, and other professionals recognize the mere fact that the space between buildings is just as important for the life of the urbanite as the buildings and that they act consequently. If the total land use is planned scrupulously to achieve an optimum use at any level, the inner city could hold just as many vertical, multi-purpose buildings of short term occupation as it could homes on ground level for families with children. Working as active parts in the technological urban context, these ground floor homes could be successful where suburbs have failed.

Comunidad y Privacidad. Ediciones Nueva Visión, Buenos Aires, 1984. p. 68

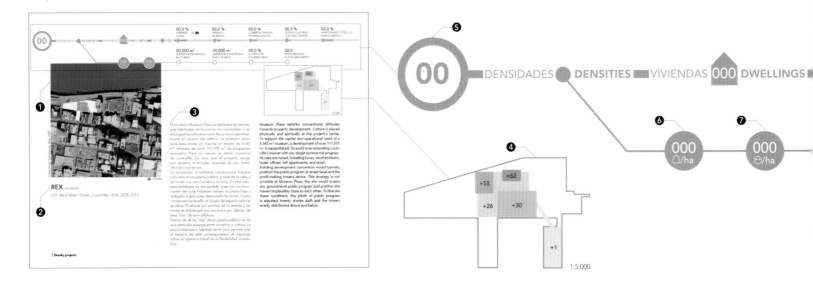

❶ IMAGEN DE SATÉLITE La parcela en su entorno, a escala 1:10.000 y situada con respecto al norte. Abarca un kilómetro cuadrado. Se añade la fuente de la imagen.

❷ Arquitectos. Página web de los arquitectos. Emplazamiento del proyecto. Fecha de inicio y final previsto.

❸ MEMORIA Texto aportado por los autores.

❹ PLANTA DE PARCELA Planta de la parcela con la huella del edificio a escala 1:2.500 o 1:5.000. En ella aparece reflejado el número de alturas sobre rasante de cada uno de los volúmenes que forman parte del proyecto.

❺ NUMERACIÓN Indica el orden de cada obra dentro de la publicación, según la densidad de población del proyecto en orden creciente.

❶ SATELLITE IMAGE Plot and surroundings at a scale of 1:10,000 and located in regard to the North. It covers one square kilometre. The source of the image is added.

❷ Architects. Architects' web site. Project location. Start and completion dates.

❸ PROJECT DESCRIPTION Text supplied by the authors.

❹ PLAN OF THE PLOT Plan of the plot with the building footprint at a scale of 1:2,500 or 1:5,000. The figures indicate the number of levels above grade of the different volumes that make up the project.

❺ NUMBERING Indicates the order of each work in the publication, according to the population density of each project from lowest to highest.

❻ DENSIDAD DE VIVIENDAS EN LA PARCELA Es el cociente entre el número de viviendas del proyecto y la superficie neta de la parcela, sin incluir los viales perimetrales. Es una densidad neta y las unidades son viviendas por hectárea.

❼ DENSIDAD DE POBLACIÓN EN LA PARCELA Se obtiene multiplicando el número de viviendas del proyecto por el número de personas que pueden habitarlas. Para calcular las personas que residen en un edificio se ha aplicado un factor de conversión (Fc) que varía en función del tamaño de la vivienda.

Fc= ** hab/vivienda
Residencias de ancianos o jóvenes, con unidades individuales:
Fc = 1,00 hab/vivienda
Vivienda estudio (un único espacio):
Fc= 1,25 hab/vivienda

❻ DENSITY OF DWELLINGS ON THE PLOT The quotient of the number of housing units and the net surface area of the plot, not including the perimetral roads. It is a net density and the unit is dwellings per hectare.

❼ RESIDENTIAL DENSITY ON THE PLOT Obtained by multiplying the number of housing units in the project by the number of people who can inhabit them. To calculate the number of people who live in a building, a factor of conversion (Fc) has been applied. It varies according to the size of the housing unit.

Fc= **inhab/dwelling
Dwellings for the elderly or young people, with individual units:
Fc = 1.00 inhab/dwelling
Studio housing (one single space):
Fc = 1.25 inhab/dwelling

00,0 %
VIVIENDA
LIVING   00 🚗 **❾**

00,0 %
TRABAJO
WORKING

00,0 %
COMERCIOS
SHOPPING

00,0 %
EQUIPAMIENTOS
CIVIC FACILITIES

00,0 %
OTROS USOS
OTHER USES

USOS ● **USES**

❽ **❿** **⓫** **⓬** **⓭**

00.000 m²
SUPERFICIE DE PARCELA
PLOT AREA

00.000 m²
SUPERFICIE CONSTRUIDA
BUILT UP AREA

00,0 %
OCUPACIÓN
COVERED AREA

00,0
EDIFICABILIDAD
FLOOR AREA RATIO

⓮ **⓯** **⓰** **⓱**

Cuando la información aparece en un sólo idioma,
todas las cifras están escritas según las convenciones de
puntuación del español.
When information appears just in one language, all
figures follow the Spanish punctuation standard (e.g.
2.000 instead of 2,000)

Vivienda de 1 dormitorio:
Fc = 1,25 hab/vivienda
Vivienda de 2 dormitorios:
Fc = 2,50 hab/vivienda
Viviendas de 3 dormitorios:
Fc = 3,75 hab/vivienda
Viviendas de 4 o más dormitorios:
Fc = 5,00 hab/vivienda
Al referirse estrictamente a la parcela, se
trata de una densidad residencial neta. Las
unidades son habitantes por hectárea.

❽ Porcentaje de superficie construida
de uso residencial.

❾ Número de plazas de aparcamiento
asignadas a los residentes.

❿ Porcentaje de superficie
construida de oficinas.

One bedroom dwelling:
Fc = 1,25 inhab/dwelling
Two bedroom dwelling
Fc = 2.50 inhab/dwelling
Three bedroom dwelling:
Fc = 3.75 inhab/dwelling
Four or more bedroom dwelling:
Fc = 5.00 inhab/dwelling
When referring strictly to the plot, this
is a net residential density. The unit is
the number of inhabitants per hectare.

❽ Percentage of residential floorspace.

❾ Number of parking spaces
assigned to dwellers.

❿ Percentage of office floorspace.

⓫ Percentage of commercial
floorspace (retail, hotels).

⓫ Porcentaje de superficie construida de
uso comercial (tiendas, hoteles).

⓬ Porcentaje de superficie construida
de equipamientos.

⓭ Porcentaje de superficie construida para
otros usos y aparcamiento público.

⓮ Superficie de parcela.

⓯ Superficie construida total en la
parcela en todas las plantas.

⓰ Porcentaje de superficie ocupada por
la edificación en la parcela analizada,
respecto a la superficie total de la parcela.

⓱ Es la relación entre la superficie construida
sobre rasante y la total de la parcela en metros
cuadrados. El cociente se expresa sin unidades.

⓬ Percentage of floorspace for civic facilities.

⓭ Percentage of floorspace for other
uses and public parking.

⓮ Plot area.

⓯ Total constructed surface area
on the plot and on all floors.

⓰ Percentage of surface area occupied by
buildings on the analysed plot, in regard
to the total surface area of the plot.

⓱ This is the relationship between the
constructed surface area above grade
and the total surface area of the
plot in square metres. The quotient
is expressed without units.

Análisis temático

Thematic analysis

Densidad de población Residential density..46

Densidad de viviendas Dwellings density.......................................52

Edificabilidad Floor area ratio...58

Usos Uses..64

DENSIDAD DE POBLACIÓN **RESIDENTIAL DENSITY**

Ordenados por densidad de población de menor a mayor, de izquierda a derecha y de arriba a abajo por página.
Arranged by residential density from lowest to highest, left to right and top to bottom on each page.

62 ☻/ha

01 **Riches Hawley Mikhail Architects**
Elmswell. United Kingdom, 2005-2008 72-75

103 ☻/ha

02 **MAB** Arquitectura
Milan. Italy, 2005-2008...76-83

118 ☻/ha

03 **AOC**
Llantwit Major. United Kingdom, 2004..84-89

139 ☻/ha

04 **MBM Arquitectes/MAB Arquitectura**
Parma. Italy, 2006-...90-99

156 ☻/ha

05 **FÜNDC**
Eindhoven. The Netherlands, 2004- 100-107

171 ☻/ha

06 **Riches Hawley Mikhail Architects**
Houghton Regis. United Kingdom, 2006-.....................................108-115

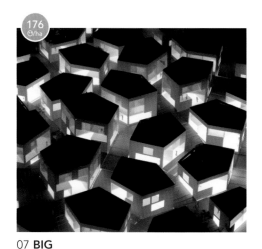

176 ⊕/ha

07 **BIG**

Holbaek. Denmark, 2006-2010 116-127

203 ⊕/ha

08 **Eric Lapierre Architecture**

Paris. France, 2007-2010 128-137

211 ⊕/ha

09 **Cino Zucchi Architetti**

Milan. Italy, 2006-2010 138-143

213 ⊕/ha

10 **Witherford Watson Mann Architects**

London. United Kingdom, 2005- 144-151

215 ⊕/ha

11 **Selgascano**

Madrid. Spain, 2007- 152-167

238 ⊕/ha

12 **ECDM Architectes**

Paris. France, 2007- 168-173

242 ⊕/ha

13 **Tatiana Bilbao/mx.a**
Guadalajara. Mexico, 2006-2010.......................................174-183

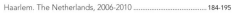

257 ⊕/ha

14 **VMX Architects**
Haarlem. The Netherlands, 2006-2010...184-195

259 ⊕/ha

15 **PLOT=BIG+JDS**
Copenhagen. Denmark, 2005-2008..196-205

306 ⊕/ha

16 **Estudio FAM**
Madrid. Spain, 2007-2009..206-209

308 ⊕/ha

17 **BIG**
Copenhagen. Denmark, 2005-..210-219

358 ⊕/ha

18 **Steven Holl Architects**
Beijing. China, 2003-2008..220-237

389 ⊕/ha

433 ⊕/ha

◯ Fase 1 Phase

437 ⊕/ha

19 **Rex Architecture**
Louisville. USA, 2005-2011...238-251

20 **Peter L. Gluck and Patners**
New York City. USA, 2007-...252-263

21 **MGM Morales, Giles**
Úbeda. Spain, 2006-...264-271

498 ⊕/ha

656 ⊕/ha

Todos los datos se refieren a la suma de los edificios A y B.
All data refer to the addition of both buildings A and B. ◯

672 ⊕/ha

22 **Atelier Thomas Pucher & Bramberger**
Tartu. Estonia, 2006-2011...272-277

23 **Cino Zucchi Architetti**
Ravenna. Italy, 2007-2009...278-283

24 **Brenac & Gonzalez**
Paris. France, 2005-2008...284-289

692 ⊕/ha

25 Kohn Pedersen Fox
New York City. USA, 2005-2009 290-293

741 ⊕/ha

26 Oppenheim Architecture+Design
Miami. USA, 2005-2009 294-301

766 ⊕/ha

27 Flexo Arquitectura
Cuevas del Almanzora. Spain, 2006- 302-305

796 ⊕/ha

28 3XN Architects
Copenhagen. Denmark, 2006-2009 306-317

852 ⊕/ha

29 BIG
Copenhaguen. Denmark, 2006-2010..318-335

919 ⊕/ha

30 Studio Gang Architects
Chicago. USA, 2006-2010 336-343

936 ⊕/ha

31 3XN Architects/UN Studio
Aarhus. Denmark, 2007-2010...344-353

944 ⊕/ha

32 Studio Gang Architects
Chicago. USA, 2004-2010...354-359

1430 ⊕/ha

33 NO.MAD, Eduardo Arroyo
Durango. Spain, 2005-2009...360-371

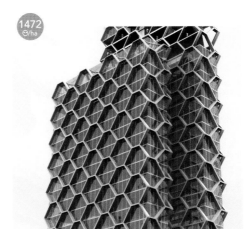

1472 ⊕/ha

34 Rojkind Arquitectos
Miguel Hidalgo. Mexico, 2005-...372-377

1511 ⊕/ha

35 Jean Nouvel
New York City. USA, 2006-2008...378-385

1985 ⊕/ha

36 X-TU Architects
Nanterre. France, 2007-2010...386-393

DENSIDAD DE VIVIENDAS **DWELLINGS DENSITY**

Ordenados por densidad de viviendas, de menor a mayor, de izquierda a derecha y de arriba a abajo por página.
Arranged by dwellings density, from lowest to highest, left to right and top to bottom on each page.
1:5.000

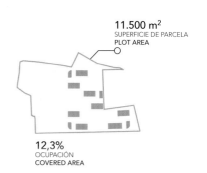

11.500 m²
SUPERFICIE DE PARCELA
PLOT AREA

12,3%
OCUPACIÓN
COVERED AREA

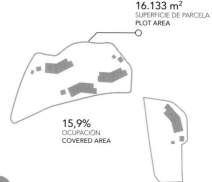

16.133 m²
SUPERFICIE DE PARCELA
PLOT AREA

15,9%
OCUPACIÓN
COVERED AREA

4.661 m²
SUPERFICIE DE PARCELA
PLOT AREA

53%
OCUPACIÓN
COVERED AREA

23 Ů/ha

01 **Riches Hawley Mikhail Architects**

Elmswell. United Kingdom, 2005-2008 72-75

30 Ů/ha

03 **AOC**

Llantwit Major. United Kingdom, 2004...84-89

43 Ů/ha

11 **Selgascano**

Madrid. Spain, 2007- 152-167

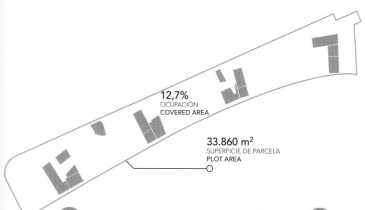

12,7%
OCUPACIÓN
COVERED AREA

33.860 m²
SUPERFICIE DE PARCELA
PLOT AREA

5.518 m²
SUPERFICIE DE PARCELA
PLOT AREA

65%
OCUPACIÓN
COVERED AREA

18.000 m²
SUPERFICIE DE PARCELA
PLOT AREA

58,3%
OCUPACIÓN
COVERED AREA

54 Ů/ha

02 **MAB** Arquitectura

Milan. Italy, 2005-2008..76-83

54 Ů/ha

09 **Cino Zucchi Architetti**

Milan. Italy, 2006-2010..138-143

56 Ů/ha

07 **BIG**

Holbaek. Denmark, 2006-2010 116-127

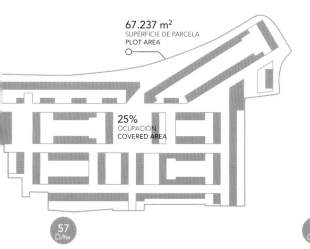

67.237 m²
SUPERFICIE DE PARCELA
PLOT AREA

25%
OCUPACIÓN
COVERED AREA

57
Δ/ha

05 FÜNDC

Eindhoven. The Netherlands, 2004-...100-107

31.740 m²
SUPERFICIE DE PARCELA
PLOT AREA

17,2%
OCUPACIÓN
COVERED AREA

57
Δ/ha

06 Riches Hawley Mikhail Architects

Houghton Regis. United Kingdom, 2006-......................................108-115

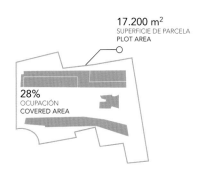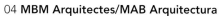

17.200 m²
SUPERFICIE DE PARCELA
PLOT AREA

28%
OCUPACIÓN
COVERED AREA

57
Δ/ha

04 MBM Arquitectes/MAB Arquitectura

Parma. Italy, 2006-...90-99

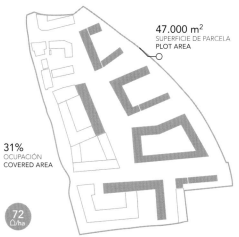

47.000 m²
SUPERFICIE DE PARCELA
PLOT AREA

31%
OCUPACIÓN
COVERED AREA

72
Δ/ha

10 Witherford Watson Mann Architects

London. United Kingdom, 2005-...144-151

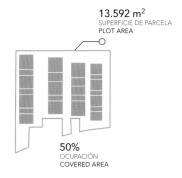

13.592 m²
SUPERFICIE DE PARCELA
PLOT AREA

50%
OCUPACIÓN
COVERED AREA

79
Δ/ha

13 Tatiana Bilbao/mx.a

Guadalajara. Mexico, 2006-2010..174-183

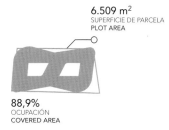

6.509 m²
SUPERFICIE DE PARCELA
PLOT AREA

88,9%
OCUPACIÓN
COVERED AREA

81
Δ/ha

12 ECDM Architectes

Paris. France, 2007-...168-173

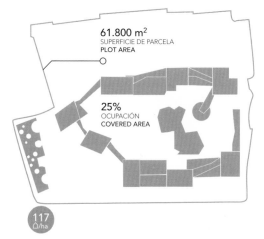

61.800 m^2
SUPERFICIE DE PARCELA
PLOT AREA

25%
OCUPACIÓN
COVERED AREA

117
□/ha

18 **Steven Holl Architects**

Beijing. China, 2003-2008 220-237

8.572 m^2
SUPERFICIE DE PARCELA
PLOT AREA

43,4%
OCUPACIÓN
COVERED AREA

128
□/ha

16 **Estudio FAM**

Madrid. Spain, 2007-2009 206-209

2.403 m^2
SUPERFICIE DE PARCELA
PLOT AREA

54,9%
OCUPACIÓN
COVERED AREA

129
□/ha

21 **MGM Morales, Giles**

Úbeda. Spain, 2006- 264-271

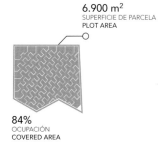

6.900 m^2
SUPERFICIE DE PARCELA
PLOT AREA

84%
OCUPACIÓN
COVERED AREA

143
□/ha

15 **PLOT=BIG+JDS**

Copenhagen. Denmark, 2005-2008 196-205

5.800 m^2
SUPERFICIE DE PARCELA
PLOT AREA

38%
OCUPACIÓN
COVERED AREA

143
□/ha

17 **BIG**

Copenhagen. Denmark, 2005- 210-219

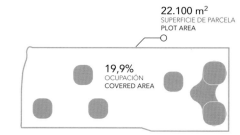

22.100 m^2
SUPERFICIE DE PARCELA
PLOT AREA

19,9%
OCUPACIÓN
COVERED AREA

143
□/ha

14 **VMX Architects**

Haarlem. The Netherlands, 2006-2010 184-195

10.900 m²
SUPERFICIE DE PARCELA
PLOT AREA

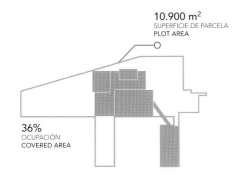

36%
OCUPACIÓN
COVERED AREA

150
Q/ha

19 **Rex Architecture**

Louisville. USA, 2005-2011 238-251

28.452 m²
SUPERFICIE DE PARCELA
PLOT AREA

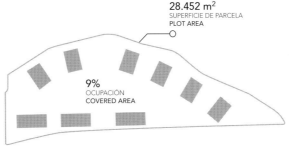

9%
OCUPACIÓN
COVERED AREA

156
Q/ha

22 **Atelier Thomas Pucher & Bramberger**

Tartu. Estonia, 2006-2011 272-277

4.537 m²
SUPERFICIE DE PARCELA
PLOT AREA

33,1%
OCUPACIÓN
COVERED AREA

185
Q/ha

23 **Cino Zucchi Architetti**

Ravenna. Italy, 2007-2009 278-283

2.972 m²
SUPERFICIE DE PARCELA
PLOT AREA

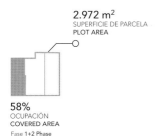

58%
OCUPACIÓN
COVERED AREA

Fase 1+2 Phase

193
Q/ha

20 **Peter L. Gluck and Patners**

New York City. USA, 2007- 252-263

17.625 m²
SUPERFICIE DE PARCELA
PLOT AREA

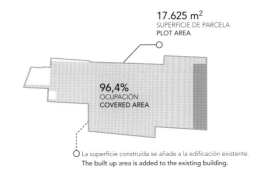

96,4%
OCUPACIÓN
COVERED AREA

 La superficie construida se añade a la edificación existente.
The built up area is added to the existing building.

200
Q/ha

08 **Eric Lapierre Architecture**

Paris. France, 2007-2010 128-137

20.000 m²
SUPERFICIE DE PARCELA
PLOT AREA

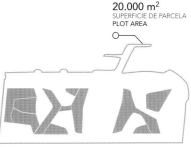

31%
OCUPACIÓN
COVERED AREA

203
Q/ha

31 **3XN Architects/UN Studio**

Aarhus. Denmark, 2007-2010 344-356

1.845 m²
SUPERFICIE DE PARCELA
PLOT AREA

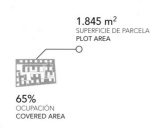

65%
OCUPACIÓN
COVERED AREA

217
⌂/ha

27 Flexo Arquitectura

Cuevas del Almanzora. Spain, 2006- 302-305

21.000 m²
SUPERFICIE DE PARCELA
PLOT AREA

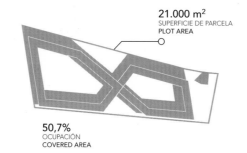

50,7%
OCUPACIÓN
COVERED AREA

239
⌂/ha

29 BIG

Copenhaguen. Denmark, 2006-2010 318-335

1.407 m²
SUPERFICIE DE PARCELA
PLOT AREA

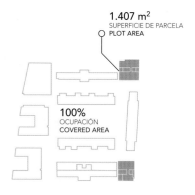

100%
OCUPACIÓN
COVERED AREA

256
⌂/ha

24 Brenac & Gonzalez

Paris. France, 2005-2008 284-289

6.000 m²
SUPERFICIE DE PARCELA
PLOT AREA

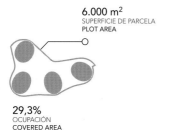

29,3%
OCUPACIÓN
COVERED AREA

280
⌂/ha

28 3XN Architects

Copenhagen. Denmark, 2006-2009 306-317

4.830 m²
SUPERFICIE DE PARCELA
PLOT AREA

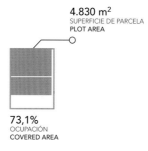

73,1%
OCUPACIÓN
COVERED AREA

300
⌂/ha

30 Studio Gang Architects

Chicago. USA, 2006-2010 336-343

---

993 m²
SUPERFICIE DE PARCELA
PLOT AREA

100%
OCUPACIÓN
COVERED AREA

322
⌂/ha

25 Kohn Pedersen Fox

New York City. USA, 2005-2009 290-293

2.081 m²
SUPERFICIE DE PARCELA
PLOT AREA

31,8%
OCUPACIÓN
COVERED AREA

432
☐/ha

33 **NO.MAD, Eduardo Arroyo**

Durango. Spain, 2005-2009 360-371

1.957 m²
SUPERFICIE DE PARCELA
PLOT AREA

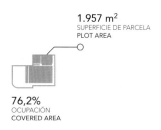

76,2%
OCUPACIÓN
COVERED AREA

577
☐/ha

26 **Oppenheim Architecture+Design**

Miami. USA, 2005-2009 294-301

16.420 m²
SUPERFICIE DE PARCELA
PLOT AREA

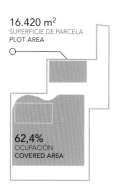

62,4%
OCUPACIÓN
COVERED AREA

592
☐/ha

32 **Studio Gang Architects**

Chicago. USA, 2004-2010 354-359

1.059 m²
SUPERFICIE DE PARCELA
PLOT AREA

73%
OCUPACIÓN
COVERED AREA

651
☐/ha

35 **Jean Nouvel**

New York City. USA, 2006-2008 378-385

2.717 m²
SUPERFICIE DE PARCELA
PLOT AREA

35%
OCUPACIÓN
COVERED AREA

662
☐/ha

34 **Rojkind Arquitectos**

Miguel Hidalgo. Mexico, 2005- 372-377

2.317 m²
SUPERFICIE DE PARCELA
PLOT AREA

82,7%
OCUPACIÓN
COVERED AREA

742
☐/ha

36 **X-TU Architects**

Nanterre. France, 2007-2010 386-393

EDIFICABILIDAD **FLOOR AREA RATIO**

◯ Ordenados por el coeficiente de edificabilidad, de menor a mayor, de izquierda a derecha y de arriba a abajo por página.
Arranged by floor area ratio, from lowest to highest, left to right and top to bottom on each page.

◑ 1:10.000

0,2

infoterra&bluesky, 2007

01 **Riches Hawley Mikhail Architects**
Elmswell. United Kingdom, 2005-2008 72-75

0,3

the geoinformation group, 2007

03 **AOC**
Llantwit Major. United Kingdom, 2004..84-89

0,5

the geoinformation group, 2007

06 **Riches Hawley Mikhail Architects**
Houghton Regis. United Kingdom, 2006-....................................108-115

0,6

scankort, 2007

07 **BIG**
Holbaek. Denmark, 2006-2010..116-127

0,6

digitalglobe, 2007

11 **Selgascano**
Madrid. Spain, 2007- 152-167

0,6

digitalglobe, 2007

02 **MAB** Arquitectura
Milan. Italy, 2005-2008..76-83

○ La superficie construida se añade a la edificación existente.
The built up area is added to the existing building.

0,6

the geoinformation group/interatlas, 2007

08 Eric Lapierre Architecture
Paris. France, 2007-2010...128-137

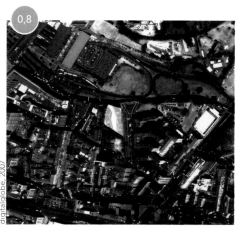

0,7

digitalglobe, 2007

05 FÜNDC
Eindhoven. The Netherlands, 2004-...100-107

0,8

digitalglobe, 2007

09 Cino Zucchi Architetti
Milan. Italy, 2006-2010..138-143

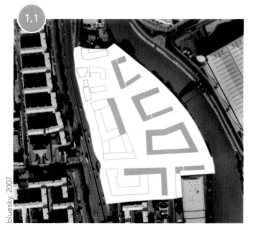

1,1

bluesky, 2007

10 Witherford Watson Mann Architects
London. United Kingdom, 2005-..144-151

1,1

21 MGM Morales, Giles
Úbeda. Spain, 2006-..264-271

1,3

digitalglobe, 2007

16 Estudio FAM
Madrid. Spain, 2007-2009..206-209

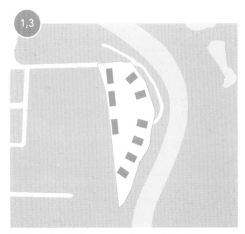

1,3

22 Atelier Thomas Pucher & Bramberger

Tartu. Estonia, 2006-2011 272-277

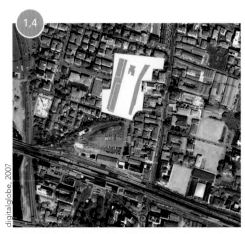

1,4

digitalglobe, 2007

04 MBM Arquitectes/MAB Arquitectura

Parma. Italy, 2006- 90-99

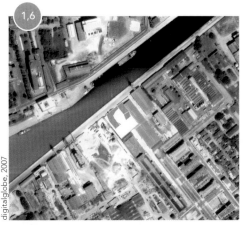

1,6

digitalglobe, 2007

23 Cino Zucchi Architetti

Ravenna. Italy, 2007-2009 278-283

1,6

digitalglobe, 2007

27 Flexo Arquitectura

Cuevas del Almanzora. Spain, 2006- 302-305

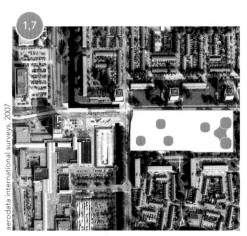

1,7

aerodata international surveys, 2007

14 VMX Architects

Haarlem. The Netherlands, 2006-2010 184-195

1,7

scankort, 2007

17 BIG

Copenhagen. Denmark, 2005- 210-219

scankort, 2007

3,0

29 BIG
Copenhaguen. Denmark, 2006-2010..318-335

scankort, 2007

3,0

31 3XN Architects/UN Studio
Aarhus. Denmark, 2007-2010..344-353

digitalglobe, 2007

3,5

18 Steven Holl Architects
Beijing. China, 2003-2008...220-237

scankort, 2007

3,6

28 3XN Architects
Copenhagen. Denmark, 2006-2009...306-317

------O Fase **1+2 Phase**

sanborn, 2007

4,0

20 Peter L. Gluck and Patners
New York City. USA, 2007-..252-263

digitalglobe, 2007

4,6

13 Tatiana Bilbao/mx.a
Guadalajara. Mexico, 2006-2010..174-183

scankort, 2007

4,8

15 PLOT=BIG+JDS
Copenhagen. Denmark, 2005-2008................................196-205

cnes/spot image, 2007

5,0

33 NO.MAD, Eduardo Arroyo
Durango. Spain, 2005-2009..................................360-371

the geoinformation group/interatlas, 2007

5,2

24 Brenac & Gonzalez
Paris. France, 2005-2008..................................284-289

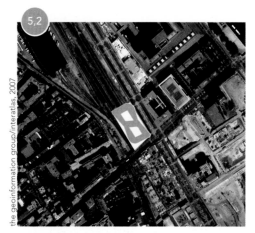

the geoinformation group/interatlas, 2007

5,2

12 ECDM Architectes
Paris. France, 2007-..................................168-173

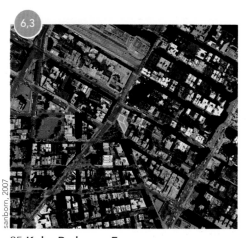

sanborn, 2007

6,3

25 Kohn Pedersen Fox
New York City. USA, 2005-2009..................................290-293

NASA

7,8

30 Studio Gang Architects
Chicago. USA, 2006-2010..................................336-343

EDIFICABILIDAD FLOOR AREA RATIO

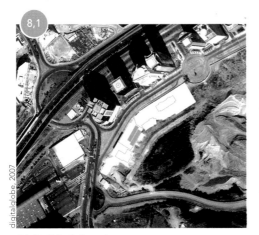

8,1

digitalglobe, 2007

34 Rojkind Arquitectos
Miguel Hidalgo. Mexico, 2005-...372-377

10,0

the geoinformation group/interatlas, 2007

36 X-TU Architects
Nanterre. France, 2007-2010..386-393

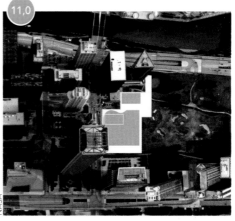

11,0

NASA

32 Studio Gang Architects
Chicago. USA, 2004-2010..354-359

11,0

sanborn/digitalglobe, 2007

35 Jean Nouvel
New York City. USA, 2006-2008...378-385

13,0

indianamap framework data, 2007

19 Rex Architecture
Louisville. USA, 2005-2011...238-251

13,3

sanborn 2007

26 Oppenheim Architecture+Design
Miami. USA, 2005-2009 294-301

USOS USES

○ Ordenados por la proporción de uso residencial, de mayor a
menor, de izquierda a derecha y de arriba a abajo por página.
**Arranged by residential use, from highest to lowest,
left to right and top to bottom on each page.**

Cuando coincide su superficie residencial, los proyectos están
ordenados por su densidad de población en orden ascendente.
**In the case of the same residential area, the projects
○ are arranged by residential density in increase order.**

01 Riches Hawley Mikhail Architects

Elmswell. United Kingdom, 2005-2008 72-75

100 %
VIVIENDA   42 🚗
LIVING

USOS ● USES   TRABAJO WORKING   COMERCIOS SHOPPING   EQUIPAMIENTOS CIVIC FACILITIES   TRABAJO WORKING

03 AOC

Llantwit Major. United Kingdom, 2004.................................84-89

100 %
VIVIENDA   14 🚗
LIVING

USOS ● USES   TRABAJO WORKING   COMERCIO SHOPPING   EQUIPAMIENTOS CIVIC FACILITIES   OTROS USOS OTHER USES

06 Riches Hawley Mikhail Architects

Houghton Regis. United Kingdom, 2006-.....................108-115

100%
VIVIENDA   97 🚗
LIVING

USOS ● USES   TRABAJO WORKING   COMERCIOS SHOPPING   EQUIPAMIENTOS CIVIC FACILITIES   OTROS USOS OTHER USES

11 Selgascano

Madrid. Spain, 2007-.................................152-167

100 %
VIVIENDA   20 🚗
LIVING

USOS ● USES   TRABAJO WORKING   COMERCIO SHOPPING   EQUIPAMIENTOS CIVIC FACILITIES   OTROS USOS OTHER USES

21 MGM Morales, Giles

Úbeda. Spain, 2006-.................................264-271

100 %
VIVIENDA   🚗
LIVING

USOS ● USES   TRABAJO WORKING   COMERCIO SHOPPING   EQUIPAMIENTOS CIVIC FACILITIES   OTROS USOS OTHER USES

22 Atelier Thomas Pucher & Bramberger

Tartu. Estonia, 2006-2011.................................272-277

100 %
VIVIENDA   460 🚗
LIVING

USOS ● USES   TRABAJO WORKING   COMERCIOS SHOPPING   EQUIPAMIENTOS CIVIC FACILITIES   OTROS USOS OTHER USES

20 Peter L. Gluck and Patners
New York City. USA, 2007-.....................252-263   USOS ● USES

100%
VIVIENDA   22 🚗
LIVING

TRABAJO   COMERCIOS   EQUIPAMIENTOS   OTROS USOS
WORKING   SHOPPING   CIVIC FACILITIES   OTHER USES

27 Flexo Arquitectura
Cuevas del Almanzora. Spain, 2006-.................302-305   USOS ● USES

100 %
VIVIENDA   🚗
LIVING

TRABAJO   COMERCIOS   EQUIPAMIENTOS   OTROS USOS
WORKING   SHOPPING   CIVIC FACILITIES   OTHER USES

28 3XN Architects
Copenhagen. Denmark, 2006-2009.................306-317   USOS ● USES

100 %
VIVIENDA   164 🚗
LIVING

TRABAJO   COMERCIOS   EQUIPAMIENTOS   OTROS USOS
WORKING   SHOPPING   CIVIC FACILITIES   OTHER USES

09 Cino Zucchi Architetti
Milan. Italy, 2006-2010.................................138-143   USOS ● USES

97,8 %
VIVIENDA   66 🚗
LIVING

TRABAJO   COMERCIOS
WORKING   SHOPPING

2,2 %
GUARDERÍA
NURSERY

OTROS USOS
OTHER USES

36 X-TU Architects
Nanterre. France, 2007-2010.....................386-393   USOS ● USES

97,1 %
VIVIENDA   148 🚗
LIVING

1,6 %
TRABAJO
WORKING

1,3 %
COMERCIOS
SHOPPING

EQUIPAMIENTOS   OTROS USOS
CIVIC FACILITIES   OTHER USES

23 Cino Zucchi Architetti
Ravenna. Italy, 2007-2009.........................278-283   USOS ● USES

96,7 %
VIVIENDA   86 🚗
LIVING

3,3 %
COMERCIOS
SHOPPING

TRABAJO   EQUIPAMIENTOS   OTORS USOS
WORKING   CIVIC FACILITIES   OTHER USES

33 NO.MAD, Eduardo Arroyo

Durango. Spain, 2005-2009.................................360-371

USOS ● USES

96,7 %		3,3 %		
VIVIENDA 193 🚗	TRABAJO	COMERCIOS	EQUIPAMIENTOS	OTROS USOS
LIVING	WORKING	SHOPPING	CIVIC FACILITIES	OTHER USES

05 FÜNDC

Eindhoven. The Netherlands, 2004-................................100-107

USOS ● USES

95,8 %		4,2 %		
VIVIENDA 494 🚗	TRABAJO	COMERCIOS	EQUIPAMIENTOS	OTROS USOS
LIVING	WORKING	SHOPPING	CIVIC FACILITIES	OTHER USES

35 Jean Nouvel

New York City. USA, 2006-2008...378-385

USOS ● USES

95,5 %		4,5 %		
VIVIENDA 🚗	TRABAJO	COMERCIOS	EQUIPAMIENTOS	OTROS USOS
LIVING	WORKING	SHOPPING	CIVIC FACILITIES	OTHER USES

07 BIG

Holbaek. Denmark, 2006-2010...116-127

USOS ● USES

95,2 %		4,8		
VIVIENDA 200 🚗	TRABAJO	COMERCIOS	EQUIPAMIENTOS	OTROS USOS
LIVING	WORKING	SHOPPING	CIVIC FACILITIES	OTHER USES

14 VMX Architects

Haarlem. The Netherlands, 2006-2010 184-195

USOS ● USES

94,5%		1,5%	4 %	
VIVIENDA 279 🚗	TRABAJO	COMERCIOS	HOSPITAL DE ANCIANOS	OTROS USOS
LIVING	WORKING	SHOPPING	HOSPITAL FOR THE ELDERLY	OTHER USES

18 Steven Holl Architects

Beijing. China, 2003-2008...220-237

USOS ● USES

87,8 %		7,2 %	2,7 %	2,3 %
VIVIENDA 870 🚗	TRABAJO	COMERCIOS	CINE/GUARDERÍA	HOTEL
LIVING	WORKING	SHOPPING	CINEMA/NURSERY	HOTEL

30 **Studio Gang Architects**
Chicago. USA, 2006-2010 336-343

87,4 % VIVIENDA 288 🚗 LIVING	**0,1 %** TRABAJO WORKING	COMERCIOS SHOPPING	EQUIPAMIENTOS CIVIC FACILITIES		**12,5 %** APARCAMIENTO PÚBLIC PUBLIC PARKING

USOS ● USES ▬▬▬▬▬▬

25 **Kohn Pedersen Fox**
New York City. USA, 2005-2009 290-293

86,4 % VIVIENDA 🚗 LIVING   TRABAJO WORKING   **13,6 %** COMERCIOS SHOPPING   EQUIPAMIENTOS CIVIC FACILITIES   OTHER USES

USOS ● USES ▬▬▬▬▬▬

02 **MAB Arquitectura**
Milan. Italy, 2005-2008 76-83

84,5 % VIVIENDA 238 🚗 LIVING   TRABAJO WORKING   **2,4 %** COMERCIOS SHOPPING   **13,1 %** GUARDERÍA/CENTRO DE DÍA/CENTRO CÍVICO NURSERY/DAY CARE CENTRE/CIVIC CENTRE

USOS ● USES ▬▬▬▬▬▬

29 **BIG**
Copenhaguen. Denmark, 2006-2010 318-335

83,3% VIVIENDA 🚗 LIVING   **16,7 %** TRABAJO WORKING   COMERCIOS SHOPPING   EQUIPAMIENTOS CIVIC FACILITIES   OTHER USES

USOS ● USES ▬▬▬▬▬▬

17 **BIG**
Copenhagen. Denmark, 2005- 210-219

79,4 % VIVIENDA 164 🚗 LIVING   TRABAJO WORKING   **20,6 %** COMERCIOS SHOPPING   EQUIPAMIENTOS CIVIC FACILITIES   OTHER USES

USOS ● USES ▬▬▬▬▬▬

16 **Estudio FAM**
Madrid. Spain, 2007-2009 206-209

78,9 % VIVIENDA 110 🚗 LIVING   TRABAJO WORKING   **8,2 %** COMERCIOS SHOPPING   **12,9 %** GUARDERÍA/C. CULTURAL/C. DE SALUD/BIBLIOTEC NURSERY/CULTURAL CENTRE/HEALTH CENTRE/LIBRA

USOS ● USES ▬▬▬▬▬▬

34 Rojkind Arquitectos
Miguel Hidalgo. Mexico, 2005-................................372-377   USOS USES

75,5 %
VIVIENDA
LIVING   🚗

TRABAJO
WORKING

10 %
COMERCIOS
SHOPPING

EQUIPAMIENTOS
CIVIC FACILITIES

14,5 %
HOTEL
HOTEL

31 3XN Architects/UN Studio
Aarhus. Denmark, 2007-2010................................344-353   USOS USES

66,7 %
VIVIENDA   400 🚗
LIVING

TRABAJO
WORKING

33,3 %
COMERCIOS
SHOPPING

EQUIPAMIENTOS
CIVIC FACILITIES

OTROS USOS
OTHER USES

32 Studio Gang Architects
Chicago. USA, 2004-2010................................354-359   USOS USES

64,5 %
VIVIENDA   🚗
LIVING

1,9 %
TRABAJO
WORKING

5 %
COMERCIOS
SHOPPING

EQUIPAMIENTOS
CIVIC FACILITIES

28,6 %
HOTEL/APARCAMIENTO
HOTEL/PUBLIC PA

10 Witherford Watson Mann Architects
London. United Kingdom, 2005-................................144-151   USOS USES

62, 2 %
VIVIENDA   254 🚗
LIVING

TRABAJO
WORKING

29,6 %
COMERCIOS
SHOPPING

EQUIPAMIENTOS
CIVIC FACILITIES

8,2 %
HOTEL
HOTEL

○ Todos los datos se refieren a la suma de los edificios A y B.
All data refer to the addition of both building A and B.

24 Brenac & Gonzalez
Paris. France, 2005-2008................................284-289   USOS USES

42,8 %
VIVIENDA   🚗
LIVING

TRABAJO
WORKING

11 %
COMERCIOS
SHOPPING

46,2 %
RESIDENCIA ANCIANOS/CENTRO MUJERES MALTRATADAS
CENTRE FOR THE ELDERLY/SHELTER FOR ABUSED WOMEN

○ La superficie construida se añade a la edificación existente.
The built up area is added to the existing building.

08 Eric Lapierre Architecture
Paris. France, 2007-2010................................128-137   USOS USES

40 %*
VIVIENDA   🚗
LIVING

TRABAJO
WORKING

COMERCIOS
SHOPPING

60 %*
APARCAMIENTO DE AUTOBUSES EXISTENTE
EXISTING BUS PARKING

26 Oppenheim Architecture+Design

Miami. USA, 2005-2009 294-301

USOS ● USES

39,9 % VIVIENDA LIVING

7,6 % TRABAJO WORKING

3,4 % COMERCIOS SHOPPING

EQUIPAMIENTOS CIVIC FACILITIES

49,1 % APARCAMIENTO PÚBLICO PUBLIC PARKING

13 Tatiana Bilbao/mx.a

Guadalajara. Mexico, 2006-2010 174-183

USOS ● USES

37,6 % VIVIENDA LIVING

TRABAJO WORKING

15,1 % COMERCIOS/HOTEL SHOPPING/HOTEL

3,6 % CINES CINEMAS

43,7 % APARCAMIENTO PÚBLICO PUBLIC PARKING

15 PLOT=BIG+JDS

Copenhagen. Denmark, 2005-2008 196-205

USOS ● USES

31,7 % VIVIENDA LIVING 80

2,1 % TRABAJO OFICINAS

0,9 % COMERCIOS SHOPPING

EQUIPAMIENTOS CIVIC FACILITIES

65,3 % APARCAMIENTO PÚBLICO PUBLIC PARKING

19 Rex Architecture

Louisville. USA, 2005-2011 238-251

USOS ● USES

27,4 % VIVIENDA LIVING

17,6 % TRABAJO WORKING

16,9 % COMERCIOS/HOTEL SHOPPING/HOTEL

10,8 % CENTRO CULTURAL CULTURAL CENTRE

27,3 % APARCAMIENTO PÚBLICO PUBLIC PARKING

04 MBM Arquitectes/MAB Arquitectura

Parma. Italy, 2006- 90-99

USOS ● USES

24,5 % VIVIENDA LIVING

21,2 % TRABAJO WORKING

6,2 % COMERCIOS SHOPPING

EQUIPAMIENTOS CIVIC FACILITIES

48,1 % APARCAMIENTO PÚBLICO PARKING

12 ECDM Architectes

Paris. France, 2007- 168-173

USOS ● USES

17,3 % VIVIENDA LIVING

58,2 % TRABAJO WORKING

24,5 % COMERCIOS SHOPPING

EQUIPAMIENTOS CIVIC FACILITIES

OTROS USOS OTHER USES

Proyectos

Projects

Número de
proyecto
Project
number

Autores Authors

Página Page

01 **Riches Hawley Mikhail Architects** 72-75

02 **MAB Arquitectura** 76-83

03 **AOC** 84-89

04 **MBM Arquitectes/MAB Arquitectura** 90-99

05 **FÜNDC** 100-107

06 **Riches Hawley Mikhail Architects** 108-115

07 **BIG** 116-127

08 **Eric Lapierre Architecture** 128-137

09 **Cino Zucchi Architetti** 138-143

10 **Witherford Watson Mann Architects** 144-151

11 **Selgascano** 152-167

12 **ECDM Architectes** 168-173

13 **Tatiana Bilbao/mx.a** 174-183

14 **VMX Architects** 184-195

15 **PLOT=BIG+JDS** 196-205

16 **Estudio FAM** 206-209

17 **BIG** 210-219

18 **Steven Holl Architects** 220-237

19 **Rex Architecture** 238-251

20 **Peter L. Gluck and Partners** 252-263

21 **MGM Morales, Giles** 264-271

22 **Atelier Thomas Pucher & Bramberger** 272-277

23 **Cino Zucchi Architetti** 278-283

24 **Brenac & Gonzalez** 284-289

25 **Kohn Pedersen Fox** 290-293

26 **Oppenheim Architecture+Design** 294-301

27 **Flexo Arquitectura** 302-305

28 **3XN Architects** 306-317

29 **BIG** 318-335

30 **Studio Gang Architects** 336-343

31 **3XN Architects/UN Studio** 344-353

32 **Studio Gang Architects** 354-359

33 **NO.MAD, Eduardo Arroyo** 360-371

34 **Rojkind Arquitectos** 372-377

35 **Jean Nouvel** 378-385

36 **X-TU Architects** 386-393

100 %
VIVIENDA   42 🚗
LIVING

TRABAJO
WORKING

COMERCIOS
SHOPPING

EQUIPAMIENTOS
CIVIC FACILITIES

OTROS USOS
OTHER USES

23 ⌂/ha   62 ⊕/ha

11.500 m²
SUPERFICIE DE PARCELA
PLOT AREA

2.320 m²
SUPERFICIE CONSTRUIDA
BUILT UP AREA

12,3 %
OCUPACIÓN
COVERED AREA

0,2
EDIFICABILIDAD
FLOOR AREA RATIO

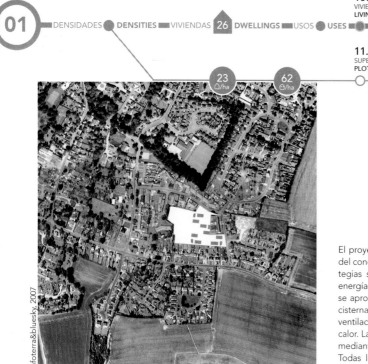

infoterra&bluesky, 2007

🌢 1:10.000

1:2.500

Riches Hawley Mikhail Architects

rhmarchitects.com

Thedwastre Close, Elmswell. United Kingdom, 2005-2008

El proyecto Three Gardens, situado en una aldea del condado de Suffolk, incorpora diferentes estrategias sostenibles de construcción, consumo de energía y relación con el entorno. El agua de lluvia se aprovecha para regar los jardines y rellenar las cisternas de los baños, mientras que el sistema de ventilación sirve para minimizar las pérdidas de calor. La calefacción y el agua caliente se obtienen mediante una caldera de biomasa.

Todas las viviendas están orientadas al sur para incrementar las ganancias solares en invierno y reducirlas en verano. La construcción se basa en una estructura de madera y un relleno proyectado a base de una mezcla de cáñamo y cal. Este innovador método de aislamiento tiene la gran ventaja de que no sólo no emite CO_2 sino que reduce la emisión del gas. Los acabados de fachada son tablillas de cedro rojo o paramentos encalados.

La organización de los edificios no es jerárquica. Los automóviles pueden acceder a la urbanización pero sin poder circular entre los edificios. Disponen de aparcamiento cerca de cada grupo de viviendas. Los muros curvos que delimitan los jardines privados proporcionan privacidad y recogimiento.

Situated in a rural village in Suffolk the Three Gardens project combines sustainable strategies for construction, lifetime energy use and landscape. Rainwater is collected to water gardens and flush toilets, whole house ventilation minimises heat loss and heat and hot water are provided by a shared biomass boiler.

Houses all face south -overshadowing is minimised and passive solar gain maximised. Construction is structural timber frame filled with a sprayed mixture of lime and hemp. This innovative insulanting material has the huge advantage of being not carbon neutral but carbon negative, locking in CO_2. Finishes are lime render and red cedar shingles and boards.

The arrangement of houses is non-hierarchical, cars can enter the site but not drive through, parking is provided near each group of houses. Curved walls define the extent of the private gardens and give a sense of privacy and enclosure.

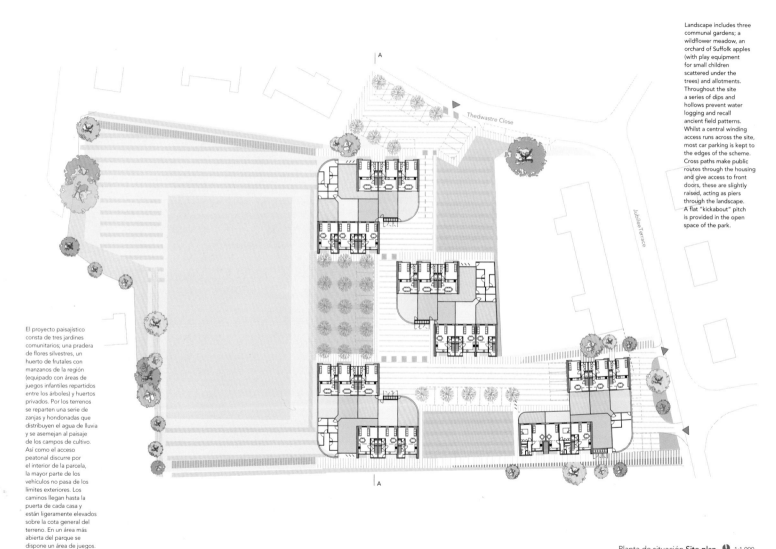

Landscape includes three communal gardens; a wildflower meadow, an orchard of Suffolk apples (with play equipment for small children scattered under the trees) and allotments. Throughout the site a series of dips and hollows prevent water logging and recall ancient field patterns. Whilst a central winding access runs across the site, most car parking is kept to the edges of the scheme. Cross paths make public routes through the housing and give access to front doors, these are slightly raised, acting as piers through the landscape. A flat "kickabout" pitch is provided in the open space of the park.

El proyecto paisajístico consta de tres jardines comunitarios; una pradera de flores silvestres, un huerto de frutales con manzanos de la región (equipado con áreas de juegos infantiles repartidos entre los árboles) y huertos privados. Por los terrenos se reparten una serie de zanjas y hondonadas que distribuyen el agua de lluvia y se asemejan al paisaje de los campos de cultivo. Así como el acceso peatonal discurre por el interior de la parcela, la mayor parte de los vehículos no pasa de los límites exteriores. Los caminos llegan hasta la puerta de cada casa y están ligeramente elevados sobre la cota general del terreno. En un área más abierta del parque se dispone un área de juegos.

Thedwastre Close

Jubilee Terrace

A

A

Planta de situación **Site plan** 🡇 1:1.000

Todas las viviendas están orientadas al sur para maximizar las ganancias de calor. Los edificios están dispuestos para evitar las sombras de unos sobre otros. Los edificios de dos plantas se ubican al Sur de los de tres plantas.
All houses face south to maximise passive solar gain. The buildings are staggered to avoid over-shadowing even in winter. Lower 2-storey buildings are to the south of the taller 3-storey buildings.

Los peatones tienen prioridad. Los caminos elevados conectan los todos la parcela y reducen la velocidad de los automóviles. Éstos acceden a una zona rodeada por las viviendas. La mayor parte de los aparcamientos está en el perímetro del terreno.
Pedestrians have priority. Raised paths connect all parts of the site and act as traffic calming. Vehicles access a 'homezone' which winds through the courtyards, most parking is to the perimeter of the site.

Todas las viviendas disponen de jardín propio, y se agrupan en edificios de 3 viviendas y grupos de 6 alrededor de sus jardines.
All houses have gardens. Houses are grouped in terraces of 3 and neighbourhoods of 6, enclosing private gardens.

3 pequeños jardines se reparten entre las agrupaciones de viviendas donde juegan los niños: se trata de pequeñas áreas junto al gran campo de juegos de la aldea.
3 small gardens are scattered between the groups of houses, small children play: it is a pocket of green space next to the larger play area for the whole village.

Tipos de viviendas Dwelling types

ESTUDIOS: 0
1 DORMITORIO: 4
2 DORMITORIOS: 13
3 DORMITORIOS: 9
4+ DORMITORIOS: 0
STUDIOS: 0
1 BEDROOM: 4
2 BEDROOMS: 13
3 BEDROOMS: 9
4+ BEDROOMS: 0

Tipo A Type

Planta segunda
Second floor plan

Planta primera
First floor plan

Planta baja
Ground floor plan

Tipo B type

Planta primera
First floor plan

Planta baja
Ground floor plan   1:500

Vista del huerto **View of orchard**

Vista de la pradera **View of the meadow**

Perspectiva aérea **Aerial perspective**

Ventilación a través de lucernarios practicables
Ventilation through opening skylights

Colectores solares en la cubierta orientada al sur
Solar collectors on south facing roof

Ventilación a través de lucernarios practicables
Ventilation through opening skylights

El agua de lluvia se recoge en depósitos
Rainwater is collected in water butts

Ventilación a través de lucernarios practicables
Ventilation through opening skylights

Colectores solares en la cubierta orientada al sur
Solar collectors on South facing roof

84,5 %
VIVIENDA 238 🚗
LIVING

TRABAJO
WORKING

2,4 %
COMERCIOS
SHOPPING

13,1 %
GUARDERÍA/CENTRO DE DÍA/CENTRO CÍVICO
NURSERY/DAY CARE CENTRE/CIVIC CENTRE

33.860 m²
SUPERFICIE DE PARCELA
PLOT AREA

29.900 m²
SUPERFICIE CONSTRUIDA
BUILT UP AREA

12,7 %
OCUPACIÓN
COVERED AREA

0,6
EDIFICABILIDAD
FLOOR AREA RATIO

54
⌂/ha

103
⬡/ha

1:5.000

digitalglobe, 2007

1:10.000

MAB Arquitectura mabarchitettura.com

Via Gallarate, Quartiere Gallaratese, Milan. Italy, 2005-2008

La intervención se sitúa en un solar estrecho y muy largo limitado por el barrio residencial Gallaratese al sur, y las áreas de futura trasformación al norte.

El espacio público estructura el proyecto. Así, el parque lineal totalmente peatonal se cierra con sus taludes verdes a la vía rápida al norte, y se abre con áreas de juego y servicios para la comunidad hacia el sur, hacia la ciudad.

En el interior del parque, cuatro bloques de viviendas y sus plazas interiores se integran con el espacio diluido del verde dejando que las plantas bajas sean porticadas y lo más transparentes posibles, favoreciendo la continuidad perceptiva del parque y el uso de los comercios.

Los edificios presentan alturas variables a lo largo del paseo peatonal, se dejan perforar por el paseo, rotan para adaptarse al recorrido, se integran con los taludes al norte y se elevan con cuatro torres en el lado sur hacia la ciudad consolidada.

Las viviendas son variaciones de cuatro tipologías distintas (en su mayoría de 3 y 4 dormitorios), cuentan con ventilación cruzada, y están dispuestas en cada bloque de forma que las zonas de día se orienten al oeste con balcones y logias, mientras que las zonas de noche miran hacia el este.

The intervention is located on a long and very narrow lot bordered to the south by the residential neighbourhood Gallaratese and to areas of future transformation to the north.

Public space structures the project. In this way, the pedestrian linear park is closed with its green slopes to the motorway to the north and opens to play areas and community services to the south, towards the city.

Inside the park, four blocks of flats and their inner plazas are integrated with the more diluted green space, allowing ground floors to be porticoed and as transparent as possible, favouring the perceptive continuity of the park and the use of those shops.

The buildings present variable heights along the pedestrian walkway and are perforated by the avenue. They then turn to adapt to the route and become part of the slopes to the north. The finally rise with four towers to the south towards the consolidated city.

The homes are variations of four different types (mostly three- and four-bedrooms) and have cross-ventilation. They are arranged in each block in a way that the areas of daytime use face the west with balconies and loggias, while the areas of night time use face west.

Vista desde la Via Appennini
View from Via Appennini

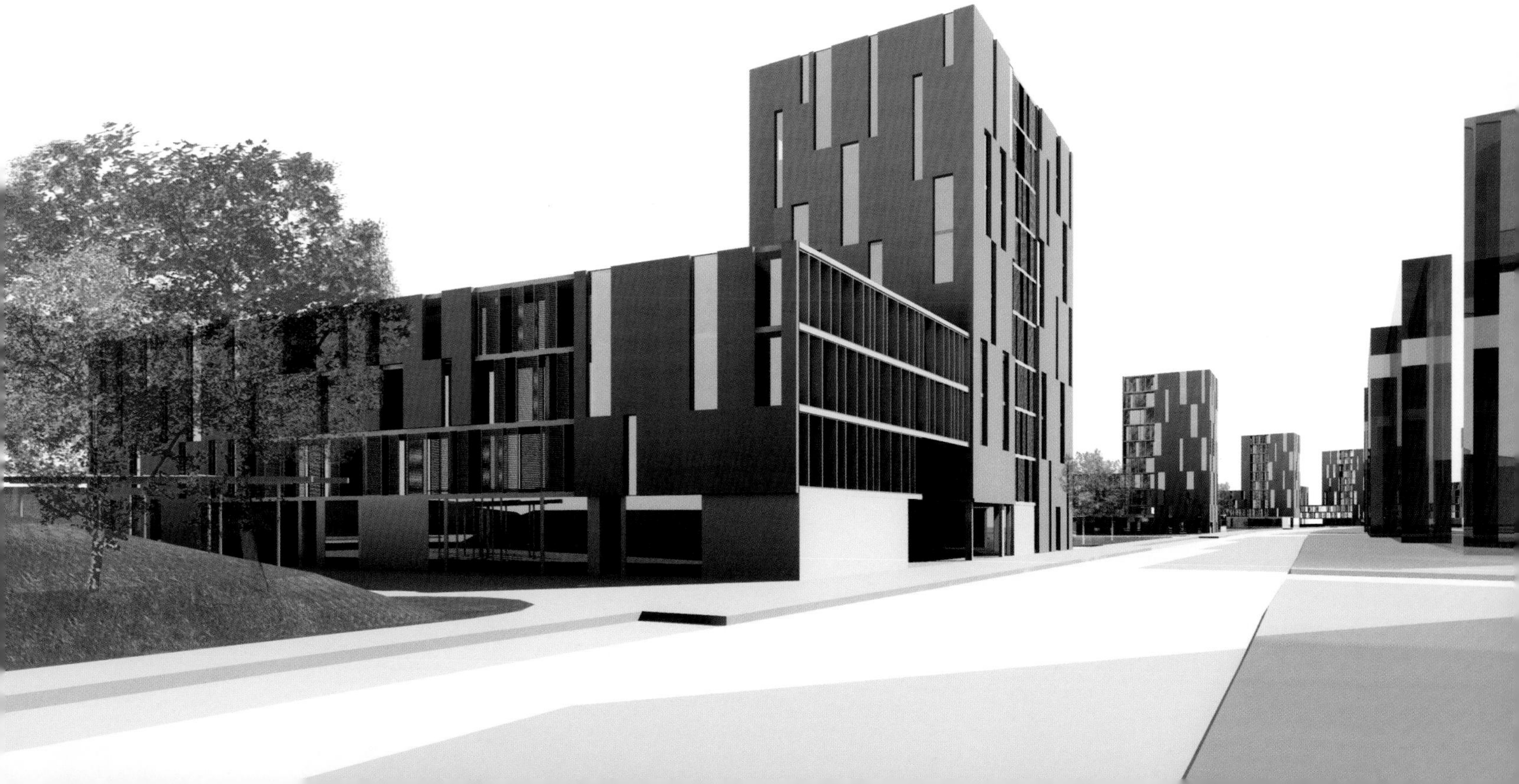

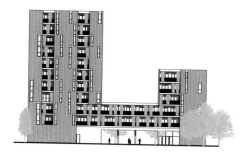

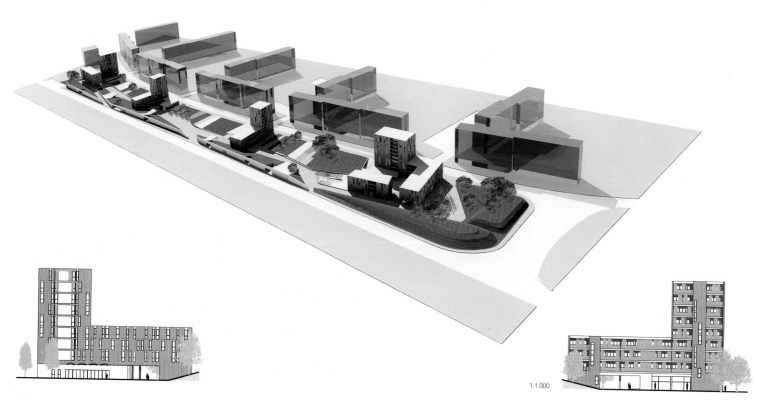

1:1.000

Sección longitudinal **Longitudinal section**

Plano de situación **Site plan** 🌢 1:1.000

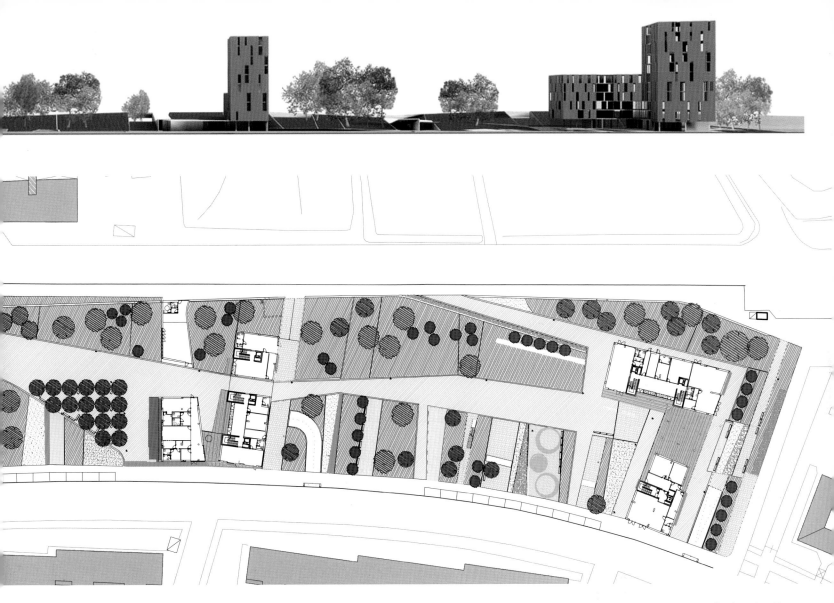

Tipo **A** Type

Tipo **T** Type

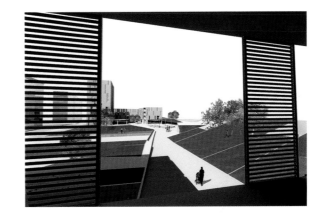

Tipo **B** Type

Tipo **D** Type   1:500

▬	TIPO **A** TYPE
▬	TIPO **B** TYPE
▬	TIPO **T** TYPE
▬	TIPO **D** TYPE

Tipos de vivienda **Dwelling Type**
ESTUDIOS: 5
1 DORMITORIO: 105
2 DORMITORIOS: 58
3 DORMITORIOS: 11
4+ DORMITORIOS: 5
STUDIOS: 5
1 BEDROOM: 105
2 BEDROOMS: 58
3 BEDROOMS: 11
4+ BEDROOMS: 5

Planta tipo **Typical floor plan** 1:5.000

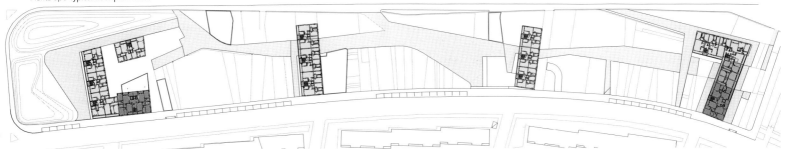

100 %
VIVIENDA   14
LIVING

TRABAJO
WORKING

COMERCIO
SHOPPING

EQUIPAMIENTOS
CIVIC FACILITIES

OTROS USOS
OTHER USES

16.133 m²
SUPERFICIE DE PARCELA
PLOT AREA

4.760 m²
SUPERFICIE CONSTRUIDA
BUILT UP AREA

15,9 %
OCUPACIÓN
COVERED AREA

0,3
EDIFICABILIDAD
FLOOR AREA RATIO

30 ☐/ha   118 ⊕/ha

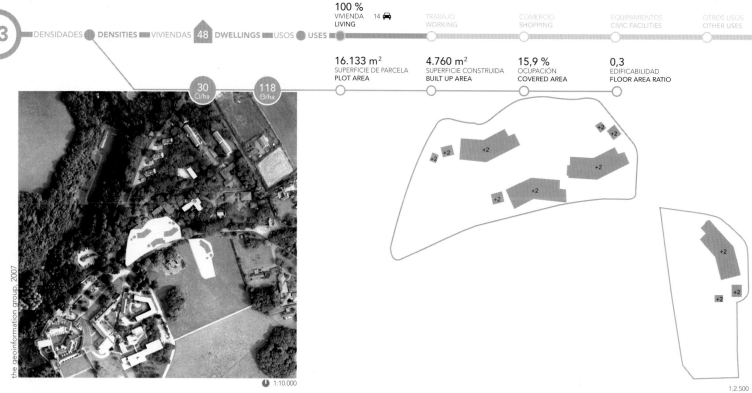

the geoinformation group, 2007

1:10.000

1:2.500

AOC theaoc.co.uk

Atlantic College, St Donat's Castle, Llantwit Major.
United Kingdom, 2004

Esta residencia de estudiantes se basa en la idea del castillo (el Atlantic College tiene su sede en un antiguo castillo) como comunidad fortificada, una estructura que define y encierra claramente una serie de espacios y usos. Cuatro familias de viviendas para estudiantes situadas en el paisaje definen una serie de jardines y praderas; se orientan respetando la posición de los árboles existentes y permiten obtener las mejores vistas. Cada uno de ellos tiene una fachada más cerrada hacia el exterior de la propiedad y otra más abierta hacia el jardín.

This students' dormitory takes the idea of the castle as a fortified village, and the form of the castle emblematic of Atlantic College - as a structure that clearly defines and encloses a recognisable flow of spaces and uses. We sited four families of student houses within the existing landscape to define an assortment of gardens and meadows. The new buildings are kinked to accommodate and embrace mature trees, and positioned so that each frames its own striking views. Each has a hard outward-facing facade, offering a tangible threshold, and a soft inner facade, overlooking the newly defined garden landscape.

En el interior de cada bloque se disponen las viviendas de dos plantas cada una a ambos lados de una calle interior, dispuestas en dos módulos articulados por un espacio interior común. En cada extremo de los bloques de vivienda para estudiantes se sitúan dos viviendas unifamiliares de mayor tamaño.

Los cuatro bloques comparten el mismo diseño y tipo de construcción, son baratos y fáciles de construir, al tiempo que su ubicación garantiza unas vistas y orientación únicas, asegurando así un carácter diferenciado.

Wrapped within each block are the student houses, arranged in two storey terraces either side of an internal street. These terraces articulate two wings, joined by the communal areas, which state a point of transition between them. At either end of each block lies the houseparent accommodation: a detached family house to one side, and a junior houseparent tower to the other. All four blocks share the same design and timber construction, ensuring they are economical and simple to build, whilst their strategic positioning guarantees unique views, orientation and consequently an individual character.

Planta de situación **Site plan** 🕛 1:2.000

Planta primera **First floor plan**

Planta baja **Ground floor plan**

Sección por el pasillo central
Section through central corridor 1:500

Tipos de viviendas **Dwelling types**

ESTUDIOS: 80
1 DORMITORIO: 0
2 DORMITORIOS: 4
3 DORMITORIOS: 0
4+ DORMITORIOS: 4
STUDIOS: 80
1 BEDROOM: 0
2 BEDROOMS: 4
3 BEDROOMS: 0
4+ BEDROOMS: 4

El bloque de dormitorio tradicional se transforma –la calle interior yuxtapone los espacios comunes y privados definidos– en una aldea en miniatura
The traditional dormitory block is transformed –the internal street juxtaposes defined communal and private spaces– its a mini village

1 of 40

1 of 4

Cada casa contribuye a tener tu propia puerta
DIY frontages to the internal street

| 24,5 %
VIVIENDA
LIVING | 21,2 %
TRABAJO
WORKING | 6,2 %
COMERCIOS
SHOPPING | EQUIPAMIENTOS
CIVIC FACILITIES | 48,1 %
APARCAMIENTO PÚBLICO
PARKING |

| 17.200 m²
SUPERFICIE DE PARCELA
PLOT AREA | 52.491 m²
SUPERFICIE CONSTRUIDA
BUILT UP AREA | 28 %
OCUPACIÓN
COVERED AREA | 1,4
EDIFICABILIDAD
FLOOR AREA RATIO |

57 Δ/ha   **139** ⊕/ha

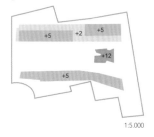

1:5.000

digitalglobe, 2007

1:10.000

MBM arquitectes mbmarquitectes.cat
MAB arquitectura mabarchitettura.com

Area Ex Boschi, Parma. Italy, 2006-

El proyecto que mostramos es la segunda fase de la remodelación del entorno de la Estación de Parma, cuya fase inicial corresponde al estudio MBM Arquitectes.

La reflexión sobre la ciudad contemporánea como lugar de convivencia de usos y actividades distintas nos ha llevado a la conclusión de que para crear un nuevo tramo de ciudad era necesario mezclar usos diferentes en los edificios. La planta baja acoge comercios, la primera, oficinas y desde la segunda hasta la cuarta hay vivienda. Los accesos a las diferentes actividades son independientes.

Esta complejidad de usos se refleja también en la imagen del proyecto. La planta baja es la planta pública, el lugar de las relaciones sociales y de las conexiones urbanas. La primera planta recupera el frente urbano a través de una galería continua de accesos a las oficinas. A partir de la segunda planta el cambio en la volumetría anuncia el cambio de uso a viviendas.

Un edificio se curva y se levanta, mientras que el otro se divide en dos núcleos distintos apoyando en la planta común de oficinas. La torre es el elemento focal de este conjunto urbano, alrededor de la cual los edificios se moldean y se alejan para encontrar un equilibrio.

The project shown is the second remodelling phase at the Parma Station. Its beginning phase corresponds to the MBM Arquitectes studio.

The reflection on the contemporary city as a place of coexistence of uses and different activities has brought us to the conclusion that in order to create a new stretch of city, combining different uses in buildings was necessary. The ground level houses businesses, the first floor offices, and on the second, third and fourth floors homes are located. The entries to different activities are independent.

This complexity of uses was also reflected in the project's image. The ground level is the public level, the area for social contact and urban connections. The first floor recovers the urban front through a continuous gallery of office entrances. The change in volumetrics beginning on the second floor announces the changing of use into homes.

One building curves and rises, while the other divides into two different nuclei supported by the common office level. The tower is the focal element in this urban setting; buildings adapt and step back to find balance.

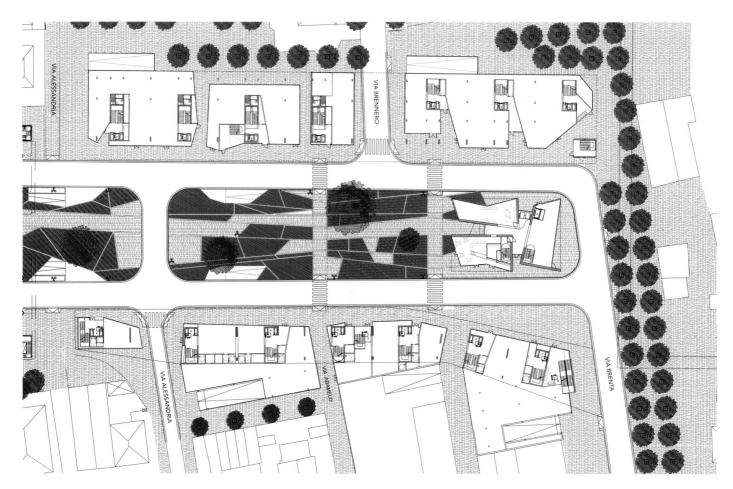

Planta baja (locales comerciales) **Ground floor plan** (shopping) ⬤ 1:1.000

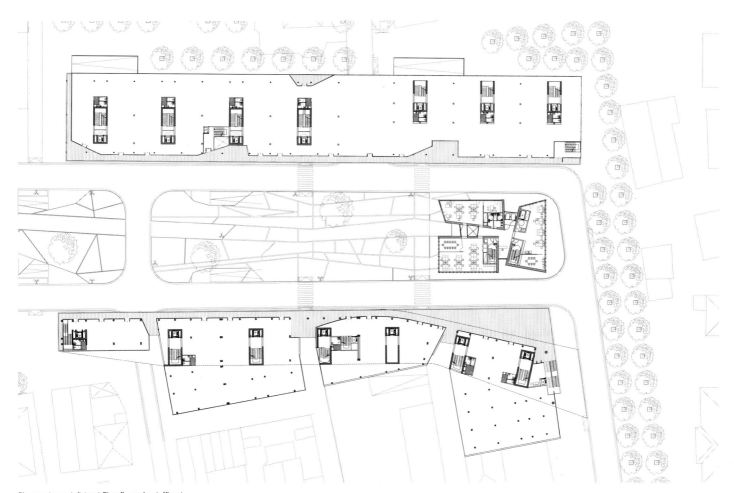

Planta primera (oficinas) **First floor plan (offices)**

Planta tipo (viviendas) **Typical floor plan (dwellings)** 1:1.000

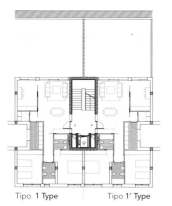

Tipo 1 Type   Tipo 1' Type

Tipo 2 Type

Tipo 3 Type   Tipo 3' Type

Tipo 4 Type   Tipo 4' Type

Tipo 5 Type   Tipo 6 Type

Tipos de viviendas
Dwellings types 1:500

ESTUDIOS: 0
1 DORMITORIO: 22
2 DORMITORIOS: 59
3 DORMITORIOS: 17
4+ DORMITORIOS: 0
STUDIOS: 0
1 BEDROOM: 22
2 BEDROOMS: 59
3 BEDROOMS: 17
4+ BEDROOMS: 0

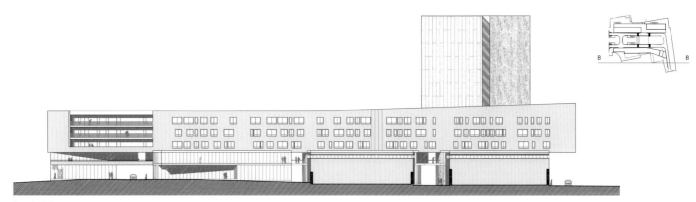

Sección **B Section**

Sección **C Section** 1:1.000

Sección **A Section** 1:1.000

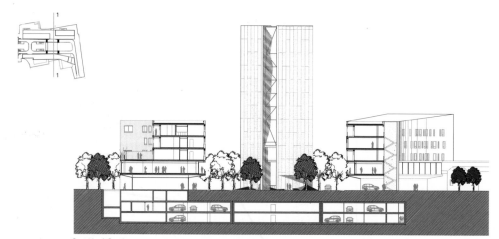

Sección **1 Section**

Plantas de la torre de oficinas
Office tower floor plan 1:500

95,8 %
VIVIENDA 494 🚗
LIVING

TRABAJO
WORKING

4,2 %
COMERCIOS
SHOPPING

EQUIPAMIENTOS
CIVIC FACILITIES

OTROS USOS
OTHER USES

67.237 m²
SUPERFICIE DE PARCELA
PLOT AREA

47.430 m²
SUPERFICIE CONSTRUIDA
BUILT UP AREA

25 %
OCUPACIÓN
COVERED AREA

0,7
EDIFICABILIDAD
FLOOR AREA RATIO

57 △/ha   156 ⊖/ha

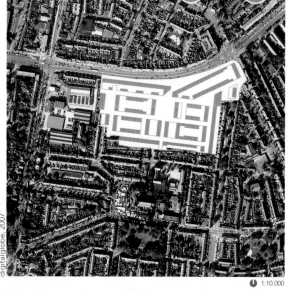

digitalglobe, 2007

🕐 1:10.000

FÜNDC fundc.com

Bloemenbuurt-Zuid, Eindhoven. The Netherlands, 2004-

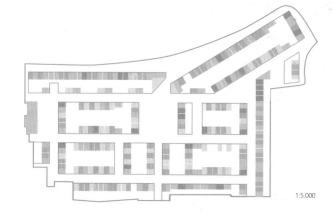

1:5.000

El barrio de Bloemenbuurt Zuid, en Eindhoven, ha quedado obsoleto y será demolido muy pronto. El tejido construido se encuentra en muy mal estado de conservación y las tipologías de vivienda no se ajustan a los distintos tamaños de las familias actuales. El carácter industrial de la ciudad de hoy ha de permitir la integración de su pasado agrícola.

Durante la elaboración del proyecto se hicieron varios encuentros con los habitantes de la zona, quienes podrán permanecer en ella, si lo desean, después de la renovación del barrio.

La máxima de "cada vivienda con su propio jardín" ha sido aceptada por el ayuntamiento y los habitantes. Para lograrlo, se plantea una nueva tipología de vivienda con jardines en altura que responde a la necesidad de aumentar el número de viviendas pero que duplica la cantidad de espacio libre público.

A whole neighbourhood of Eindhoven, Bloemenbuurt Zuid, is obsolete and going to be demolished: the built tissue is in poor conservation state and the housing typologies are not fitting today's dissimilar family sizes needs.

The industrial essence of the city must blend with its agricultural past. Several gatherings were conducted to explore the desires of the existing inhabitants which can keep living in the renewed neighbourhood, if they wish.

The motto "every house with a garden" has been accepted by municipality and inhabitants. But the only way of integrating program, plot size and the private garden common wish is to propose a new housing typology with elevated gardens which would allow for an increment in the amount of dwellings while doubling the open space.

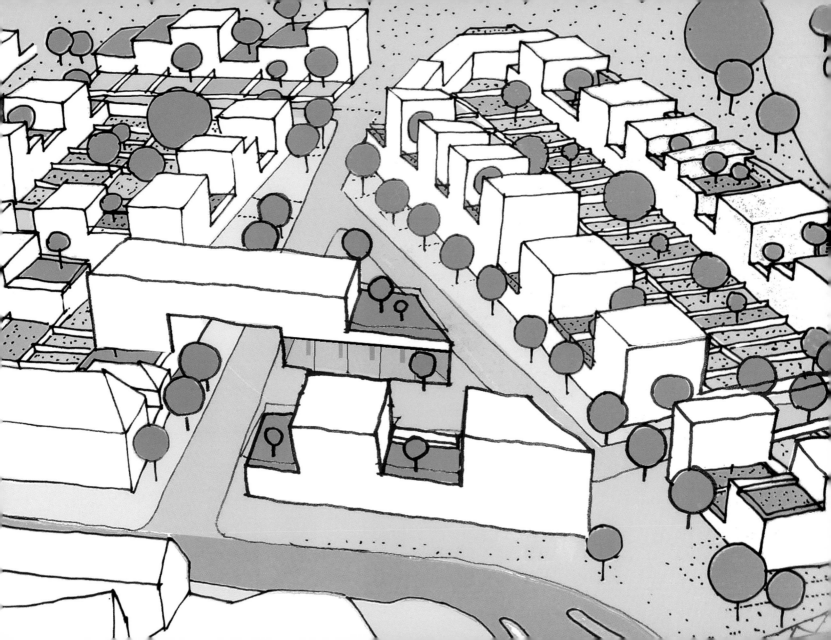

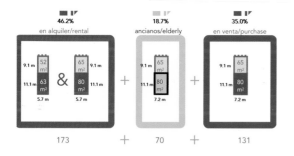

46.2%
en alquiler/rental

18.7%
ancianos/elderly

35.0%
en venta/purchase

| 52 m² | & | 65 m² | | 65 m² | | 65 m² |
| 63 m² | | 80 m² | | 80 m² | | 80 m² |

9.1 m   9.1 m   9.1 m   9.1 m
11.1 m   11.1 m   11.1 m   11.1 m
5.7 m   5.7 m   7.2 m   7.2 m

173   +   70   +   131

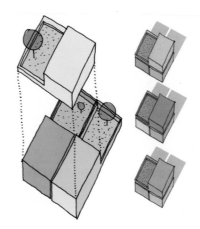

Tipología **Typology**

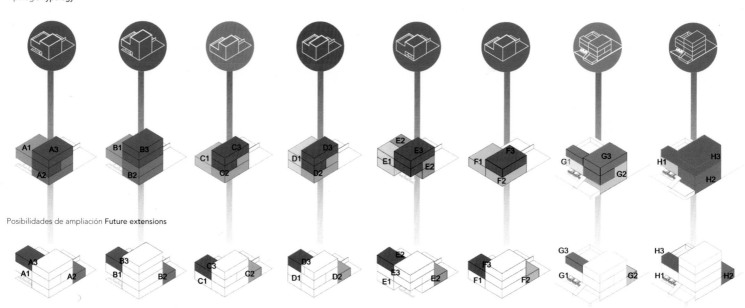

Posibilidades de ampliación **Future extensions**

Planta baja **Ground floor plan** ⬇ 1:2.500

Planta primera **First floor plan** 1:2.500

Sección **A Section** 1:1.000

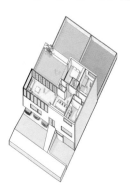

Tipo B Type

Tipo G Type

Planta baja **Ground floor plan**

Planta primera **First floor plan**

Planta segunda **Second floor plan**

Alzado a la calle **Street elevation**

Planta tercera **Third floor plan**

Alzado al jardín **Garden elevation**

Alzado lateral **Side elevation**

Tipo **G Type**

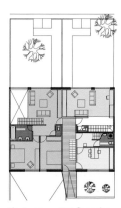

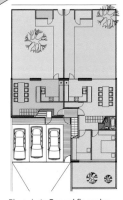

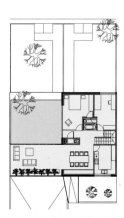

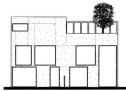

Alzado al jardín **Garden elevation**

Alzado a la calle **Street elevation** 1:500

Planta baja **Ground floor plan**

Planta primera **First floor plan**

Planta segunda **Second floor plan**

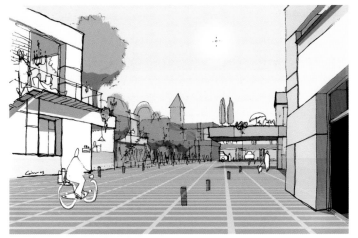

Vistas del eje norte-sur **North-South axis view**

Tipo **C Type**

Tipos de viviendas Dwelling types
ESTUDIOS: 0
1 DORMITORIO: 32
2 DORMITORIOS: 254
3 DORMITORIOS: 76
4+ DORMITORIOS: 18
STUDIOS: 0
1 BEDROOM: 32
2 BEDROOMS: 254
3 BEDROOMS: 76
4+ BEDROOMS: 18

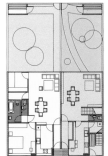

Planta baja **Ground floor plan**

Alzado a la calle **Street elevation**

Alzado al jardín **Garden elevation**

Alzado lateral **Side elevation** 1:500

Planta primera **First floor plan**

Planta segunda Variante 1
Second floor plan **Type 1**

P2 Variante 2
Type 2

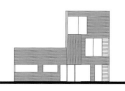

P2 Variante 3
Type 3

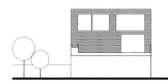

100% VIVIENDA LIVING	97 🚗	TRABAJO WORKING	COMERCIOS SHOPPING	EQUIPAMIENTOS CIVIC FACILITIES	OTROS USOS OTHER USES

31.740 m²	16.540 m²	17,2 %	0,5
SUPERFICIE DE PARCELA PLOT AREA	SUPERFICIE CONSTRUIDA BUILT UP AREA	OCUPACIÓN COVERED AREA	EDIFICABILIDAD FLOOR AREA RATIO

57 ⌂/ha   171 ⊙/ha

the geoinformation group, 2007

1:10.000

1:2.500

Riches Hawley Mikhail Architects

rhmarchitects.com

Kingsland Close, Houghton Regis. United Kingdom, 2006-

El proyecto consta de 180 viviendas a las afueras de Luton, una ciudad dormitorio de Londres. El proyecto requería, dentro de un esquema de alta densidad, apartamentos que fuesen tan atractivos para las familias como una vivienda unifamiliar.

A partir de los ejemplos escandinavos de áreas comunes, el proyecto proporciona jardines compartidos que son el centro de la comunidad. En estos espacios puede haber barbacoas, mesas de picnic o huertos fácilmente accesibles desde las viviendas, desde las que se tiene un control de las actividades o de los juegos de los niños.

The project consists of 180 residential units in a run-down suburb of the satellite town of Luton. The brief asks how flats could be as desirable as houses for families in a high-density suburban scheme.

Referencing Scandinavian models of shared communal space, the project proposes two private shared gardens that form the centre of the new community. In these spaces there could be barbeques, sheltered picnic tables and areas for growing vegetables, all directly accessed from your home.

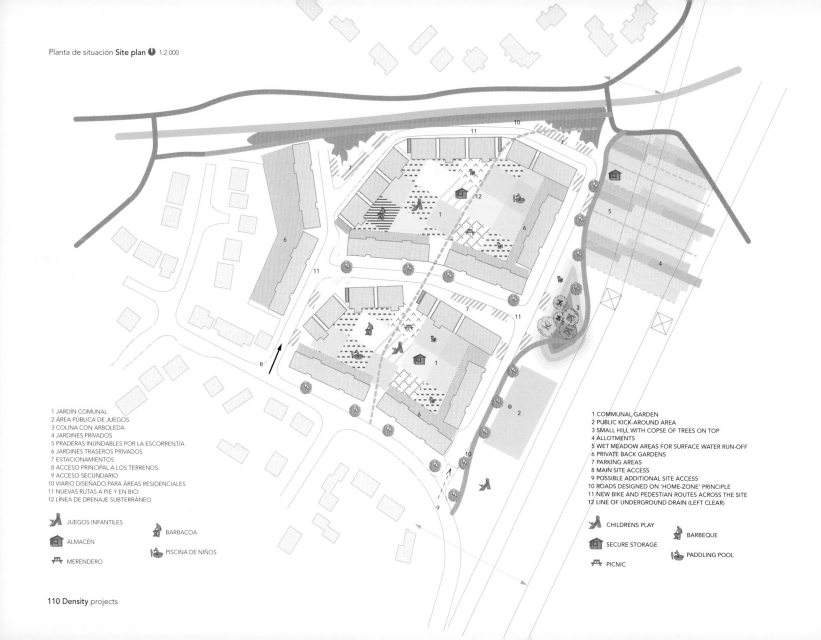

Planta de situación **Site plan** 🔄 1:2.000

1 JARDÍN COMUNAL
2 ÁREA PÚBLICA DE JUEGOS
3 COLINA CON ARBOLEDA
4 JARDINES PRIVADOS
5 PRADERAS INUNDABLES POR LA ESCORRENTÍA
6 JARDINES TRASEROS PRIVADOS
7 ESTACIONAMIENTOS
8 ACCESO PRINCIPAL A LOS TERRENOS
9 ACCESO SECUNDARIO
10 VIARIO DISEÑADO PARA ÁREAS RESIDENCIALES
11 NUEVAS RUTAS A PIE Y EN BICI
12 LÍNEA DE DRENAJE SUBTERRÁNEO

JUEGOS INFANTILES

ALMACÉN

MERENDERO

BARBACOA

PISCINA DE NIÑOS

1 COMMUNAL GARDEN
2 PUBLIC KICK-AROUND AREA
3 SMALL HILL WITH COPSE OF TREES ON TOP
4 ALLOTMENTS
5 WET MEADOW AREAS FOR SURFACE WATER RUN-OFF
6 PRIVATE BACK GARDENS
7 PARKING AREAS
8 MAIN SITE ACCESS
9 POSSIBLE ADDITIONAL SITE ACCESS
10 ROADS DESIGNED ON 'HOME-ZONE' PRINCIPLE
11 NEW BIKE AND PEDESTIAN ROUTES ACROSS THE SITE
12 LINE OF UNDERGROUND DRAIN (LEFT CLEAR)

CHILDRENS PLAY

SECURE STORAGE

PICNIC

BARBEQUE

PADDLING POOL

La concertación con los usuarios y la colaboración del artista Nils Norman determinó tanto el diseño como los contenidos y la gestión del jardín común. Las tipologías propuestas son viviendas unifamiliares adosadas de madera, con jardín privado o bien apartamentos con grandes terrazas orientadas al sur y con vistas al jardín comunitario. El sistema de paneles prefabricados de madera permitirá construir a gran velocidad, y se logrará maximizar las ganancias solares optimizando el aislamiento de las viviendas. Las calles que rodean al conjunto son fáciles de recorrer y de contemplar desde los balcones. Están entendidas como espacios para ser ocupados y conducen hasta un parque público y una red de pistas para bicicletas que unen los espacios verdes circundantes.

Overlooking gives a benign surveillance, children can play in safety. An active consultation process with residents and the artist Nils Norman would evolve the design, content and long term support of the communal garden. The dwellings are a mix of timber clad terraced houses with their own gardens, and flats with large balconies, that all face south across the shared space. Prefabricated timber panel systems speed up construction. Solar gain is maximised and houses highly insulated. The streets that bound the gardens are easily understood and navigated. Overlooked by terraces and balconies they are designed for occupation not purely access. They lead through to a public park and cycle tracks linking together surrounding green spaces.

Planta baja **Ground floor plan**

Planta primera **First floor plan**

Sección **A Section** 1:500

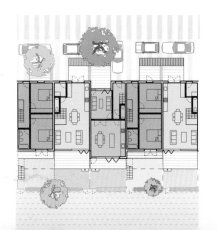

Planta baja **Ground floor plan**

Planta primera **First floor plan**

Planta segunda **Second floor plan**

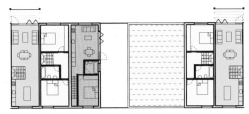

Planta tercera **Third floor plan** 1:500

Planta segunda **Second floor plan** 1:500

Tipos de vivienda **Dwelling types**

ESTUDIOS: 0
1 DORMITORIO: 22
2 DORMITORIOS: 80
3 DORMITORIOS: 61
4+ DORMITORIOS: 17
STUDIOS: 0
1 BEDROOM: 22
2 BEDROOMS: 80
3 BEDROOMS: 61
4+ BEDROOMS: 17

APARTAMENTO DE 2 DORMITORIOS
2 BEDROOM FLAT

APARTAMENTO DE 3 DORMITORIOS
3 BEDROOM FLAT

ÁTICO DE 2 DORMITORIOS
2 BEDROOM MAISONETTE

ÁTICO DE 2 DORMITORIOS
2 BEDROOM MAISONETTE

APARTAMENTO DE 1 DORMITORIO
1 BEDROOM FLAT

VIVIENDA PROTEGIDA
SUPPORTED DWELLING

CASA DE 3 DORMITORIOS
3 BEDROOM HOUSE

CASA DE 3 DORMITORIOS
3 BEDROOM HOUSE

4 BEDROOM HOUSE
CASA DE 4 HABITACIONES

APARTAMENTO DE 2 DORMITORIOS
2 BEDROOM FLAT

APARTAMENTO DE 2 DORMITORIOS
2 BEDROOM FLAT

APARTAMENTO DE 2 DORMITORIOS
2 BEDROOM FLAT

P3

P2

P1

P0

1:5.000

Density projects 113

95,2 %
VIVIENDA   200
LIVING

TRABAJO
WORKING

4,8 %
COMERCIOS
SHOPPING

EQUIPAMIENTOS
CIVIC FACILITIES

OTROS USOS
OTHER USES

18.000 m²
SUPERFICIE DE PARCELA
PLOT AREA

10.500 m²
SUPERFICIE CONSTRUIDA
BUILT UP AREA

58,3 %
OCUPACIÓN
COVERED AREA

0,58
EDIFICABILIDAD
FLOOR AREA RATIO

56 Δ/ha   176 ⊕/ha

scankort, 2007

1:10.000

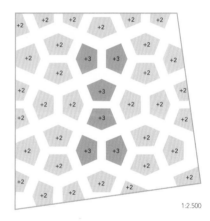

1:2.500

BIG big.dk

Holbæk Harbour, Holbaek. Denmark, 2006-2010

¿Se pueden combinar las ventajas que proporciona la gran escala de un frente marítimo con la intimidad que requiere la escala humana?

Para conseguirlo, nuestro proyecto propone una *kasbah* elevada sobre una colina artificial que aloja el aparcamiento, procurando a cada vivienda de vistas al mar. Los volúmenes construidos se articulan de tal manera que dan lugar a un laberinto de pequeños espacios abiertos y comunes para el juego y la interacción social entre vecinos.

How can you combine the large scale qualities of an urban waterfront with the intimacy of the human scale?

To do so, our project consists of a dense *kasbah* of interlocking geometric forms that twists and turns to differentiate the site into spaces for living and play is raised on a slow hill of parking to provide each apartment with a panoramic view of the sea. The twisted and turned placing on the site creates a labyrinth of small, open spaces and hiding places for life, play and socialising between the houses.

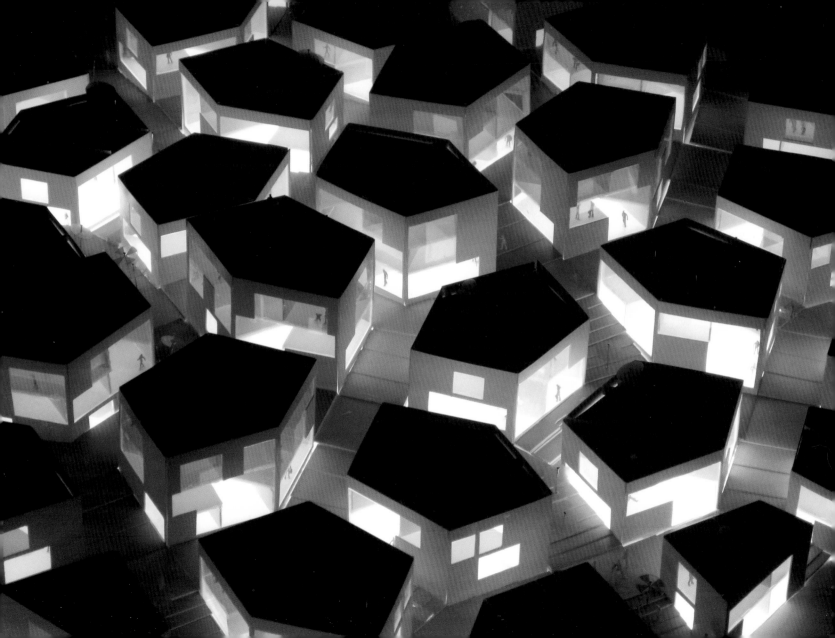

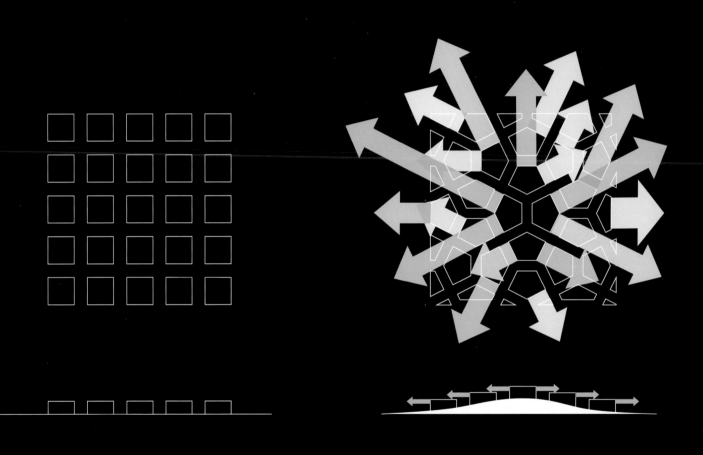

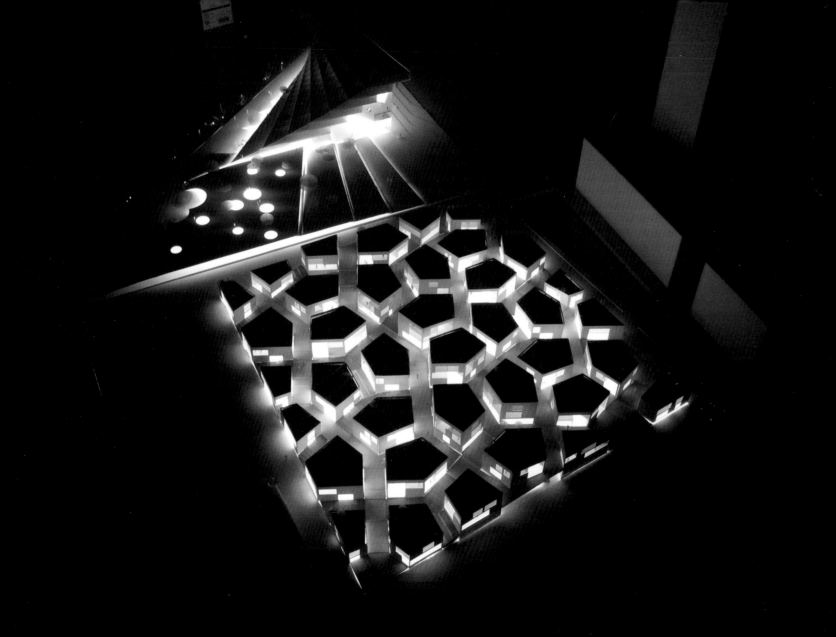

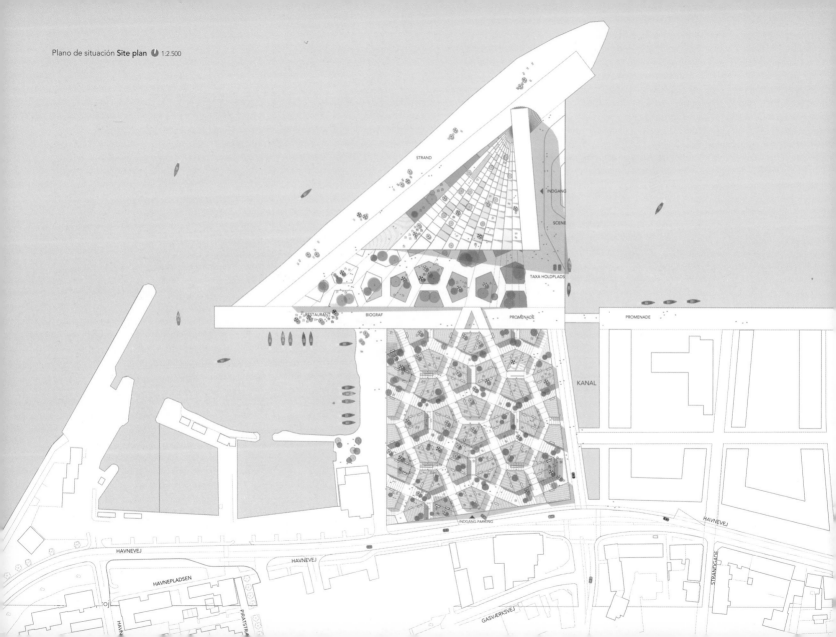

Plano de situación **Site plan** 1:2.500

STRAND

INDGANG

SCENE

TAXA HOLDPLADS

RESTAURANT   BIOGRAF   PROMENADE   PROMENADE

KANAL

INDGANG PARKING   HAVNEVEJ

HAVNEVEJ

HAVNEVEJ

HAVNEPLADSEN

STRANDGADE

PIRATSTRÆ

GASVÆRKSVEJ

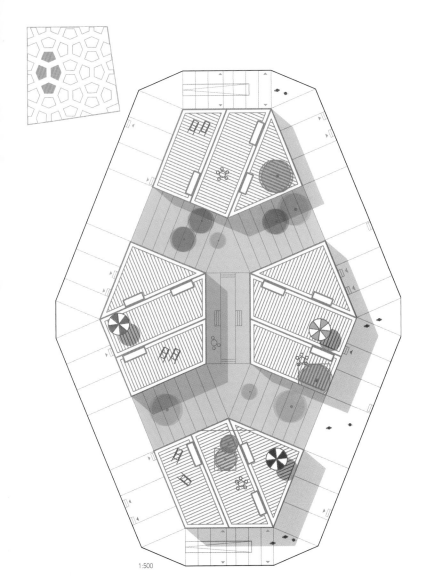

1:500

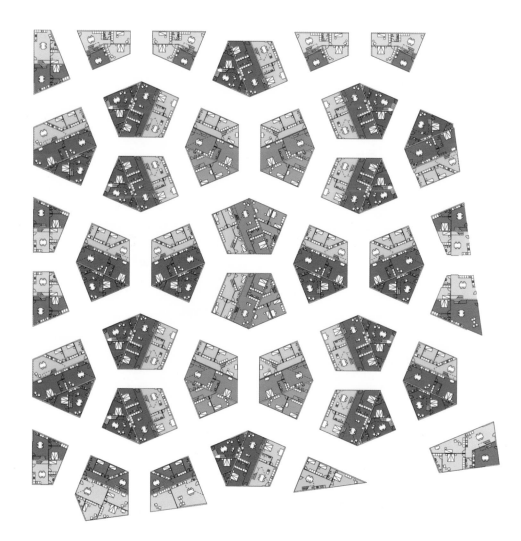

Planta primera **First floor plan** 1:1.000

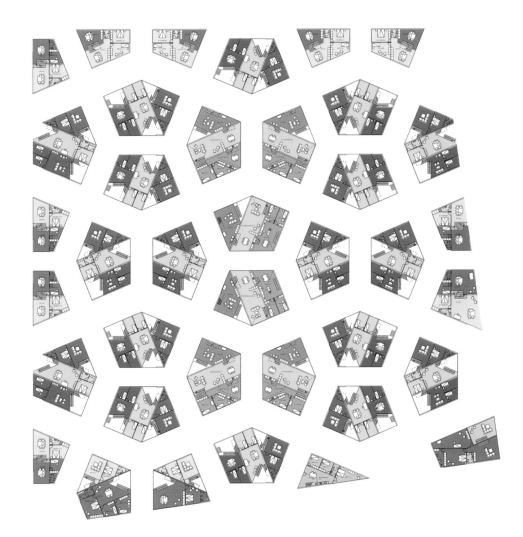

Planta segunda **Second floor plan**

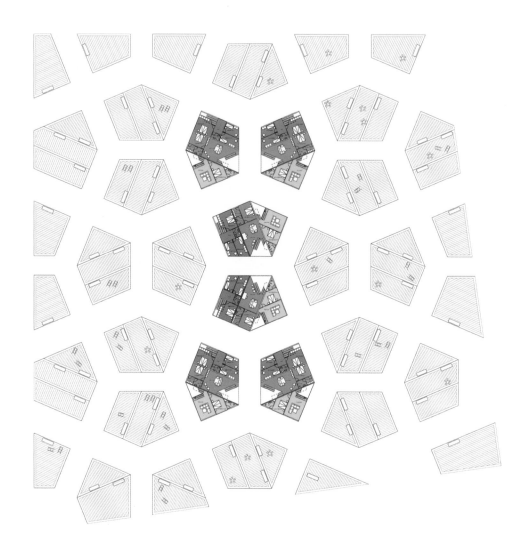

Planta tercera **Third floor plan** 1:1.000

 + + =

Tipos de viviendas **Dwelling types** 1:500

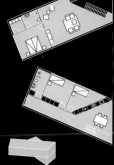

Tipo **A1** Type

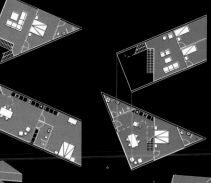

Tipo **A2** Type

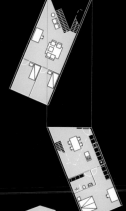

Tipo **A3** Type

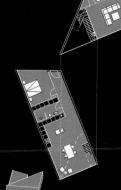

Tipo **B1** Type

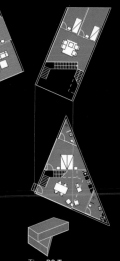

Tipo **B2** Type

Tipo **B3** Type

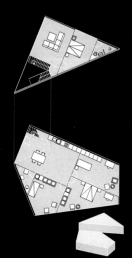

Tipo **E1** Type

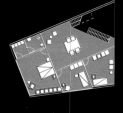
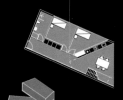

Tipo **E2** Type

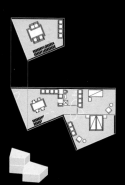

Tipo **F1** Type

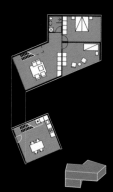

Tipo **F2** Type

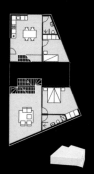

Tipo **G1** Type

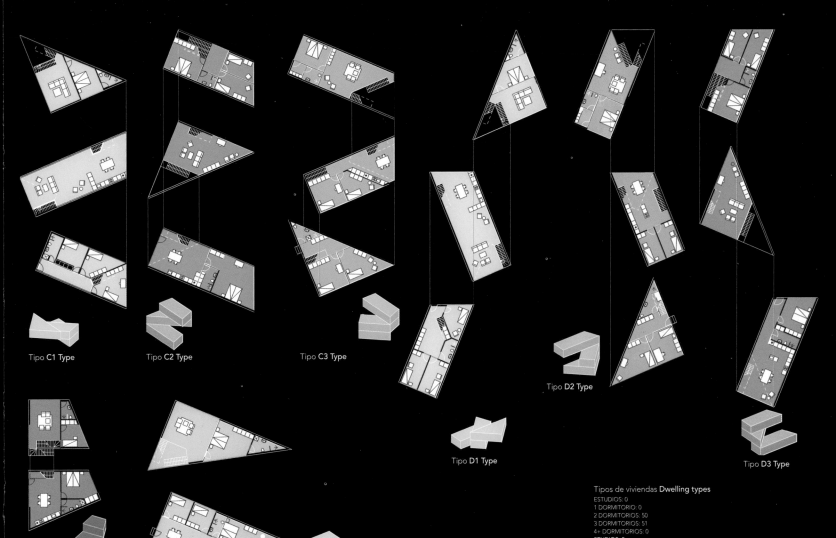

Tipo **C1** Type

Tipo **C2** Type

Tipo **C3** Type

Tipo **D1** Type

Tipo **D2** Type

Tipo **D3** Type

Tipo **G2** Type

Tipo **H** Type

Tipos de viviendas **Dwelling types**
ESTUDIOS: 0
1 DORMITORIO: 0
2 DORMITORIOS: 50
3 DORMITORIOS: 51
4+ DORMITORIOS: 0
STUDIOS: 0
1 BEDROOM: 0
2 BEDROOMS: 50
3 BEDROOMS: 51
4+ BEDROOMS: 0

40 %*
VIVIENDA
LIVING

TRABAJO
WORKING

COMERCIOS
SHOPPING

60 %*   APARCAMIENTO DE AUTOBUSES EXISTENTE
EXISTING BUS PARKING

17.625 m²
SUPERFICIE DE PARCELA
PLOT AREA

+10.880* m²
SUPERFICIE CONSTRUIDA*
BUILT UP AREA

96,4 %
OCUPACIÓN
COVERED AREA

+0,6*
EDIFICABILIDAD
FLOOR AREA RATIO

*La superficie contruida se añade a la edificación existente
The built up area is added to the exisitng building

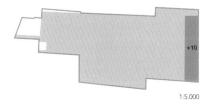

1:5.000

the geoinformation group/interatlas, 2007

1:10.000

Eric Lapierre Architecture

Rue de la Tombe-Issoire, Paris. France, 2007-2010

La nueva residencia de estudiantes se levanta sobre el aparcamiento existente de los autobuses públicos de París e incluye 350 habitaciones individuales. El emplazamiento está muy próximo a la Ciudad Universitaria de París, donde Le Corbusier construyó los pabellones de Suiza y Brasil, y en frente del pabellón holandés de Willem Dudok. La estructura es de acero y el edificio está prefabricado. Se trata de una composición sencilla, una retícula de módulos de habitaciones de la que se extraen algunos para obtener espacios que alojan las zonas comunes y las circulaciones. En el lado de la calle, el vacío que se obtiene da lugar a un gran espacio piranesiano en diagonal, que conecta el acceso con el principal espacio colectivo en cubierta y por el que discurre un funicular y una gran escalera.

En el lado más privado, el gran hueco está modelado para dar lugar a terrazas que acogen los usos comunitarios. Como tales espacios colectivos, se relacionan con la vida urbana de la avenida cercana, mientras que las habitaciones se dedican al estudio y el reposo. De ellas, el 25% disponen de doble exposición por el pasillo. Todas disponen de vistas al exterior a través de la fachada de vidrio y de un balcón privado: el parque Montsouris al este y los tejados de París al oeste.

The student's dormitory is built above an existing parking for parisian public buses. It houses 350 students in individual flats. The site is close to Cité Universitaire, where Le Corbusier built Swiss and Brasilian Pavilions, and faces the Willem Dudok's 1929 Dutch Pavilion. The building is made of steel and totally prefabricated. It is a linear structure filled with individual flats from which we have removed some to create voids dedicated to collective life and movement. On the street side, void creates a huge piranesian diagonal which connects entrance on the ground floor to main collective space on the roof, through stairs and funicular.

On the private side void is shaped as series of terraces for collective uses. As collective spaces are dedicated to movement and connected to urban energy of the close boulevard, flats are dedicated to concentration and quietness: 25 per cent of them have double exposure through a gangway. All of them look to open space through a glazed facade and a private balcony: the Parc Montsouris to the east, and the parisian roof landscape to the west.

Intervención artística en fachada **Art intervention on the facade**

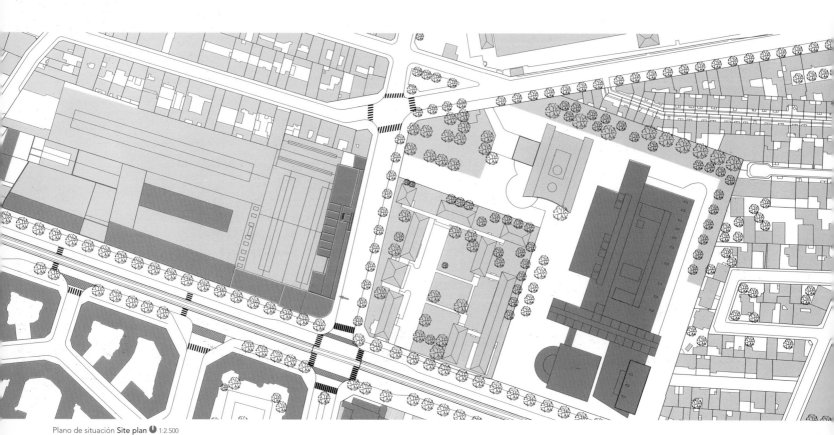

Plano de situación **Site plan** ◑ 1:2.500

Vista de la fachada norte desde la rue de la Tombe-Issorie
View of the North facade from rue de la Tombe-Issoire

Alzado norte **North elevation**

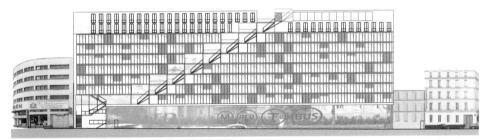

Alzado este **East elevation**

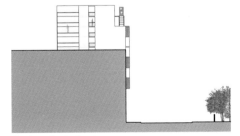

Alzado sur **South elevation**

Alzado oeste **West elevation** 1:1.000

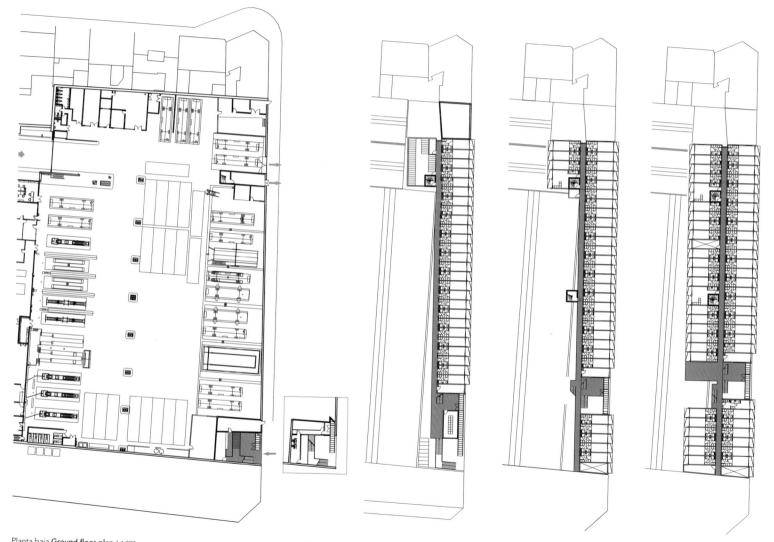

Planta baja **Ground floor plan** 1:1.000

Entreplanta **Mezzanine plan**　　　Planta primera **First floor plan**　　　Planta segunda **Second floor plan**　　　Planta tercera **Third floor plan**

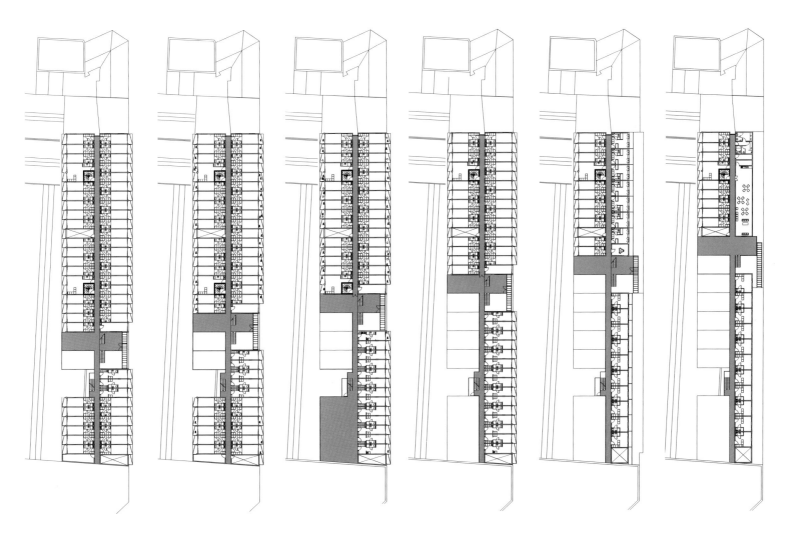

Planta cuarta **Fourth floor plan**   Planta quinta **Fifth floor plan**   Planta sexta **Sixth floor plan**   Planta séptima **Seventh floor plan**   Planta optava **Eighth floor plan**   Planta novena **Ninth floor plan**

Planta tipo (planta sexta) **Typical foor plan (sixth floor plan)**

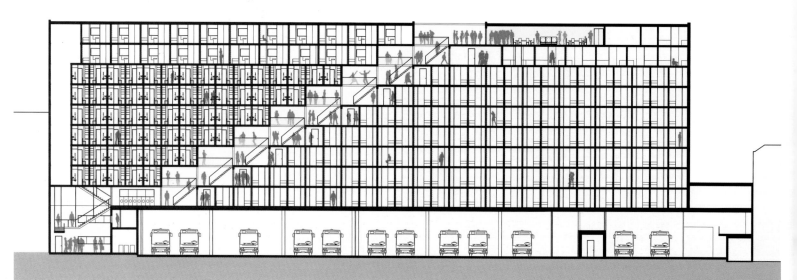

Sección longitudinal **A long section** 1:500

Habitación no pasante
Single exposition room

Habitación pasante
Double exposition room

Habitación doble
Double room

Habitación para discapacitado
Disable room

Habitación en ático
Penthouse room 1:500

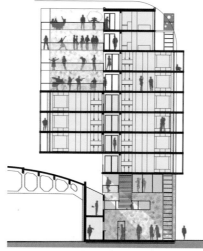

Sección transversal **B cross section** 1:500

Habitación pasante
Double exposition room

97,8 %
VIVIENDA 66 🚗
LIVING

TRABAJO
WORKING

COMERCIOS
SHOPPING

2,2 %
GUARDERÍA
NURSERY

OTROS USOS
OTHER USES

5.518 m²
SUPERFICIE DE PARCELA
PLOT AREA

4.620 m²
SUPERFICIE CONSTRUIDA
BUILT UP AREA

65 %
OCUPACIÓN
COVERED AREA

0,8
EDIFICABILIDAD
FLOOR AREA RATIO

54
⌂/ha

211
☺/ha

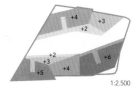

1:2.500

digitalglobe, 2007

🌐 1:10.000

Cino Zucchi Architetti zucchiarchitetti.com

Via Vigano/Via Rosales, Milan. Italy, 2006-2010

El edificio propuesto interpreta la normativa del plan haciendo hincapié en la integración de la nueva secuencia de edificios y espacios públicos con la estructura de la ciudad existente, en la búsqueda de la calidad urbana y la creación de un complejo residencial de gran calidad medioambiental. La disposición de los edificios y su perfil aterrazado buscan la orientación solar más favorable, así como las vistas hacia las zonas comunes. El proyecto reafirma la huella histórica de la manzana tradicional en que se ubica, al tiempo que se adapta a las necesidades de la vivienda contemporánea. Por su parte, la composición de las fachadas exteriores de los bloques genera una textura urbana muy rica donde la relación entre el suelo y el cielo determina las diferentes soluciones de vivienda, respetando la pluralidad de los espacios exteriores privados. Asimismo, el diseño del patio de manzana común recoge la tradición histórica de los patios interiores milaneses.

El cuidadoso estudio de las dimensiones, distribución, estructura e instalaciones técnicas genera la gran flexibilidad y calidad de las viviendas, cuya distribución puede variar enormemente a lo largo del tiempo.

La elección de los materiales y los detalles constructivos sirve para evidenciar la especial atención que se ha puesto en el confort y en el respeto a criterios de sostenibilidad.

The proposed building layout interprets the master plan guidelines maximizing the positive interaction between the existing structure of the city, the new sequence of buildings and public spaces, the pursuit of urban quality and the creation of a residential complex of high environmental quality. The disposition of the building masses and the inner terraced profile follow the path of the sun and the views from and toward the collective amenities.

The confirmation of the historical imprint of the perimeter block is enriched by new features, creating a contemporary environment which conjugates the resources of inner city living with the spatial needs of contemporary lifestyles.

The articulation of the outer fronts generate a rich urban texture, where the relationship with the ground and the sky orientates a series of living solutions watching a plurality of private outdoor spaces. The design of the inner common garden treasures Milan's deeply rooted historical tradition of the inner courtyard.

A careful study on dimensions, distribution, structure and technical installations generates the very high flexibility and living quality of the apartments, whose partition can strongly vary over time.

The choice of materials and construction details remarks the high attention for comfort and environmental sustainability criteria.

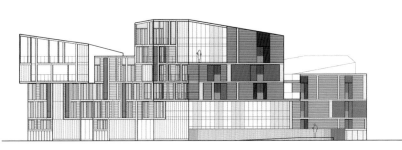

Alzado norte **North elevation** —————————

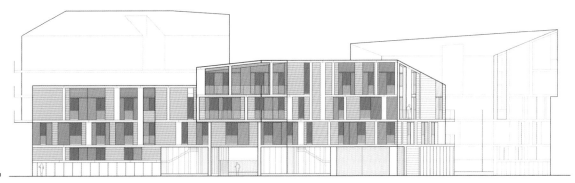

Alzado oeste **West elevation** —————————

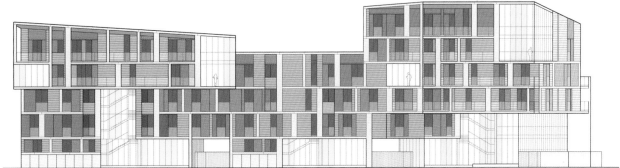

Alzado este **East elevation** 1:500 —————————

Planta baja **Ground floor plan** ⬇ 1:500

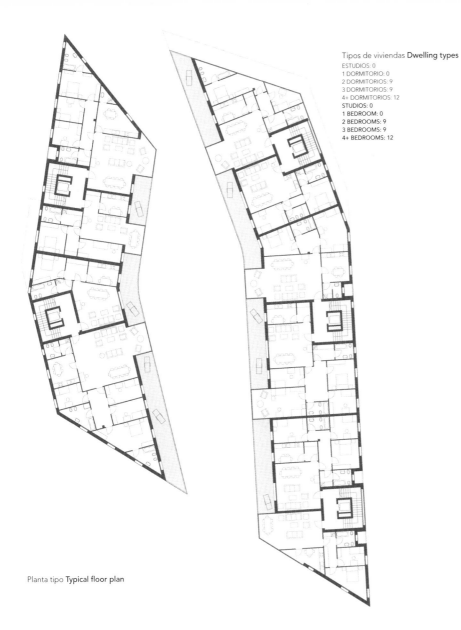

Planta tipo **Typical floor plan**

Tipos de viviendas **Dwelling types**
ESTUDIOS: 0
1 DORMITORIO: 0
2 DORMITORIOS: 9
3 DORMITORIOS: 9
4+ DORMITORIOS: 12
STUDIOS: 0
1 BEDROOM: 0
2 BEDROOMS: 9
3 BEDROOMS: 9
4+ BEDROOMS: 12

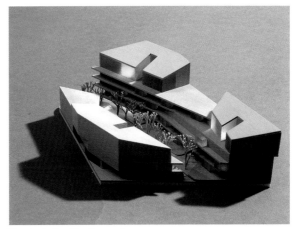

Vista desde el sur **View from south**

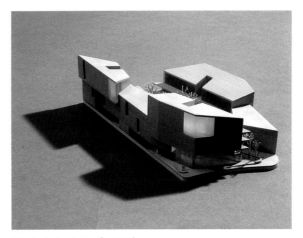

Vista desde el norte **View from north**

62,2 %
VIVIENDA 254 🚗
LIVING

29,6 %
COMERCIOS
SHOPPING

8,2 %
HOTEL
HOTEL

TRABAJO
WORKING

EQUIPAMIENTOS
CIVIC FACILITIES

47.000 m²
SUPERFICIE DE PARCELA
PLOT AREA

50.097 m²
SUPERFICIE CONSTRUIDA
BUILT UP AREA

31 %
OCUPACIÓN
COVERED AREA

1,1
EDIFICABILIDAD
FLOOR AREA RATIO

72 ⌂/ha   213 ⊖/ha

bluesky, 2007

⊙ 1:10.000

Witherford Watson Mann Architects

marchitects.co.uk

Ailsa Street, London. United Kingdom, 2005-

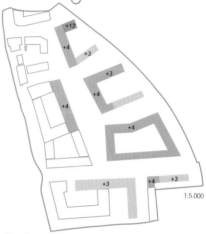

1:5.000

Ailsa Street ocupa unas 4,7 hectáreas al Este de Londres, en una zona conocida como Lea Valley, que quedó aislada de los barrios vecinos cuando se construyó la autopista A12 en los años 60. Al quedar incomunicada, el área se fue ocupando por vertederos de chatarra y otros residuos.

En este contexto, las autoridades de Londres encargaron a Witherford Watson Mann la redacción de un proyecto para el desarrollo de la zona apoyado en la normativa CPO, una herramienta en manos de las autoridades locales que les permite hacerse con terrenos privados para lograr transformaciones económicas y sociales. Los objetivos del proyecto son: retener e intensificar los usos comerciales en la zona, construir viviendas para familias con espacio libre privado en la mayoría de ellas, dotar al área de equipamientos a escala local, promover el transporte público y conexiones a nivel local.

Ailsa Street is a 4.7 hectare site in the lower Lea Valley in East London that became isolated from Poplar when the A12 road was created in the 1960's. Once cut off from the surrounding urban fabric, the site has become increasingly treated as a *back*, occupied by scrap dealers, refuse recycling and fly tippers. The London Development Agency commissioned Witherford Watson Mann to produce a development framework to support a CPO procedure that would see the long term comprehensive redevelopment of the entire site with the aims of: retaining and intensifying the commercial use of the site; creating residential development with the provision of a significant proportion of family accommodation, with private external space for the majority of units; making provision of local amenity space; making a contribution to public transport and local movement infrastructure links.

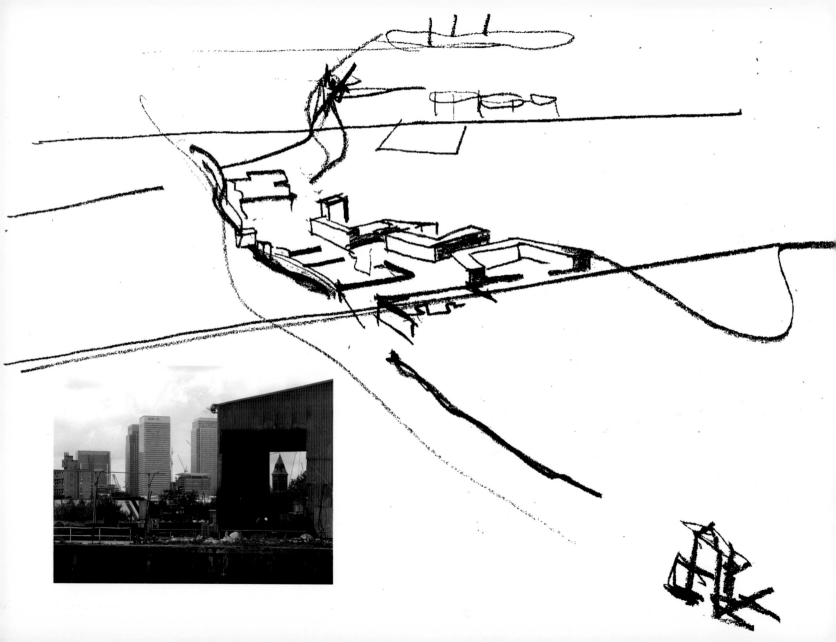

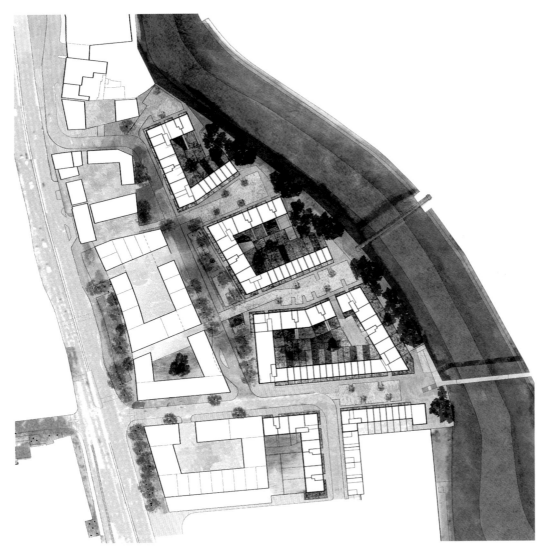

Planta de situación **Site plan** 🔽 1:2.500

Planta segunda **Second floor plan** 1:1.000

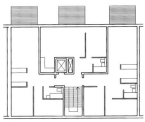

Plantas segunda y tercera
Second and third floor plan

Tipos de viviendas **Dwelling types**

ESTUDIOS: 0
1 DORMITORIO: 56
2 DORMITORIOS: 149
3 DORMITORIOS: 81
4+ DORMITORIOS: 54
STUDIOS: 0
1 BEDROOM: 56
2 BEDROOMS: 149
3 BEDROOMS: 81
4+ BEDROOMS: 54

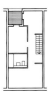

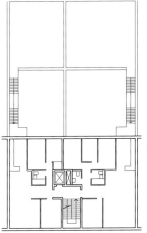

Planta primera
First floor plan

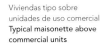

Planta baja
Ground floor plan

Viviendas tipo sobre
unidades de uso comercial
**Typical maisonette above
commercial units**

Apartamentos tipos en torno al
hueco de escaleras/ascensor
**Typical apartment cluster around
common stair/lift core** 1:500

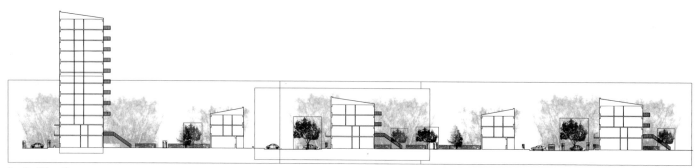

Sección **N-S section**

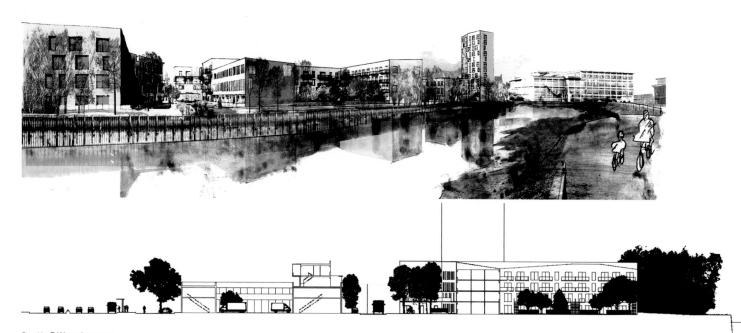

Sección **E-W section** 1:1.000

100 %
VIVIENDA   20 🚗
LIVING

TRABAJO
WORKING

COMERCIO
SHOPPING

EQUIPAMIENTOS
CIVIC FACILITIES

OTROS USOS
OTHER USES

4.661 m²
SUPERFICIE DE PARCELA
PLOT AREA

2.820 m²
SUPERFICIE CONSTRUIDA
BUILT UP AREA

53 %
OCUPACIÓN
COVERED AREA

0,6
EDIFICABILIDAD
FLOOR AREA RATIO

43 ⌂/ha   215 ⌖/ha

+3

1:2.500

digitalglobe, 2007

🎥 1:10.000

Selgascano selgascano.com

Calle Embalse del Manzanares, Madrid. Spain, 2007-

El único material que nos interesa de este proyecto son las plantas. El resto de los materiales vienen obligados: la malla metálica para sujetar las plantas y que se enreden en ella, los tableros prefabricados de hormigón de la estructura y los cierres entre viviendas, el vidrio en fachada para disfrutar de las vistas al verde y de la mayor luz posible, y los suelos continuos de goma.

El proyecto de jardinería trata básicamente de conseguir una fachada vegetal con enredaderas.

Las especies escogidas responden por un lado, a las condiciones medioambientales y climáticas de Vallecas, y por otro se distribuyen en las fachadas en función del soleamiento de cada una de ellas.

Para cada fachada se ha realizado un estudio de soleamiento, y para las condiciones más extremas de sombreado se ha determinado una proporción sol/sombra que se ha utilizado también para determinar la proporción de especies de sol y de sombra que tiene cada fachada.

A lo largo de la fachada, las especies de sol y las de sombra se mezclan, diferenciándose únicamente por la forma en que están ancladas a la malla. La propuesta se complementa con una plantación de arbolado.

Tanto los árboles como las enredaderas se riegan con un sistema de goteo.

The only materials in this project that interest us are the plants. The rest of the materials are obligatory, the metal mesh to hold up the plants and let them climb, the prefabricated concrete slabs of the structure and window closures, the glass on the facade to be able to enjoy the views of the greenery and the highest amount of light possible, and finally the continuous rubber floors.

The landscaping project is basically meant to create a green facade with climbing plants.

The plant types chosen respond to the environmental and climatic conditions of Vallecas (Madrid) as they also are distributed on the facades according to the amount of sunlight that each side receives.

For each facade, a sunlight study was carried out. For the most extreme shade conditions, a sun-shade proportion was determined and was also used to decide the proportion of plant types requiring sun or shade on each facade.

Along the facade, these plant types are combined, only different in the way that they are anchored to the mesh. The planting of trees complements the proposal.

Both the trees and the climbing plants are watered using a drip system.

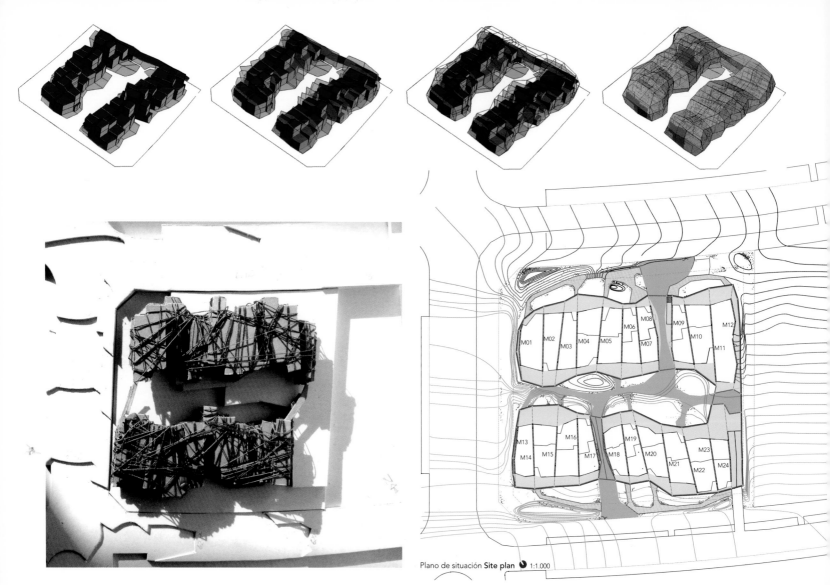

Plano de situación **Site plan** 1:1.000

M01 M02 M03 M04 M05 M06 M07 M08 M09 M10 M11 M12
M13 M14 M15 M16 M17 M18 M19 M20 M21 M22 M23 M24

M12   M24

M11   M23

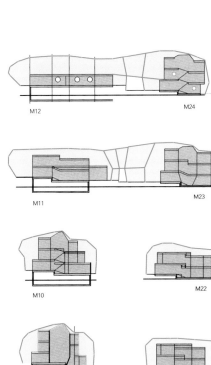

M10   M22

M09   M21

M08   M20

M07   M19

M06   M18

M05   M17

M04   M16

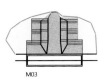

M03   M15

M02   M14

Secciones de muros **Wall sections** 1:1.000   M01   M13

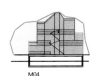

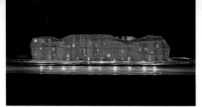

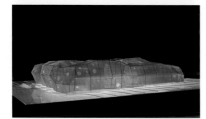

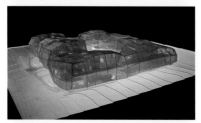

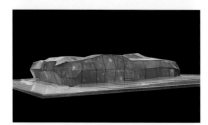

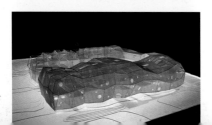

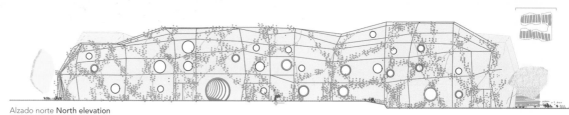

Alzado norte **North elevation**

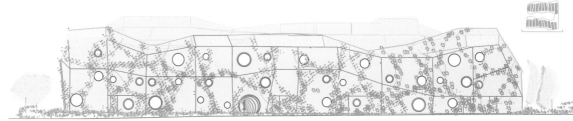

Alzado sur **South elevation**

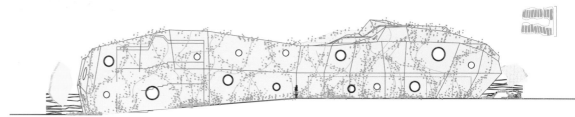

Alzado este **East elevation**

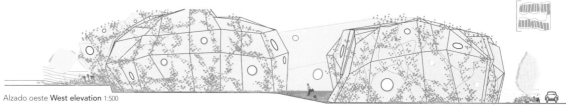

Alzado oeste **West elevation** 1:500

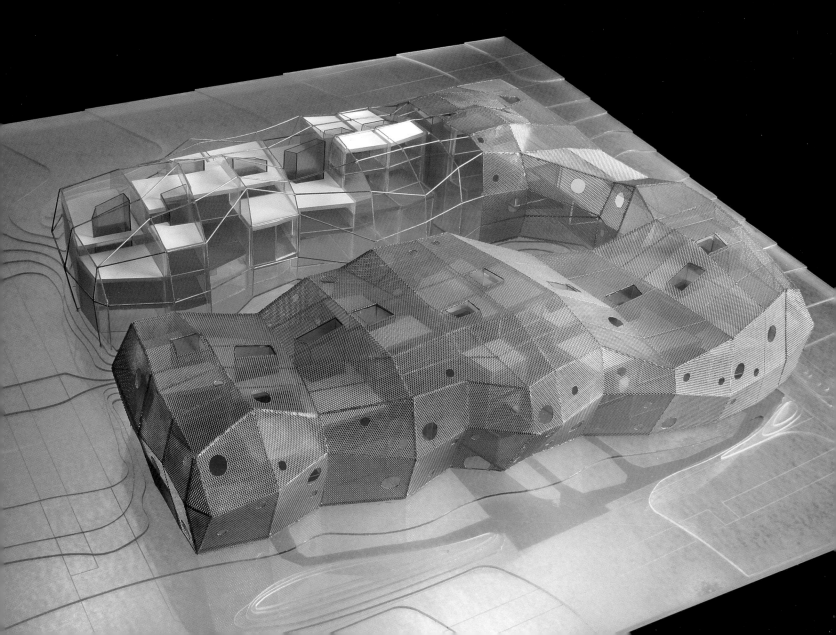

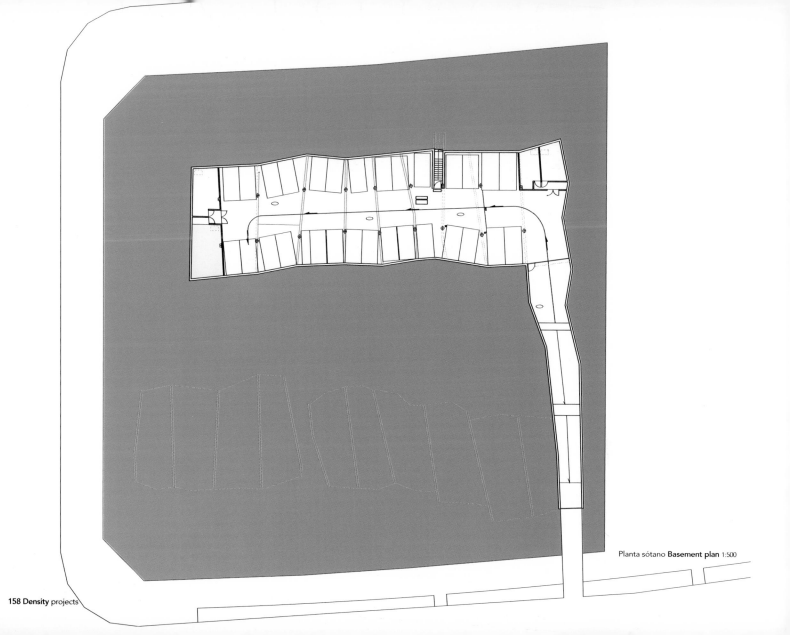

Planta sótano **Basement plan** 1:500

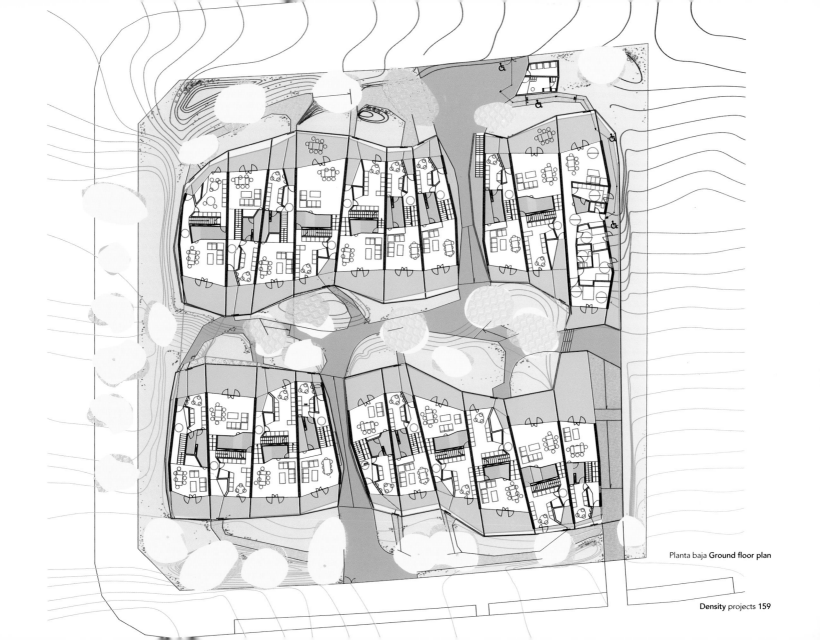

Planta baja **Ground floor plan**

Planta primera **First floor plan** 1:500

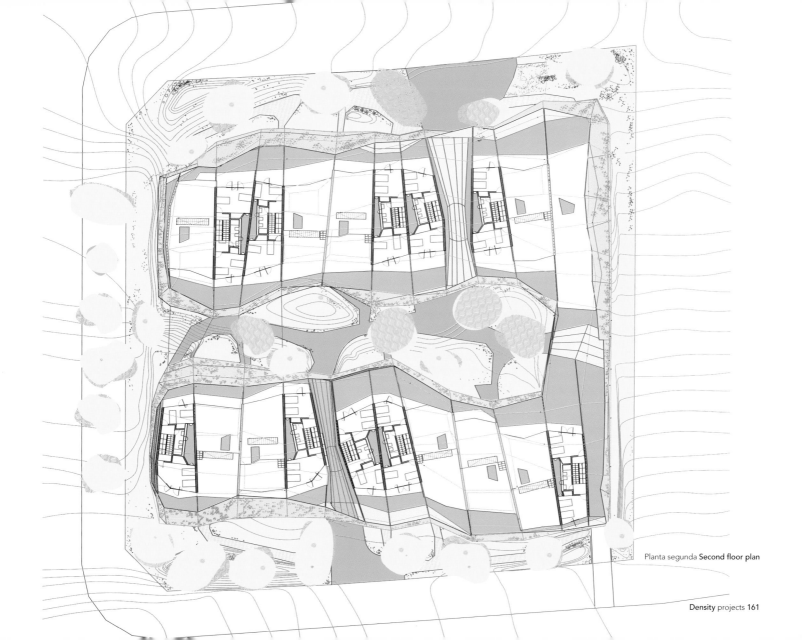

Planta segunda **Second floor plan**

Planta de cubiertas **Roof plan** 1:500

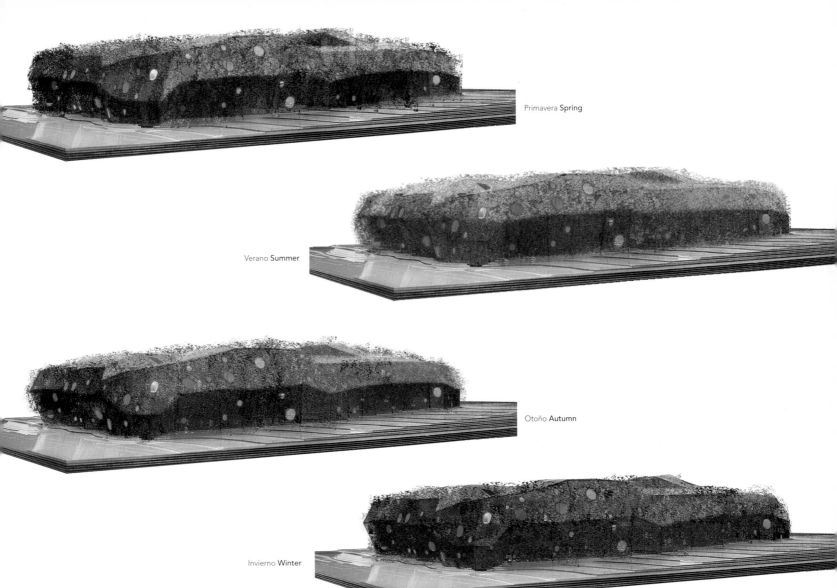

Primavera **Spring**

Verano **Summer**

Otoño **Autumn**

Invierno **Winter**

1:500

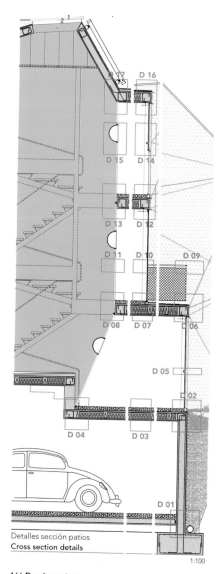

Detalles sección patios
Cross section details

1:100

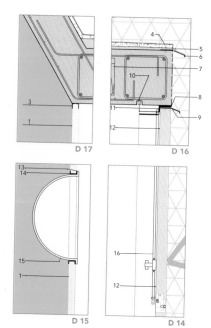

D 17

D 16

D 15

D 14

Detalle constructivo de la fachada
Facade constructive detail 1:20

1 PANEL DE POLICARBONATO
  CELULAR TRANSLÚCIDO
2 PERFIL ACERO UPN 100
3 PERFIL ACERO GALVANIZADO DE 3 mm
  DE ESPESOR ANCLADO AL FORJADO
4 CAPA DE RECUBRIMIENTO ELÁSTICO
  COMO PROTECCIÓN A LA INTEMPERIE
  Y ACABADO FINAL CON PINTURA
  PIGMENTADA DE POLIURETANO
5 HORMIGÓN DE PENDIENTE CON ÁRIDO
  ALIGERADO, DE UN ESPESOR MÁXIMO
  DE 11 cm Y PENDIENTE DEL 1,5%
6 PERFIL DE ACERO GALVANIZADO
  DE 3 mm DE ESPESOR PLEGADO
  FORMANDO VIERTEAGUAS
7 AISLAMIENTO DE POLIESTIRENO
  EXPANDIDO
8 CINTA ADHESIVA DE NEOPRENO
  DE 6 mm DE ESPESOR
9 PERFIL DE ACERO GALVANIZADO
  DE 3 mm DE ESPESOR PLEGADO
  FORMANDO GOTERÓN
10 CORTINERO DE 40 x 30 mm DE
  SECCIÓN REALIZADO METIENDO
  BERENJENO EN LOSA DE HORMIGÓN
11 PERFIL EN L DE ACERO GALVANIZADO
  DE 70 DE ANCHO x 30 mm DE
  ALTO Y 3 mm DE ESPESOR
12 PANEL *SÁNDWICH* PREFABRICADO DE
  60 mm DE ESPESOR, LACADO EN COLOR
13 CINTA ADHESIVA DE NEOPRENO
  DE 3 mm DE ESPESOR
14 PERFIL ACERO GALVANIZADO
  DE 3 mm DE ESPESOR
15 MEDIA ESFERA DE METACRILATO
16 HERRAJE DE ACERO INOXIDABLE
17 PAVIMENTO DE COLOR EN PVC
18 CAPA DE NIVELACIÓN
19 PERFIL ACERO LAMINADO 75 mm DE ALTO
  x 90 mm DE ANCHO Y 9 mm DE ESPESOR

1 TRANSLUCENT CELLULAR
  POLYCARBONATE PANEL
2 UPN 100 STEEL PROFILE
3 3 mm THICK GALVANIZED STEEL
  PROFILE, ATTACHED TO SLAB
4 ELASTIC PROTECTIVE COATING
  AND POLYURETHANE COLOURED
  PAINT FINISHING
5 1,5 % SLOPE OF CONCRETE FILLED WITH
  ARLITE (MAXIMUM DEPTH IS 11 cm)
6 3 mm THICK BENDED
  GALVANISED STEEL GUTTER
7 EXPANDED POLYESTIRENE
  INSULATION LAYER
8 6 mm THICK NEOPRENE ADHESIVE TAPE
9 3 mm THICK BENDED
  GALVANISED STEEL DRIP
10 40 x 30 mm CURTAIN CHANNEL
  MADE BY MEANS OF INSERTING A
  LISTEL INTO THE CONCRETE SLAB
11 70 mm WIDE x 30 mm TALL x 3 mm
  THICK GALVANIZED STEEL PROFILE
12 60 mm THICK, COLOR LACQUERED,
  SANDWICH PANEL
13 3 mm THICK NEOPRENE ADHESIVE TAPE
14 3 mm THICK GALVANISED STEEL PROFILE
15 METACRILATE HEMISPHERICAL WINDOW
16 STAINLESS STEEL FRAME
17 COLORED PVC FLOORING
18 CEMENT LAYER
19 75 mm TALL x 90 mm WIDE x 9 mm
  THICK LAMINATED STEEL PROFILE

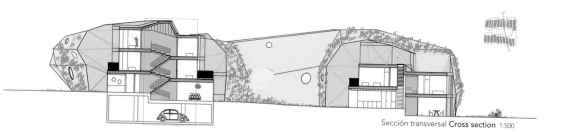

Sección transversal **Cross section** 1:500

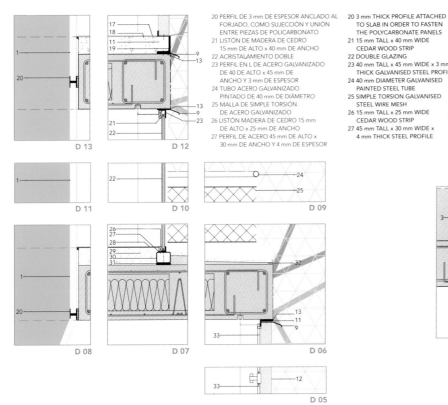

20 PERFIL DE 3 mm DE ESPESOR ANCLADO AL FORJADO, COMO SUJECCIÓN Y UNIÓN ENTRE PIEZAS DE POLICARBONATO
21 LISTÓN DE MADERA DE CEDRO 15 mm DE ALTO x 40 mm DE ANCHO
22 ACRISTALAMIENTO DOBLE
23 PERFIL EN L DE ACERO GALVANIZADO DE 40 DE ALTO x 45 mm DE ANCHO Y 3 mm DE ESPESOR
24 TUBO ACERO GALVANIZADO PINTADO DE 40 mm DE DIÁMETRO
25 MALLA DE SIMPLE TORSIÓN DE ACERO GALVANIZADO
26 LISTÓN MADERA DE CEDRO 15 mm DE ALTO x 25 mm DE ANCHO
27 PERFIL DE ACERO 45 DE ALTO x 30 mm DE ANCHO Y 4 mm DE ESPESOR

20 3 mm THICK PROFILE ATTACHED TO SLAB IN ORDER TO FASTEN THE POLYCARBONATE PANELS
21 15 mm TALL x 40 mm WIDE CEDAR WOOD STRIP
22 DOUBLE GLAZING
23 40 mm TALL x 45 mm WIDE x 3 mm THICK GALVANISED STEEL PROFILE
24 40 mm DIAMETER GALVANISED PAINTED STEEL TUBE
25 SIMPLE TORSION GALVANISED STEEL WIRE MESH
26 15 mm TALL x 25 mm WIDE CEDAR WOOD STRIP
27 45 mm TALL x 30 mm WIDE x 4 mm THICK STEEL PROFILE

28 PAVIMENTO DE COLOR EN PVC
29 CAPA DE NIVELACIÓN
30 TUBO DE ACERO
31 BANDA DE NEOPRENO
32 HORMIGÓN DE PENDIENTE ALIGERADO CON ÁRIDO TIPO ARLITA, DE UN ESPESOR MÁXIMO DE 11 cm Y PENDIENTE DEL 2%
33 HERRAJE DE ACERO INOXIDABLE
34 IMPERMEABILIZACIÓN DE LÁMINA DE PVC PROTEGIDA CONTRA RAÍCES Y SELLADA EN EL EXTREMO
35 GRAVILLA
36 LÁMINA DE POLIETILENO RÍGIDO COMO CAPA SEPARADORA DRENANTE
37 LÁMINA GEOTEXTIL DE 2 mm DE ESPESOR
38 CAPA DE GRAVA DE 400 mm DE ESPESOR
39 DREN. DE 200 mm DE DIÁMETRO

28 COLORED PVC FLOORING
29 CEMENT LAYER
30 STEEL TUBE
31 NEOPRENE BAND
32 2% SLOPE OF CONCRETE FILLED WITH ARLITE (MAXIMUM DEPTH IS11 cm)
33 STAINLESS STEEL FRAME
34 PVC SEALED WATERPROOF LAYER AND ROOT BARRIER
35 GRAVEL LAYER
36 RIGID POLYETHYLENE AS DRAINING LAYER
37 2 mm THICK GEOTEXTILE MEMBRANE
38 400 mm THICK GRAVEL LAYER
39 200 mm DIAMETER DRAIN PIPE

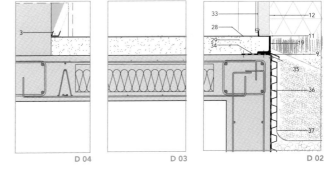

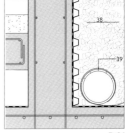

Tipos de viviendas **Dwelling types**
ESTUDIOS: 0
1 DORMITORIO: 0
2 DORMITORIOS: 0
3 DORMITORIOS: 0
4+ DORMITORIOS: 20
STUDIOS: 0
1 BEDROOM: 0
2 BEDROOMS: 0
3 BEDROOMS: 0
4+ BEDROOMS: 20

1:20

12

DENSIDADES ● **DENSITIES** ■ VIVIENDAS **53** DWELLINGS ■ USOS ● **USES** ■

| 17,3 % VIVIENDA LIVING | 58,2 % TRABAJO WORKING | 24,5 % COMERCIOS SHOPPING | EQUIPAMIENTOS CIVIC FACILITIES | OTROS USOS OTHER USES |

81 ☐/ha   238 ☺/ha

| 6.509 m² SUPERFICIE DE PARCELA PLOT AREA | 34.439 m² SUPERFICIE CONSTRUIDA BUILT UP AREA | 88,9 % OCUPACIÓN COVERED AREA | 5,2 EDIFICABILIDAD FLOOR AREA RATIO |

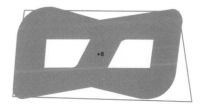

1:2.500

the geoinformation group/interatlas, 2007

1:10.000

ECDM Architectes combarel-marrec.com

Avenue de France/Rue Neuve Tolbiac, Paris. France, 2007

El objetivo del proyecto es crear una mezcla vertical de usos con el fin de mejorar y optimizar cada función en este típico programa urbano.

La gran cantidad de programa comercial requerida condujo al aprovechamiento máximo de la parcela, ocupando toda la planta baja a excepción de los accesos a las oficinas y las viviendas. Por su parte, las plantas de oficinas proporcionan una gran variedad tipológica, gracias a su anchura variable y a que son totalmente divisibles. La fluidez del espacio de oficinas se ve favorecida por la curvatura de las fachadas, que permite evitar las problemáticas particiones en las esquinas.

El programa residencial se concentra en las plantas superiores, para aprovechar al máximo la luz y las vistas. La mayoría de las viviendas dispone del amplio espacio exterior que proporciona la cubierta verde.

The purpose of the project was to create a real vertical mix in order to optimise and improve each function of this typical urban program.

The density of the commercial program led to spread the building up to the maximum capacity of the plot. The entire ground floor is allocated to the commerce except halls of offices and dwellings. Office floors offer a large typological diversity by their non-constant width although they are totally divisible. The fluidity of office floors is increased by the curved facades that avoid the partitioning problematic in angles.

The residential area hangs out on top of the building to take maximum advantage of light and views. There, the majority of apartments enjoy a large exterior space and a quality environment thanks to the green roof.

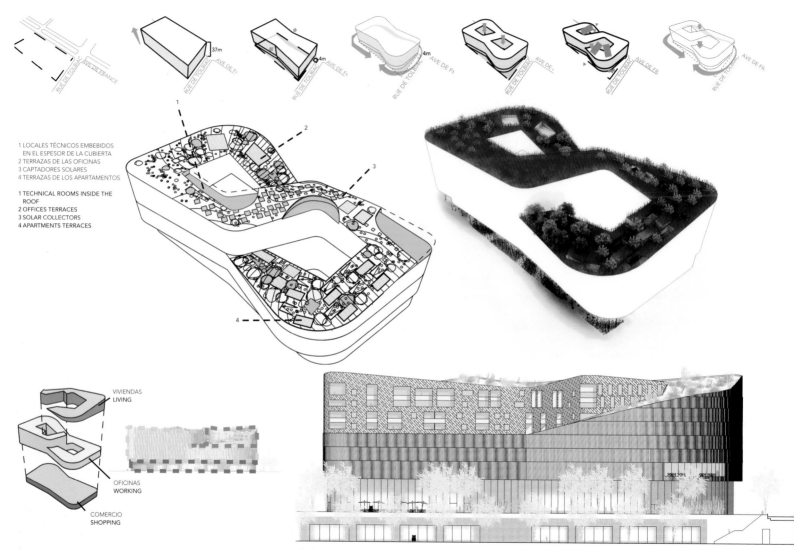

1 LOCALES TÉCNICOS EMBEBIDOS
  EN EL ESPESOR DE LA CUBIERTA
2 TERRAZAS DE LAS OFICINAS
3 CAPTADORES SOLARES
4 TERRAZAS DE LOS APARTAMENTOS

1 TECHNICAL ROOMS INSIDE THE
  ROOF
2 OFFICES TERRACES
3 SOLAR COLLECTORS
4 APARTMENTS TERRACES

37m

4m

4m

RUE DE TOLBIAC AVE DE FRANCE
RUE DE TOLBIAC AVE DE F
RUE DE TOLBIAC AVE DE F
RUE DE TOLBIAC AVE DE F
RUE DE TOLBIAC AVE DE
RUE DE TOLBIAC AVE DE FR
RUE DE TOLBIAC AVE OE FR

VIVIENDAS
LIVING

OFICINAS
WORKING

COMERCIO
SHOPPING

Alzado oeste **West elevation** 1:1.000

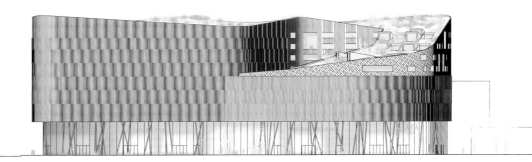

Alzado este **East elevation** 1:1.000

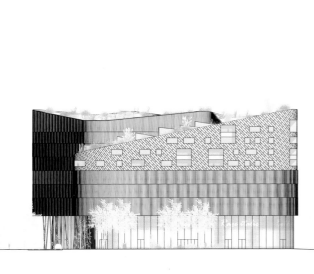

Alzado norte **North elevation**

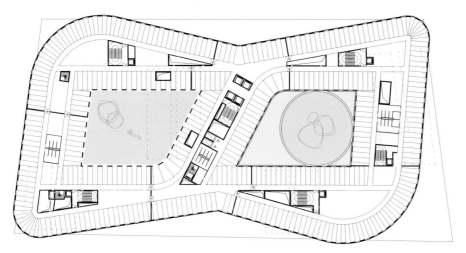

Planta de oficinas con diferentes posibilidades de distribución
Office floor plan with different possibilities of distribution

Tipo 1 **Type**

Seccion A **Section**

Planta inferior
Lower floor plant

Planta superior
Upper floor plant

Planta de la cubierta
Roof plant

1:500

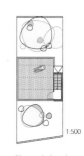

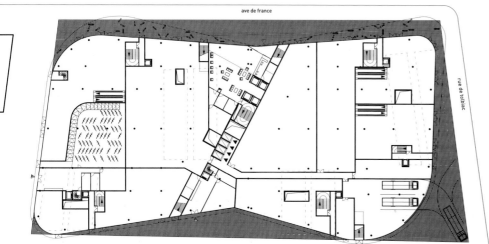

ave de france

rue de tolbiac

Planta baja **Ground floor plan** 1:1.000

Tipos de viviendas **Dwelling types**
ESTUDIOS: 0
1 DORMITORIO: 8
2 DORMITORIOS: 29
3 DORMITORIOS: 6
4+ DORMITORIOS: 10
STUDIOS: 0
1 BEDROOM: 8
2 BEDROOMS: 29
3 BEDROOMS: 6
4+ BEDROOMS: 10

Tipo 2 **Type**

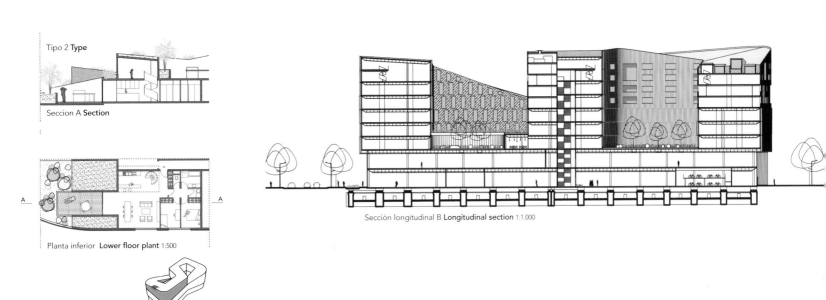

Seccion A **Section**

Planta inferior **Lower floor plant** 1:500

Sección longitudinal B **Longitudinal section** 1:1.000

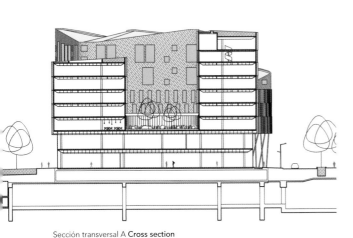

Sección transversal A **Cross section**

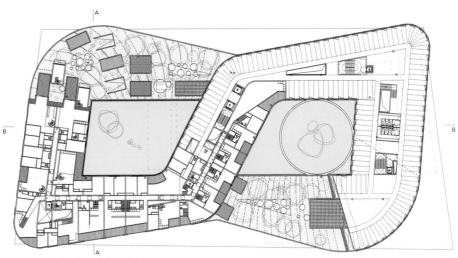

Planta séptima **Seventh floor plan** 1:1.000

DENSIDADES ● **DENSITIES** ■ VIVIENDAS **108** **DWELLINGS** ■ USOS ● **USES** ■

79 Ⓓ/ha   **242** Ⓓ/ha

37,6 %
VIVIENDA
LIVING

TRABAJO
WORKING

15,1 %
COMERCIOS/HOTEL
SHOPPING/HOTEL

3,6 %
CINES
CINEMAS

43,7 %
APARCAMIENTO PÚBLICO
PUBLIC PARKING

13.592 m²
SUPERFICIE DE PARCELA
PLOT AREA

62.250 m²
SUPERFICIE CONSTRUIDA
BUILT UP AREA

50 %
OCUPACIÓN
COVERED AREA

4,6
EDIFICABILIDAD
FLOOR AREA RATIO

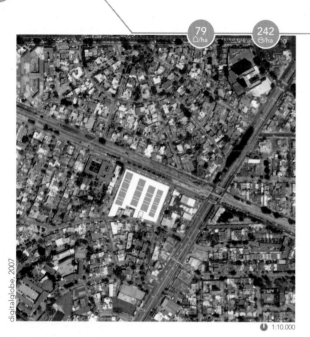

digitalglobe, 2007

Ⓓ 1:10.000

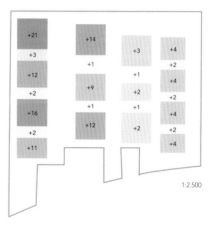

1:2.500

Tatiana Bilbao/mx.a mxa.com.mx

Avenida Inglaterra 3089, Guadalajara. Mexico, 2006-2010

El programa de este centro multiusos se divide en cuatro bloques: el bloque 1, de cuatro torres, alberga viviendas de lujo; el bloque 2, con tres torres más bajas, comprende un hotel y un *apar-thotel*; el bloque 3 aloja una galería de arte y por último, el bloque 4 contiene cuatro salas de cine de arte y ensayo.

Los cuatro bloques van disminuyendo en altura y la ubicación irregular de sus volúmenes da lugar a un ambiente urbano en el área, que dota al proyecto de identidad y coherencia.

The program of this mixed-use centre is divided in four blocks: block 1 with four towers containing higher standard living; block 2 with three lower towers for the eco-hotel and apartments with halftime hotel service; block 3 with three volumes for a gallery and block 4 with four boxes for an art movie cinema.

The 4 blocks and their towers rise up from block 4 to block 1. In their irregular positioning they create an urban atmosphere within the area, which gives the complex an identity and coherence.

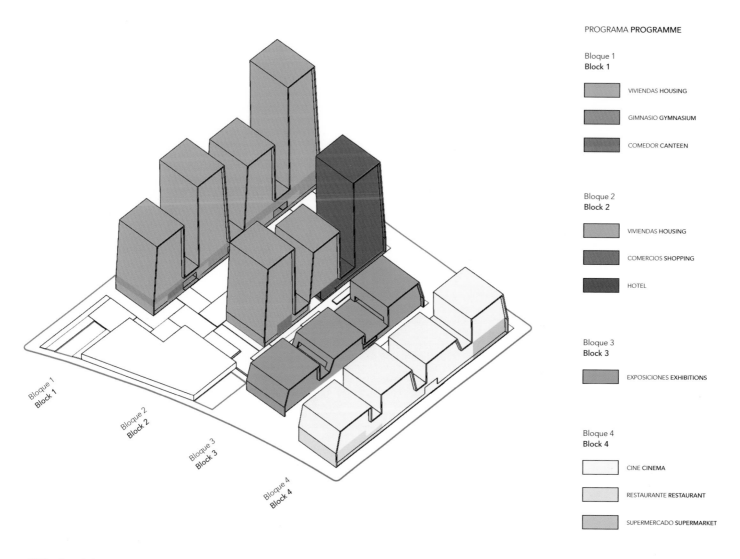

PROGRAMA **PROGRAMME**

Bloque 1
Block 1

VIVIENDAS **HOUSING**

GIMNASIO **GYMNASIUM**

COMEDOR **CANTEEN**

Bloque 2
Block 2

VIVIENDAS **HOUSING**

COMERCIOS **SHOPPING**

HOTEL

Bloque 3
Block 3

EXPOSICIONES **EXHIBITIONS**

Bloque 4
Block 4

CINE **CINEMA**

RESTAURANTE **RESTAURANT**

SUPERMERCADO **SUPERMARKET**

Bloque 1
Block 1

Bloque 2
Block 2

Bloque 3
Block 3

Bloque 4
Block 4

AV. INGLATERRA

CALLE ANDRES CAVO

CALLE MISIONES

CALLE SAN GABRIEL

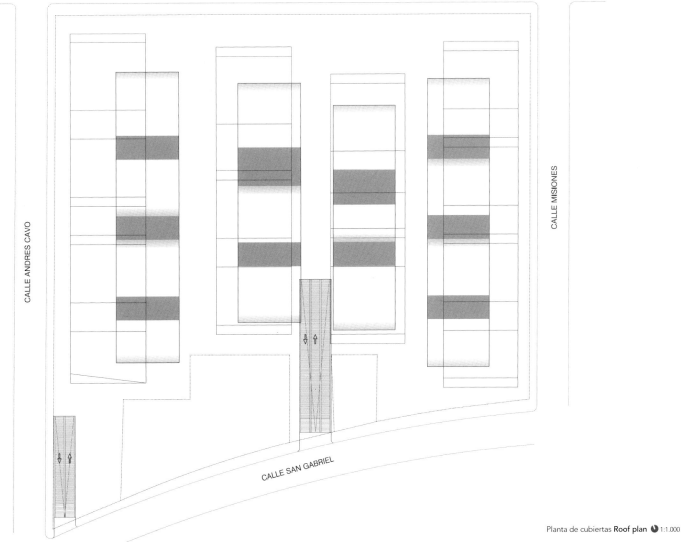

Planta de cubiertas **Roof plan** 🌓 1:1.000

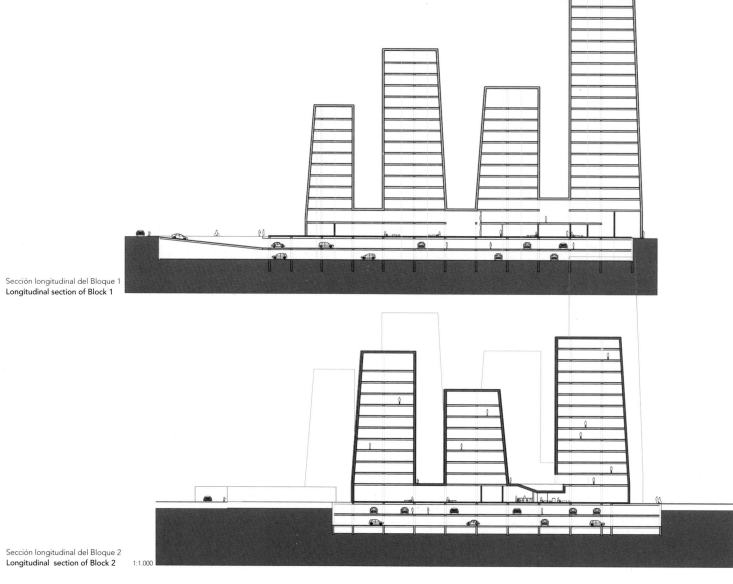

Sección longitudinal del Bloque 1
Longitudinal section of Block 1

Sección longitudinal del Bloque 2
Longitudinal section of Block 2   1:1.000

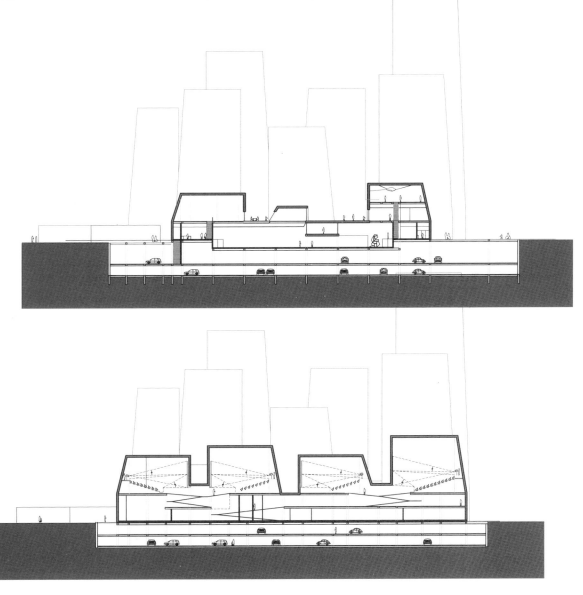

Sección longitudinal del Bloque 3
Longitudinal section of Block 3

Sección longitudinal del Bloque 4
Longitudinal section of Block 4

AV. INGLATERRA

1 VESTÍBULO
2 USOS MÚLTIPLES
3 ALMACÉN
4 CIRCULACIÓN PRINCIPAL
5 SALA DE EXPOSICIONES
6 COMEDOR
7 RECEPCIÓN
8 SALA DE CONFERENCIAS
9 OFICINA
10 VESTÍBULO
11 TIENDA
12 RAMPA DE ESTACIONAMIENTO
13 VESTÍBULO
14 BAR
15 ACCESO DE EMPLEADOS
16 COCINA
17 ALMACÉN
18 BAR
19 TAQUILLAS
20 TERRAZA DE ACCESO
21 ACCESO
22 SUPERMERCADO
23 MURO DE ESCALADA

1 LOBBY
2 MULTIPLE PURPOSE ROOM
3 STORAGE
4 MAIN CIRCULATION
5 EXHIBITION SPACE
6 CANTEEN
7 RECEPTION
8 CONFERENCE ROOM
9 OFFICE
10 LOBBY
11 SHOP
12 PARKING RAMP
13 LOBBY
14 BAR
15 SERVICE ENTRANCE
16 KITCHEN
17 STORAGE
18 BAR
19 BOX OFFICE
20 ACCESS TERRACE
21 ENTRANCE
22 SUPERMARKET
23 SCALING WALL

CALLE ANDRES CAVO

CALLE MISIONES

CALLE SAN GABRIEL

Planta baja **Ground floor plan** 1:1.000

1 VACÍO
2 SALA DE FITNESS
3 MURO DE ESCALADA
4 GIMNASIO
5 SPA
6 SAUNA
7 SALA DE RELAJACIÓN
8 TERRAZA
9 PISCINA
10 APARTAMENTO
11 RAMPA DE ESTACIONAMIENTO
12 ALMACÉN
13 TALLERES
14 SALA JUNTAS
15 DIRECCIÓN
16 RECEPCIÓN
17 ÁREA DE TRABAJO
18 TIENDA
19 VESTÍBULO
20 CAFETERÍA
21 ALMACEN

1 VOID
2 FITNESS ROOM
3 SCALING WALL
4 GYM
5 SPA
6 SAUNA
7 WELLNES ROOM
8 TERRACE
9 POOL
10 APARTMENT
11 PARKING RAMP
12 STORAGE
13 WORKSHOPS
14 MEETING ROOM
15 DIRECTOR'S OFFICE
16 RECEPTION
17 WORKING SPACE
18 SHOP
19 LOBBY
20 CAFÉ
21 STORAGE

CALLE ANDRES CAVO

CALLE MISIONES

CALLE SAN GABRIEL

Planta primera **First floor plan**

1 APARTAMENTO
2 TERRAZA
3 PISCINA
4 MEDIATECA
5 SALA 4 CAPACIDAD
  200 PERSONAS
6 SALA 3 CAPACIDAD
  150 PERSONAS
7 SALA 2 CAPACIDAD
  150 PERSONAS
8 SALA 1 CAPACIDAD
  150 PERSONAS

1 APARTMENT
2 TERRACE
3 POOL
4 MEDIA LIBRARY
5 HALL 4 (200 SEATS)
6 HALL 3 (150 SEATS)
7 HALL 2 (150 SEATS)
8 HALL 1 (150 SEATS)

CALLE ANDRES CAVO

CALLE MISIONES

CALLE SAN GABRIEL

Planta segunda **Second floor plan** 1:1.000

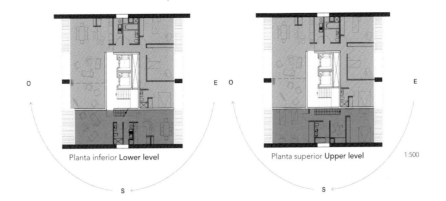

Tipos de vivienda **Dwelling types**

ESTUDIOS: 0
1 DORMITORIO: 0
2 DORMITORIOS: 67
3 DORMITORIOS: 35
4+ DORMITORIOS: 6
STUDIOS: 0
1 BEDROOM: 0
2 BEDROOMS: 67
3 BEDROOMS: 35
4+ BEDROOMS: 6

O — E   O — E

Planta inferior **Lower level**   Planta superior **Upper level**   1:500

S   S

94,5%
VIVIENDA 279 🚗
LIVING

TRABAJO
WORKING

1,5%
COMERCIOS
SHOPPING

4 %
HOSPITAL DE ANCIANOS
HOSPITAL FOR THE ELDERLY

OTROS USOS
OTHER USES

22.100 m²
SUPERFICIE DE PARCELA
PLOT AREA

45.800 m²
SUPERFICIE CONSTRUIDA
BUILT UP AREA

19,9 %
OCUPACIÓN
COVERED AREA

1,7
EDIFICABILIDAD
FLOOR AREA RATIO

143 ☖/ha   257 🜂/ha

aerodata international surveys, 2007

🌑 1:10.000

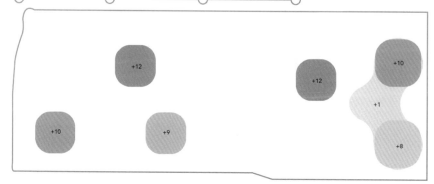

1:2.500

VMX Architects vmxarchitects.nl

Schalkwijk, Haarlem. The Netherlands, 2006-2010

El programa comprende 118 apartamentos en venta y 50 en régimen de alquiler para mayores, 100 habitaciones para ancianos y 48 habitaciones de cuidado intensivo. La gran diversidad tipológica permite así la interacción entre los diferentes grupos de edad.

El diseño retoma las cualidades más beneficiosas del urbanismo de posguerra donde se ubica, en concreto el carácter público del espacio entre los edificios, los jardines comunitarios y la luz. Los edificios de vivienda se agrupan alrededor de aparcamientos semienterrados. Por su parte, los edificios que alojan las viviendas de ancianos se agrupan sobre un zócalo de servicios, que incluye salas de recreo, oficinas, consultas médicas, café y áreas comerciales.

El vínculo entre las 6 torres se obtiene mediante los espacios compartidos, las áreas protegidas y el parque. Así se crea un espacio común para los distintos grupos de edad. La variedad de tipos se consigue a partir de la forma circular, que proporciona privacidad y vistas.

The program includes 118 apartments to sell, 50 to rent for seniors, 100 units for elderly people and 48 intensive care rooms. Therefore, the large diversity in housing types interaction between different age groups.

The design takes its starting point in the qualities of the post-war neighbourhood where it is located, more specifically the public character, the green and the light. The towers of the apartments to sell are free-standing but grouped around an open courtyard above the half-sunken parking garage. The towers of the care complex are connected by a shared program on the ground floor, including recreational rooms, offices, examinations rooms and a large centre with a café, restaurant and shops. The six towers are thus tied together by shared spaces, protected areas, and the elements of the park. Hereby a coherent public space is created for the different user groups. A large variation of housing types has been made possible within a coherent shape, where the circular exterior of the tower offers privacy and views.

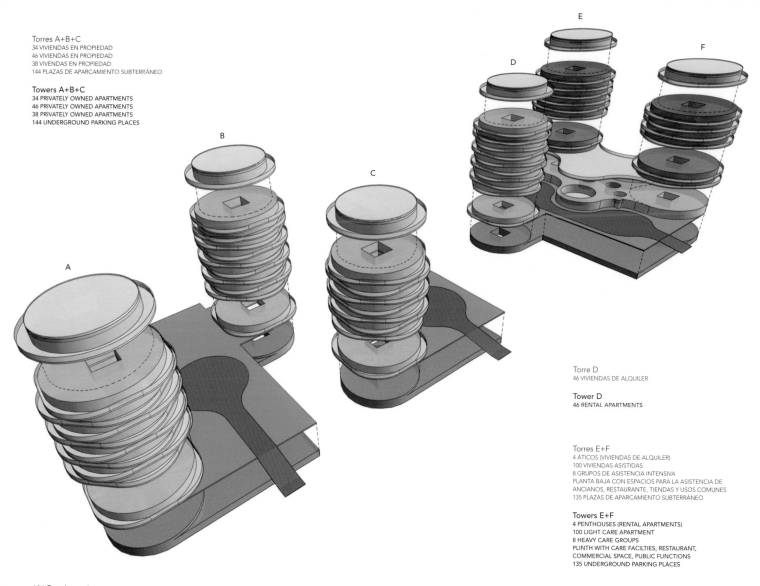

Torres A+B+C
34 VIVIENDAS EN PROPIEDAD
46 VIVIENDAS EN PROPIEDAD
38 VIVENDAS EN PROPIEDAD
144 PLAZAS DE APARCAMIENTO SUBTERRÁNEO

Towers A+B+C
34 PRIVATELY OWNED APARTMENTS
46 PRIVATELY OWNED APARTMENTS
38 PRIVATELY OWNED APARTMENTS
144 UNDERGROUND PARKING PLACES

E

D

F

B

C

A

Torre D
46 VIVIENDAS DE ALQUILER

Tower D
46 RENTAL APARTMENTS

Torres E+F
4 ÁTICOS (VIVIENDAS DE ALQUILER)
100 VIVIENDAS ASISTIDAS
8 GRUPOS DE ASISTENCIA INTENSIVA
PLANTA BAJA CON ESPACIOS PARA LA ASISTENCIA DE
ANCIANOS, RESTAURANTE, TIENDAS Y USOS COMUNES
135 PLAZAS DE APARCAMIENTO SUBTERRÁNEO

Towers E+F
4 PENTHOUSES (RENTAL APARTMENTS)
100 LIGHT CARE APARTMENT
8 HEAVY CARE GROUPS
PLINTH WITH CARE FACILTIES, RESTAURANT,
COMMERCIAL SPACE, PUBLIC FUNCTIONS
135 UNDERGROUND PARKING PLACES

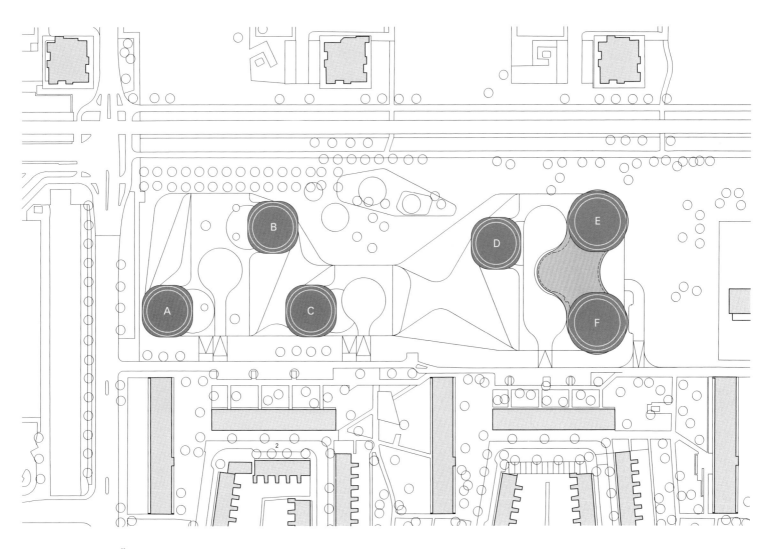

Plano de situación **Site plan** ⬇ 1:2.000

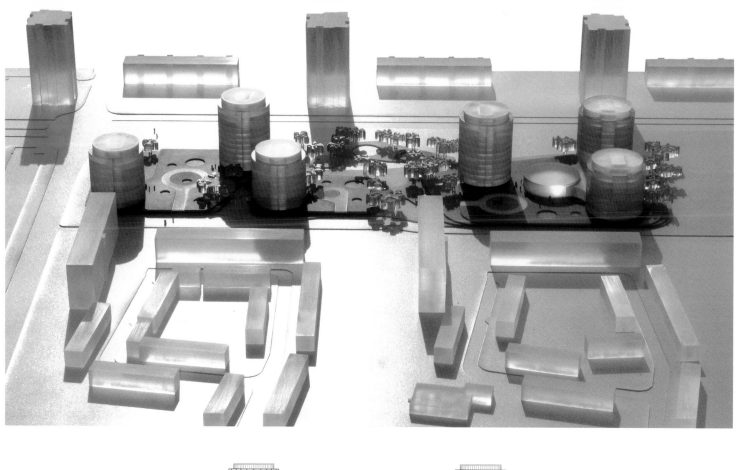

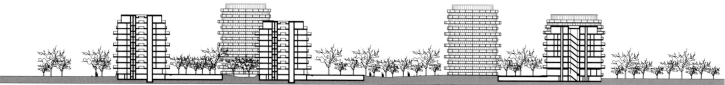

Sección longitudinal **A Long section** 1:2.000

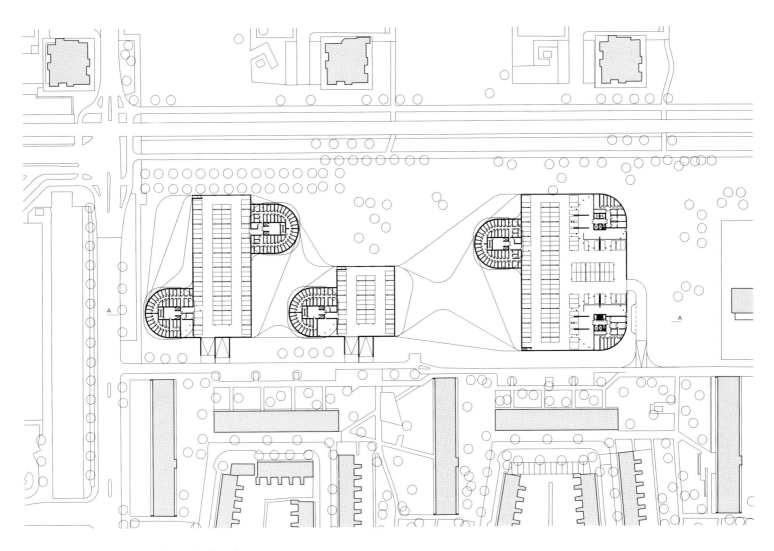

Plano del aparcamiento subterráneo **Underground parking plan** 1:2.000

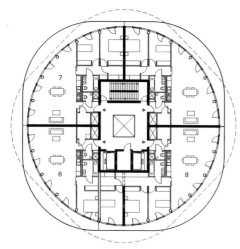

Planta segunda **Second floor plan**

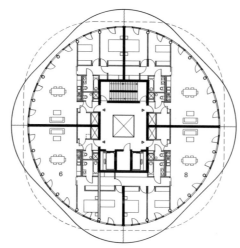

Planta tercera **Third floor plan**

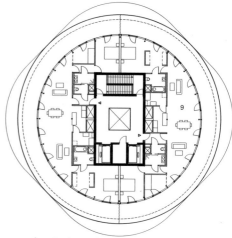

Ático **Penthouse plan**

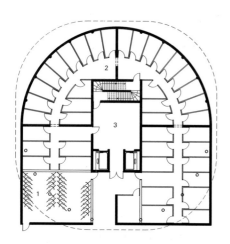

Sótano **Basement plan** 1:500

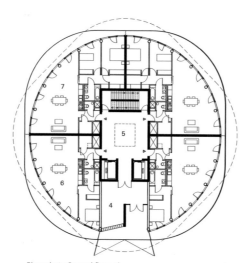

Planta baja **Ground floor plan**

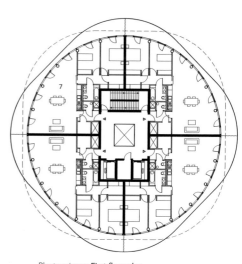

Planta primera **First floor plan**

190 **Density** projects

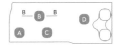

Torres A+B+C+D
1 APARCAMIENTO DE BICICLETAS
2 TRASTEROS
3 ACCESO AL SÓTANO
4 ACCESO PRINCIPAL
5 VIVIENDA PEQUEÑA
6 VIVIENDA NORMAL
8 VIVIENDA GRANDE
9 ÁTICO

Towers A+B+C+D
1 BICYCLE PARKING
2 STORAGE
3 BASEMENT ENTRANCE
4 MAIN ACCESS
5 LOBBY
6 SMALL APARTMENT
7 STANDARD APARTMENT
8 LARGE APARTMENT
9 PENTHOUSE

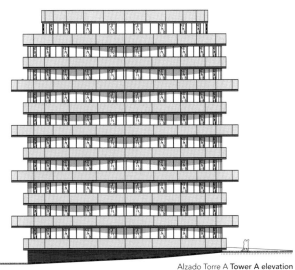

Alzado Torre A **Tower A elevation**

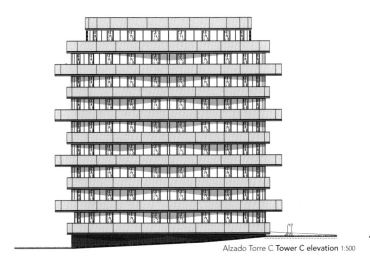

Alzado Torre C **Tower C elevation** 1:500

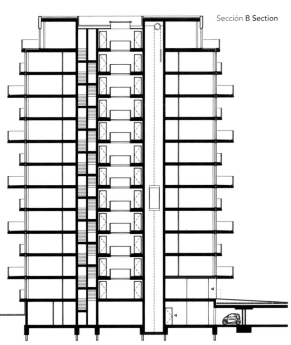

Sección **B Section**

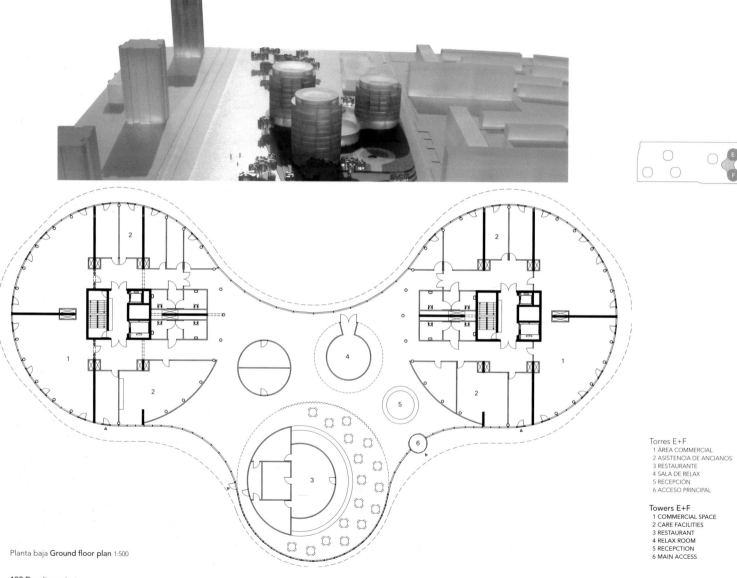

Planta baja **Ground floor plan** 1:500

Torres E+F
1 ÁREA COMMERCIAL
2 ASISTENCIA DE ANCIANOS
3 RESTAURANTE
4 SALA DE RELAX
5 RECEPCIÓN
6 ACCESO PRINCIPAL

Towers E+F
1 COMMERCIAL SPACE
2 CARE FACILITIES
3 RESTAURANT
4 RELAX ROOM
5 RECEPTION
6 MAIN ACCESS

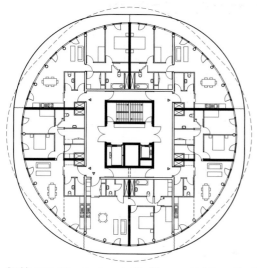

Posible conversión en apartamentos **Possible conversion into apartments**

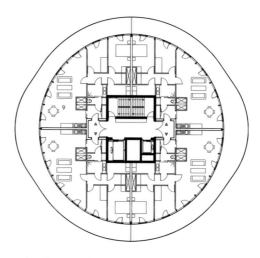

Ático **Penthouse plan**

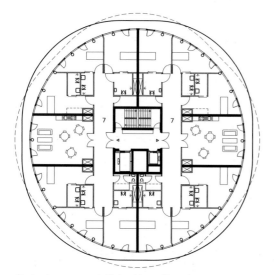

Planta primera y segunda **First and second floor plan**

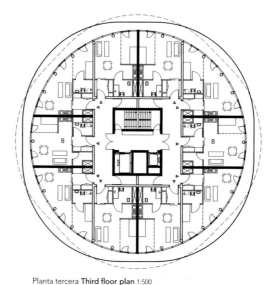

Planta tercera **Third floor plan** 1:500

Torres E+F
7 GRUPO DE CUIDADOS INTENSIVOS
8 VIVIENDA ASISTIDA
9 VIVIENDA DE ALQUILER

Towers E+F
7 HEAVY CARE GROUP
8 LIGHT CARE APARTMENT
9 RENTAL APARTMENT

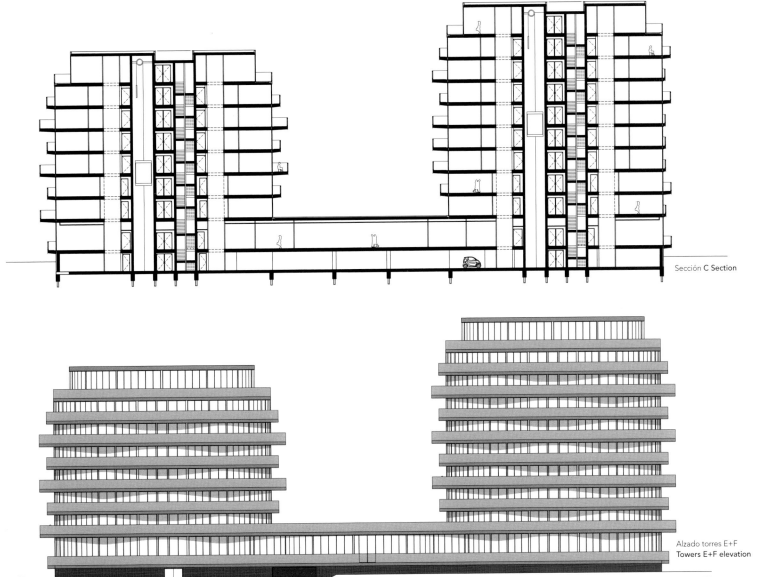

Sección **C** Section

Alzado torres E+F
Towers E+F elevation

1:500

31,7 %	2,1 %	0,9 %	EQUIPAMIENTOS	65,3 %
VIVIENDA 80 🚗	TRABAJO	COMERCIOS	CIVIC FACILITIES	APARCAMIENTO PÚBLICO
LIVING	OFICINAS	SHOPPING		PUBLIC PARKING

6.900 m²	32.930 m²	84 %	4,8
SUPERFICIE DE PARCELA	SUPERFICIE CONSTRUIDA	OCUPACIÓN	EDIFICABILIDAD
PLOT AREA	BUILT UP AREA	COVERED AREA	FLOOR AREA RATIO

120 ⬠/ha   **259** ⬠/ha

scankort, 2007

🕐 1:10.000

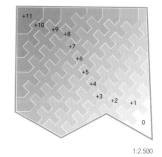

1:2.500

PLOT=BIG+JDS big.dk, jdsarchitects.com

Ørestads Boulevard 55, Copenhagen. Denmark, 2005-2008

El proyecto Mountain Dwellings es la segunda generación de las viviendas VM (el cliente, el tamaño y la calle coinciden). El programa sin embargo varía en cuanto que se trata de dos tercios de aparcamiento y un tercio de vivienda. Para resolver este requerimiento nos planteamos la posibilidad de que el aparcamiento se convirtiese en base de las viviendas, semejante a una colina de hormigón cubierto por una fina capa de viviendas deslizándose desde el undécimo piso hasta el primero. Así pues, en vez de plantear el proyecto sobre dos edificios separados, decidimos integrar ambos programas en una relación simbiótica. El aparcamiento requiere una conexión directa con la calle, mientras que las viviendas necesitan de vistas, aire y luz natural, de modo que todos los apartamentos disponen de grandes terrazas orientadas al sol, y plazas de aparcamiento en el décimo piso.

The Mountain Dwellings are the 2nd generation of the VM Houses (same client, same size and same street). The program, however, is 2/3 parking and 1/3 living. What if the parking area became the foundation of the homes –like a concrete hillside covered by a thin layer of housing, cascading from the 1st to the 11th floor? Rather than doing two separate buildings next to each other –a parking and a housing block– we decided to merge the two functions into a symbiotic relationship. The parking area needs to be connected to the street and the homes require sunlight, fresh air and a view, thus all apartments have roof gardens facing the sun, amazing views and street parking on the 10th floor.

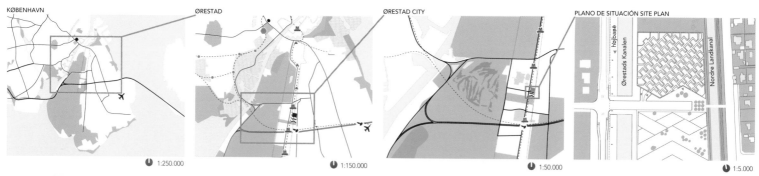

KØBENHAVN

ØRESTAD

ØRESTAD CITY

PLANO DE SITUACIÓN SITE PLAN

1:250.000

1:150.000

1:50.000

1:5.000

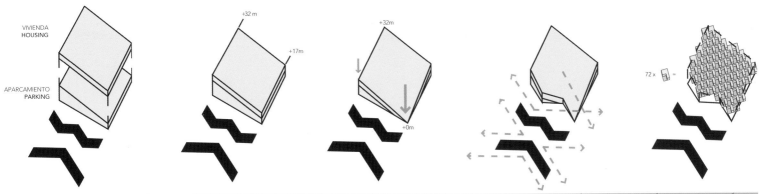

VIVIENDA
HOUSING

APARCAMIENTO
PARKING

+32 m

+17m

+32m

+0m

72 x

Tipos de viviendas **Dwelling types**
ESTUDIOS: 0
1 DORMITORIO: 33
2 DORMITORIOS: 40
3 DORMITORIOS: 10
4+ DORMITORIOS: 0
STUDIOS: 0
1 BEDROOM: 33
2 BEDROOMS: 40
3 BEDROOMS: 10
4+ BEDROOMS: 0

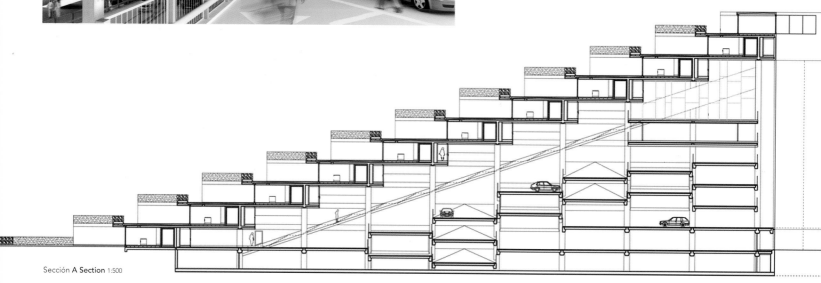

Sección **A Section** 1:500

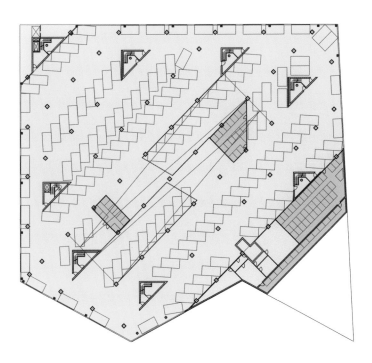

Planta sótano **Basement plan**

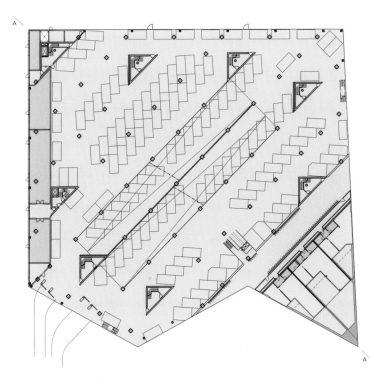

Planta baja **Ground floor plan** 1:1.000

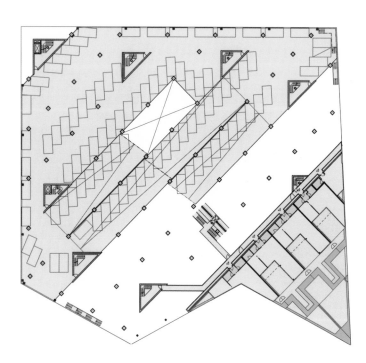

Planta primera **First floor plan**

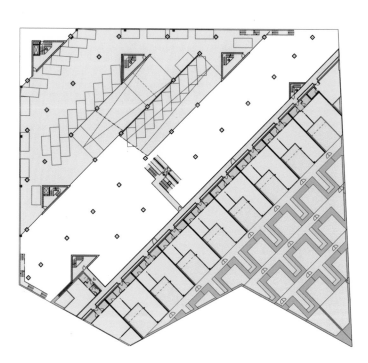

Planta tercera **Third floor plan**

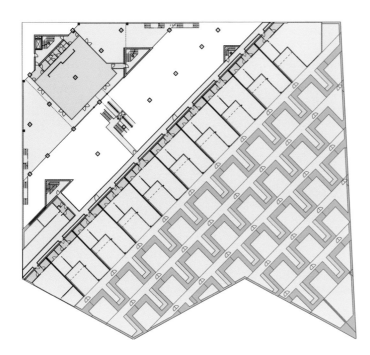

Planta quinta **Fifth floor plan**

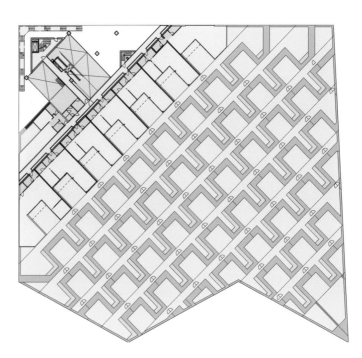

Planta séptima **Seventh floor plan**

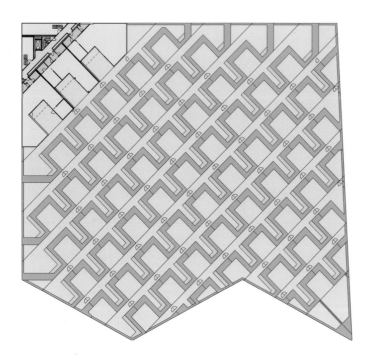

Planta novena **Ninth floor plan**

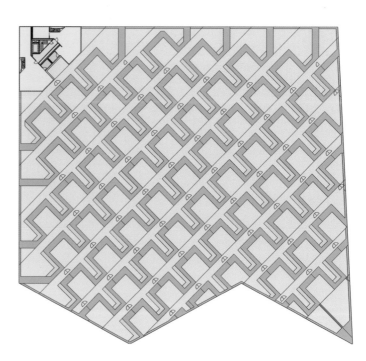

Planta décima **Tenth floor plan**

78,9 %
VIVIENDA 110 🚗
LIVING

TRABAJO
WORKING

8,2 %
COMERCIOS
SHOPPING

12,9 %
GUARDERÍA/C. CULTURAL/C. DE SALUD/BIBLIOTECA
NURSERY/CULTURAL CENTRE/HEALTH CENTRE/LIBRARY

8.572 m²
SUPERFICIE DE PARCELA
PLOT AREA

10.881 m²
SUPERFICIE CONSTRUIDA
BUILT UP AREA

43,4 %
OCUPACIÓN
COVERED AREA

1,3
EDIFICABILIDAD
FLOOR AREA RATIO

128 ⌂/ha   306 ⊕/ha

1:2.500

digitalglobe, 2007

🔵 1:10.000

Estudio FAM estudiofam.com

Calle Bravo Murillo 105, Madrid. Spain, 2007-2009

La singularidad de la manzana y su configuración actual, ha dejado una parcela hacia la que se vuelcan todos los patios traseros y medianas de los edificios, en algunos casos de más de cuatro plantas. La propuesta tiene como objeto reestablecer ese interior para conformar una manzana uniforme y completa. Las viviendas nuevas se adosan a las construcciones existentes configurando patios para volcar los elementos húmedos de las viviendas y permitir su ventilación.

Generamos un vacío urbano que aporta espacios ajardinados y dotaciones tanto para la comunidad de viviendas como para el barrio. Este espacio público queda entreabierto y conectado al barrio, asumiendo con descaro una condición de interior-exterior. Todas las viviendas orientan sus estancias más importantes hacia este exterior, siendo la fachada más importante y la que da sentido a la tipología de vivienda.

Todas las viviendas poseen una terraza configurada por una doble piel de vidrio y lamas de madera. Este ámbito se justifica como elemento de riqueza espacial de las viviendas, pues puede ser respetado como terraza o habitarse. Este elemento permite un movimiento de la fachada con diferentes alzados, que genera un espacio dinámico desde el interior de la parcela.

The singularity of the city block and its current configuration have created a plot that all of the back patios and centres of buildings with up to four storeys can pour into. The objective of the proposal is to reestablish that interior to create a uniform and complete block. The new homes are adjacent to existing construction and thus create patios that are home to the wet areas of the homes and allow ventilation.

We generate an urban void that contributes landscaped areas and resources for both the housing community as well as the neighbourhood. This public space remains half-opened and connects to the neighbourhood, blatantly assuming an inside-outside condition. The most important living areas of all of the homes face this outside, which is the most important facade and the one that classifies the building's typology. All of the homes have a terrace made of a double skin of glass and wood slats. This area is justified as an element of spatial richness of the homes, and thus can be respected as a terrace or as a habitable area. This element allows a movement of the facade with different elevations to generate a dynamic space from the inside of the plot.

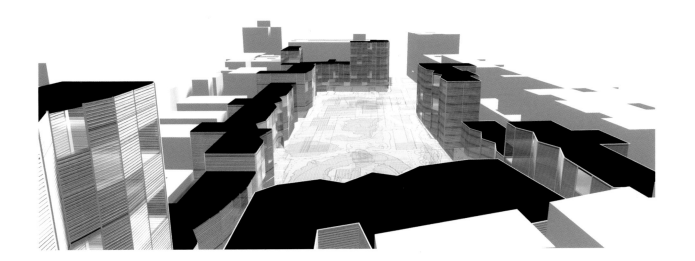

centro cultural josé espronceda

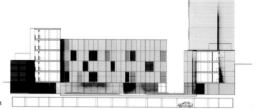

Sección transversal A Cross section

A

CALLE DE ALMANSA

CALLE DE GARELLANO

CALLE DE BRAVO MURILLO

B

B

1

4

2

3

A

CALLE DEL DOCTOR SANTERO

Planta baja
Ground floor plan

1:1.000

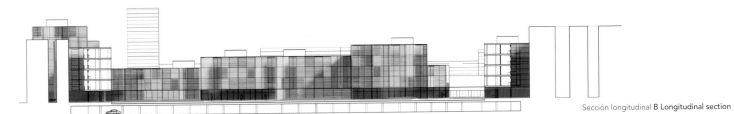

Sección longitudinal B Longitudinal section

CALLE DE ALMANSA

CALLE DE BRAVO MURILLO

CALLE DEL DOCTOR SANTERO

Tipos de viviendas
Dwelling types

ESTUDIOS: 0
1 DORMITORIO: 17
2 DORMITORIOS: 86
3 DORMITORIOS: 7
4+ DORMITORIOS: 0
STUDIOS: 0
1 BEDROOM: 17
2 BEDROOMS: 86
3 BEDROOMS: 7
4+ BEDROOMS: 0

Planta tipo **Type floor plan**

DENSIDADES ● **DENSITIES** ■ VIVIENDAS 83 **DWELLINGS** ■ USOS ● **USES** ■

79,4 %
VIVIENDA 164 🚗
LIVING

TRABAJO
WORKING

20,6 %
COMERCIOS
SHOPPING

EQUIPAMIENTOS
CIVIC FACILITIES

OTROS USOS
OTHER USES

143 △/ha
308 ⬙/ha

5.800 m²
SUPERFICIE DE PARCELA
PLOT AREA

10.200 m²
SUPERFICIE CONSTRUIDA
BUILT UP AREA

38 %
OCUPACIÓN
COVERED AREA

1,7
EDIFICABILIDAD
FLOOR AREA RATIO

scankort, 2007

1:10.000

+14

1:2.500

BIG big.dk

Njalsgade 19-27, Copenhagen. Denmark, 2005-

El proyecto propone rebasar los límites del volumen de la manzana respetando la normativa urbanística. Así, mediante la expansión del volumen del edificio hasta el máximo permitido se crea una arquitectura semejante a la de algunas catedrales, con agujas y cubiertas inclinadas.

Como el volumen generado es demasiado profundo para alojar viviendas, su interior contiene un atrio de uso público: una sala de estar para la comunidad.

El volumen se deforma para permitir que dos plazas públicas ocupen el espacio a ambos lados del edificio, mientras que la inclinación de las fachadas permite que la luz solar penetre sin ensombrecer las construcciones vecinas. Por último, una gran rampa comunica el atrio interior con la plaza pública que ocupa parte de la parcela.

How can we go beyond the traditional perimeter block but still stay within the letter of the building code?

By inflating a block of apartments to the limit of the maximum urban volume, we generate a cathedral like architecture of sloping roofs and spires. Too deep to be inhabited, the prismatic volume contains a public cavity –the courtyard as a collective living room. The volume is deformed as to liberate spaces for *plazas* at both sides and slanted in order to let light flow unimpeded to the neighbouring buildings. A tilted ramp leads from the inside out transforming itself into a street corridor with public accessibility.

Vista de la fachada oeste
West elevation view

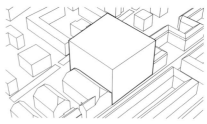

1 EXTRUSIÓN DE LA SUPERFICIE DE PARCELA DISPONIBLE **EXTRUSION OF THE AVAILABLE PLOT**

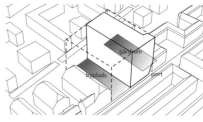

2 RECORTE PARCIAL DEL VOLUMEN CAPAZ PARA DAR LUGAR AL ESPACIO PÚBLICO, EL PATIO DE MANZANA Y LAS ÁREAS DE ACCESO **PARTIAL REMOVAL OF THE VOLUME, IN ORDER TO INCREASE PUBLIC SPACE, A COURTYARD, AND ACCESS SPACE**

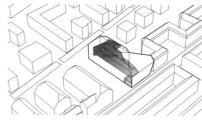

3 RECORTE DEL VOLUMEN PARA PERMITIR QUE LOS EDIFICIOS CERCANOS RECIBAN LUZ NATURAL **VOLUME IS CUT OUT SO THAT THE ADJACENT BUILDINGS RECEIVE MORE DAYLIGHT**

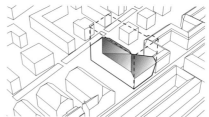

4 VACIADO INTERIOR DEL VOLUMEN PARA PERMITIR LA ENTRADA DE LUZ NATURAL **VOLUME IS CUT OUT TO LET DAYLIGHT ENTER INSIDE THE BUILDING**

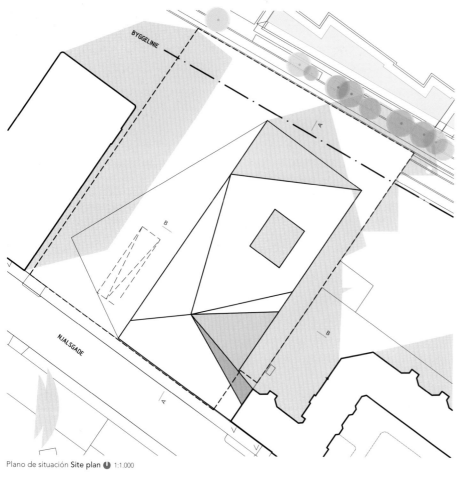

Plano de situación **Site plan** 🌓 1:1.000

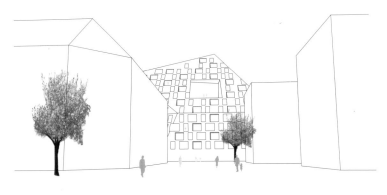

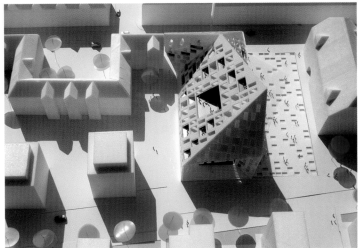

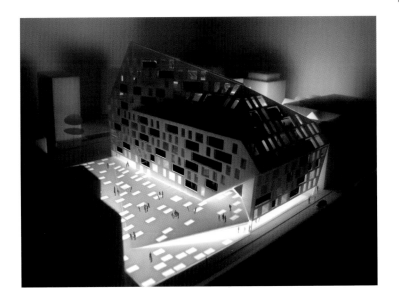

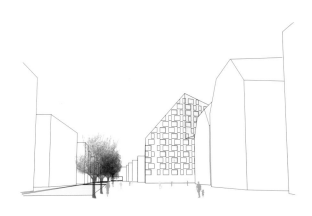

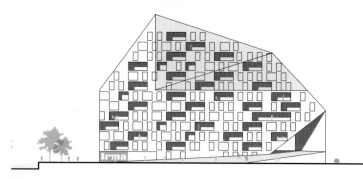

Alzado este **East elevation**

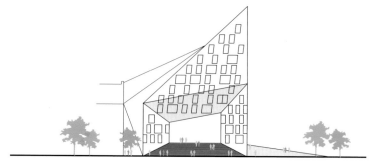

Alzado norte **North elevation**

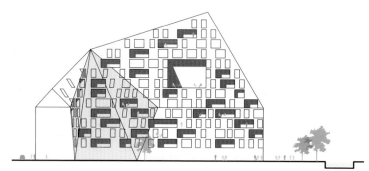

Alzado oeste **West elevation**

Alzado sur **South elevation**

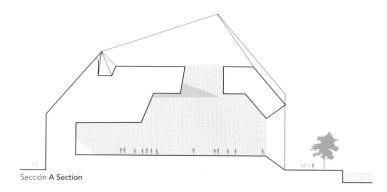

Sección **A Section**

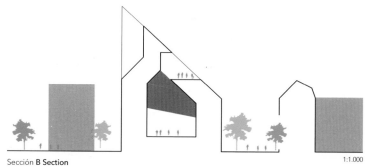

Sección **B Section**

1:1.000

214 Density projects

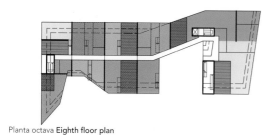

Planta octava Eighth floor plan

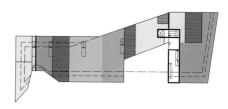

Planta novena Ninth floor plan

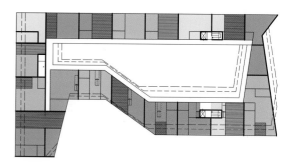

Planta cuarta Fourth floor plan

Planta quinta Fifth floor plan

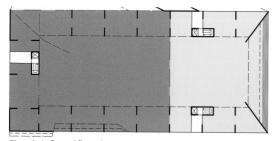

Planta baja Ground floor plan

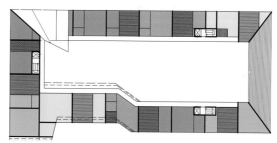

Planta primera First floor plan

Planta duodécima **Twelfth floor plan**

Tipo **1 Type**

Planta decimotercera **Thirteenth floor plan**

Planta décima **Tenth floor plan**

Tipo **2 Type**

Planta undécima **Eleventh floor plan**

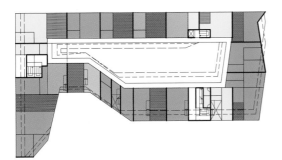

Planta sexta **Sixth floor plan**

Tipo **3 Type** 1:500

ESTUDIOS: 0
1 DORMITORIO: 33
2 DORMITORIOS: 40
3 DORMITORIOS: 10
4+ DORMITORIOS: 0
STUDIOS: 0
1 BEDROOM: 33
2 BEDROOMS: 40
3 BEDROOMS: 10
4+ BEDROOMS: 0

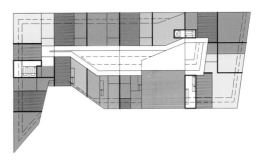

Planta séptima **Seventh floor plan**

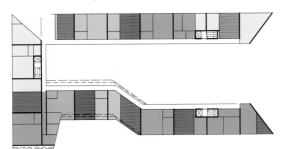

Planta segunda **Second floor plan**

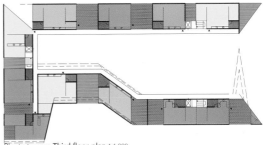

Planta tercera **Third floor plan** 1:1.000

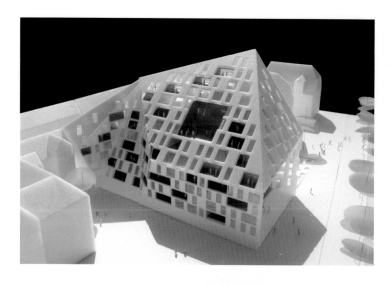

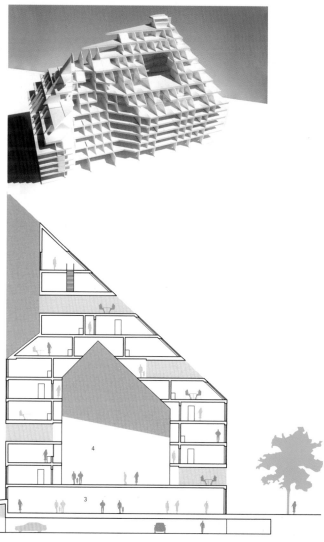

Sección **B Section**
1:500

1 PLAZA
2 APARCAMIENTO
3 GALERÍA INTERIOR
4 SUPERMERCADO

1 SQUARE
2 PARKING GARAGE
3 ATRIUM
4 SUPERMARKET

87,8 %
VIVIENDA 870 🚗
LIVING

TRABAJO
WORKING

7,2 %
COMERCIOS
SHOPPING

2,7 %
CINE/GUARDERÍA
CINEMA/NURSERY

2,3 %
HOTEL
HOTEL

61.800 m²
SUPERFICIE DE PARCELA
PLOT AREA

221.000 m²
SUPERFICIE CONSTRUIDA
BUILT UP AREA

25 %
OCUPACIÓN
COVERED AREA

3,5
EDIFICABILIDAD
FLOOR AREA RATIO

117 △/ha   358 ⊕/ha

digitalglobe, 2007

🕐 1:10.000

1:5.000

Steven Holl Architects stevenholl.com

East Xiba River Road, Beijing. China, 2003-2008

La recreación de un espacio cinematográfico tanto al exterior y como al interior de este proyecto es la idea que impulsa este complejo multiusos situado junto a la antigua muralla de Pekín. Actualmente, la ciudad crece a base de edificios-objeto aislados entre sí. Por el contrario, este proyecto pretende crear una ciudad dentro de la ciudad capaz de atender las necesidades de sus habitantes. Para ello, las ocho torres están unidas a la altura del vigésimo piso por un anillo de equipamientos.

Las caras inferiores de este anillo están coloreadas con pintura fosforescente, y en la plaza inferior, las fuentes alimentadas por el estanque central producen una niebla que se ilumina de distintos colores. Por su parte, sobre la fachada del edificio que aloja los cines se proyectan imágenes de las películas que pueden verse al interior.

La vivienda colectiva en China ha estado tradicionalmente muy estandarizada y resulta repetitiva. El proyecto, sin embargo, investiga la individualización de la vida urbana, y para ello se ofrece un amplio abanico de tipologías de vivienda. Cada apartamento goza de doble exposición y respeta los principios del Feng-Shui. Al exterior, se creado una parque semipúblico que consta de 5 colinas temáticas.

Filmic urban space: around, over and through multifaceted spatial layers, is one of the central aims of this Hybrid Building complex sited adjacent to the old city wall of Beijing.

Current development in Beijing is almost entirely -object buildings- and free standing towers. This -city within a city- envisions urban space as the central aim –as well as all the activities and programs that can support the daily life of its inhabitants. The eight towers are linked at the twentieth floor by a ring of services.

The undersides of the cantilevered portions are colored membranes in night light glow. Misting fountains from the water retention basin activate the night light in colorful clouds, while the floating Cineplex centerpiece has partial images of its ongoing films projected on its undersides and reflected in the water.

Mass housing in China has historically been stand-ardized and repetitive. However, this new vertical urban sector aspires to individuation in urban living. Hundreds of different apartment layouts in a huge variety of types will be available. Every apartment has two exposures with no interior hallways. Principles of Feng-Shui are followed throughout the complex.
Outside the buildings, a semi-public park, out of five landscape mounds is formed, each one fusing with recreational function

Espacio **Space**

HORIZONTALIDAD **HORIZONTALITY**

Pekín antesde los 80 **Beijing Before 1980s**

VERTICALIDAD **VERTICALITY**

Pekín después de los 80 **Beijing After 1980s**

VERTICAL-HORIZONTALIDAD **VERTICAL HORIZONTALITY**

Propuesta **Proposed**

CIUDAD DE OBJETOS
CITY OF OBJECTS

CIUDAD DE ESPACIOS
CITY OF SPACES

Barrio **Neighborhood**

Ciudad de calles densas
y patios
**City of Dense Streets
and Courtyards**

Barrios tradicionales
Traditional Neighborhoods

Ciudad de bolsas residuales
causa del nuevo desarrollo de
viviendas y una privatización
sin coordinación
**City of Pockets Caused by
New Residential Development
and Uncoordinated privatization**

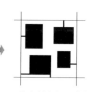

ALTERNATIVAS **ALTERNATIVES**

?

Comunidad abierta y programa híbrido **Open Community and Hybrid Programing**

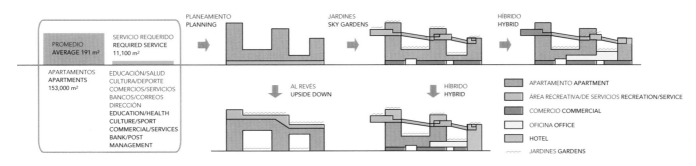

PROMEDIO AVERAGE 191 m²	SERVICIO REQUERIDO REQUIRED SERVICE 11,100 m²	
APARTAMENTOS APARTMENTS 153,000 m²	EDUCACIÓN/SALUD CULTURA/DEPORTE COMERCIOS/SERVICIOS BANCOS/CORREOS DIRECCIÓN EDUCATION/HEALTH CULTURE/SPORT COMMERCIAL/SERVICES BANK/POST MANAGEMENT	

PLANEAMIENTO
PLANNING

JARDINES
SKY GARDENS

HÍBRIDO
HYBRID

AL REVÉS
UPSIDE DOWN

HÍBRIDO
HYBRID

APARTAMENTO **APARTMENT**

ÁREA RECREATIVA/DE SERVICIOS **RECREATION/SERVICE**

COMERCIO **COMMERCIAL**

OFICINA **OFFICE**

HOTEL

JARDINES **GARDENS**

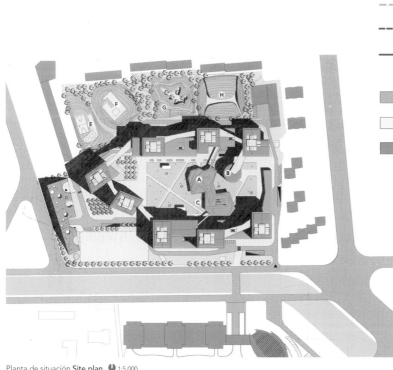

Planta de situación **Site plan** 🕐 1:5.000

Diagrama de circulación peatonal **Pedestrian circulation**

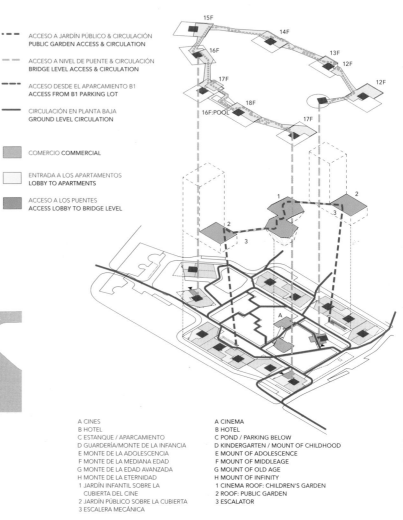

- - - ACCESO A JARDÍN PÚBLICO & CIRCULACIÓN
PUBLIC GARDEN ACCESS & CIRCULATION

- - - ACCESO A NIVEL DE PUENTE & CIRCULACIÓN
BRIDGE LEVEL ACCESS & CIRCULATION

- - - ACCESO DESDE EL APARCAMIENTO B1
ACCESS FROM B1 PARKING LOT

── CIRCULACIÓN EN PLANTA BAJA
GROUND LEVEL CIRCULATION

COMERCIO **COMMERCIAL**

ENTRADA A LOS APARTAMENTOS
LOBBY TO APARTMENTS

ACCESO A LOS PUENTES
ACCESS LOBBY TO BRIDGE LEVEL

A CINES
B HOTEL
C ESTANQUE / APARCAMIENTO
D GUARDERÍA/MONTE DE LA INFANCIA
E MONTE DE LA ADOLESCENCIA
F MONTE DE LA MEDIANA EDAD
G MONTE DE LA EDAD AVANZADA
H MONTE DE LA ETERNIDAD
1 JARDÍN INFANTIL SOBRE LA
  CUBIERTA DEL CINE
2 JARDÍN PÚBLICO SOBRE LA CUBIERTA
3 ESCALERA MECÁNICA

A CINEMA
B HOTEL
C POND / PARKING BELOW
D KINDERGARTEN / MOUNT OF CHILDHOOD
E MOUNT OF ADOLESCENCE
F MOUNT OF MIDDLEAGE
G MOUNT OF OLD AGE
H MOUNT OF INFINITY
1 CINEMA ROOF: CHILDREN'S GARDEN
2 ROOF: PUBLIC GARDEN
3 ESCALATOR

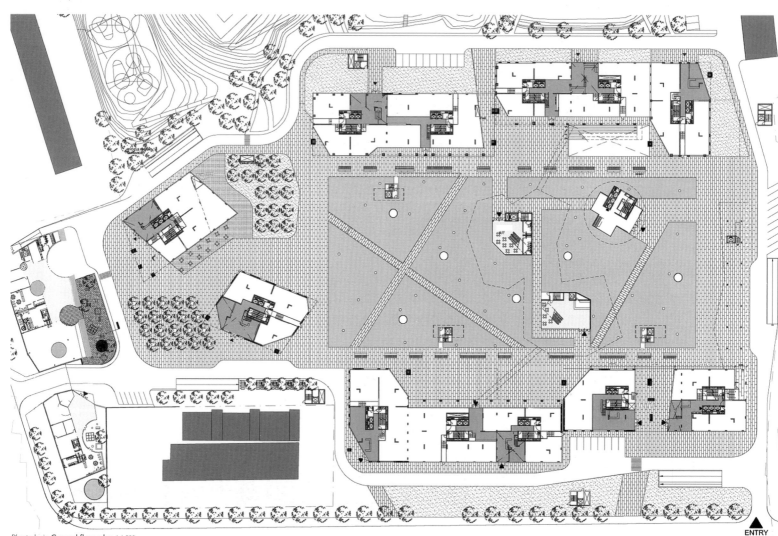

Planta baja **Ground floor plan** 1:1.500

▲
ENTRY

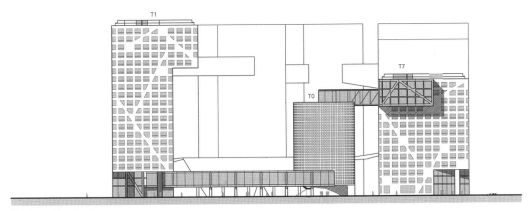

Alzado este **East elevation**

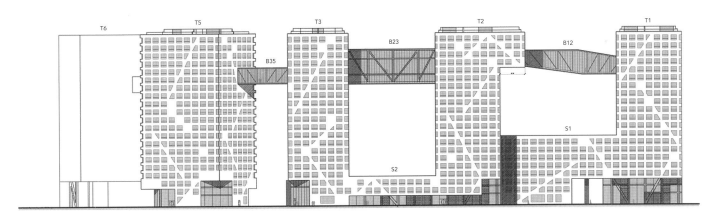

Pasaje de la plaza **Plaza passage**

Alzado sur **South elevation** 1:1.500

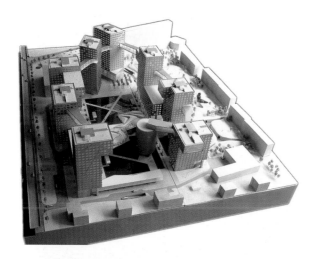

Parque semipúblico con 5 colinas temáticas
Semi-public park, with five mounds, each one fusing with recreational functions

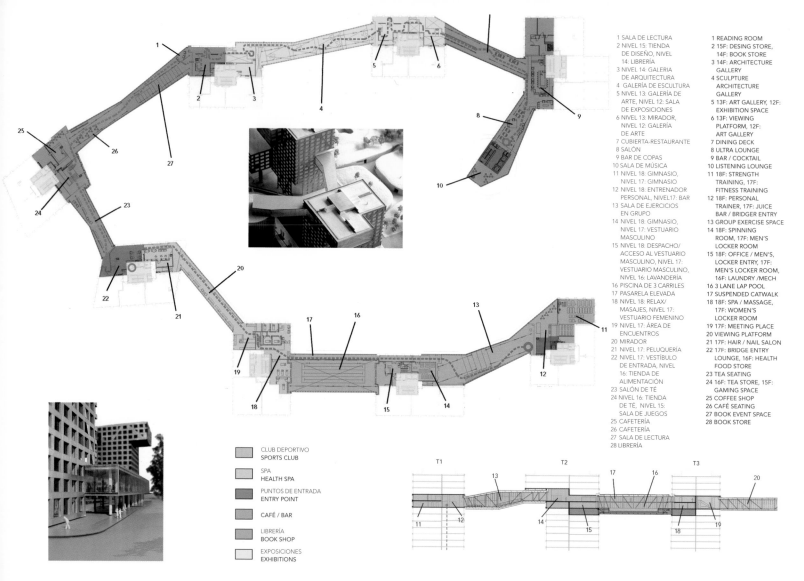

1 SALA DE LECTURA
2 NIVEL 15: TIENDA DE DISEÑO, NIVEL 14: LIBRERÍA
3 NIVEL 14: GALERIA DE ARQUITECTURA
4 GALERÍA DE ESCULTURA
5 NIVEL 13: GALERÍA DE ARTE, NIVEL 12: SALA DE EXPOSICIONES
6 NIVEL 13: MIRADOR, NIVEL 12: GALERÍA DE ARTE
7 CUBIERTA-RESTAURANTE
8 SALÓN
9 BAR DE COPAS
10 SALA DE MÚSICA
11 NIVEL 18: GIMNASIO, NIVEL 17: GIMNASIO
12 NIVEL 18: ENTRENADOR PERSONAL, NIVEL17: BAR
13 SALA DE EJERCICIOS EN GRUPO
14 NIVEL 18: GIMNASIO, NIVEL 17: VESTUARIO MASCULINO
15 NIVEL 18: DESPACHO/ ACCESO AL VESTUARIO MASCULINO, NIVEL 17: VESTUARIO MASCULINO, NIVEL 16: LAVANDERÍA
16 PISCINA DE 3 CARRILES
17 PASARELA ELEVADA
18 NIVEL 18: RELAX/ MASAJES, NIVEL 17: VESTUARIO FEMENINO
19 NIVEL 17: ÁREA DE ENCUENTROS
20 MIRADOR
21 NIVEL 17: PELUQUERÍA
22 NIVEL 17: VESTÍBULO DE ENTRADA, NIVEL 16: TIENDA DE ALIMENTACIÓN
23 SALÓN DE TÉ
24 NIVEL 16: TIENDA DE TÉ, NIVEL 15: SALA DE JUEGOS
25 CAFETERÍA
26 CAFETERÍA
27 SALA DE LECTURA
28 LIBRERÍA

1 READING ROOM
2 15F: DESING STORE, 14F: BOOK STORE
3 14F: ARCHITECTURE GALLERY
4 SCULPTURE ARCHITECTURE GALLERY
5 13F: ART GALLERY, 12F: EXHIBITION SPACE
6 13F: VIEWING PLATFORM, 12F: ART GALLERY
7 DINING DECK
8 ULTRA LOUNGE
9 BAR / COCKTAIL
10 LISTENING LOUNGE
11 18F: STRENGTH TRAINING, 17F: FITNESS TRAINING
12 18F: PERSONAL TRAINER, 17F: JUICE BAR / BRIDGER ENTRY
13 GROUP EXERCISE SPACE
14 18F: SPINNING ROOM, 17F: MEN'S LOCKER ROOM
15 18F: OFFICE / MEN'S, LOCKER ENTRY, 17F: MEN'S LOCKER ROOM, 16F: LAUNDRY /MECH
16 3 LANE LAP POOL
17 SUSPENDED CATWALK
18 18F: SPA / MASSAGE, 17F: WOMEN'S LOCKER ROOM
19 17F: MEETING PLACE
20 VIEWING PLATFORM
21 17F: HAIR / NAIL SALON
22 17F: BRIDGE ENTRY LOUNGE, 16F: HEALTH FOOD STORE
23 TEA SEATING
24 16F: TEA STORE, 15F: GAMING SPACE
25 COFFEE SHOP
26 CAFÉ SEATING
27 BOOK EVENT SPACE
28 BOOK STORE

CLUB DEPORTIVO
SPORTS CLUB

SPA
HEALTH SPA

PUNTOS DE ENTRADA
ENTRY POINT

CAFÉ / BAR

LIBRERÍA
BOOK SHOP

EXPOSICIONES
EXHIBITIONS

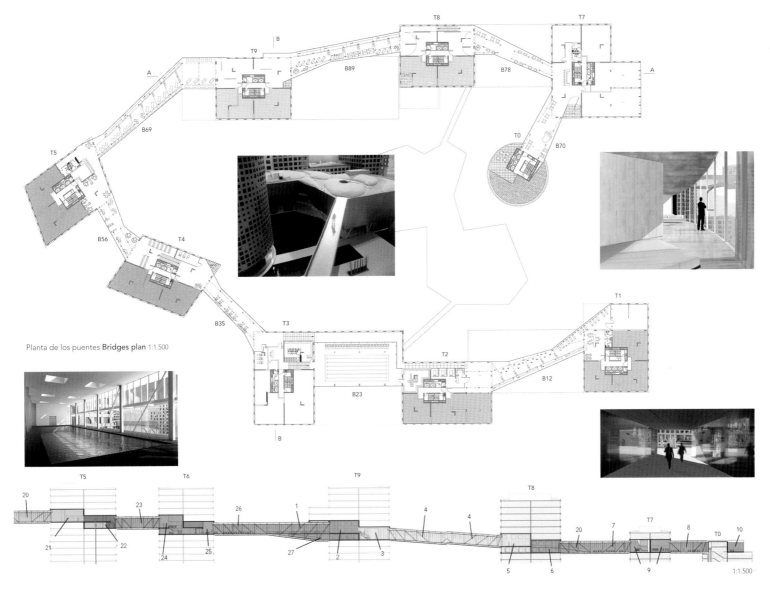

Planta de los puentes **Bridges plan** 1:1.500

1:1.500

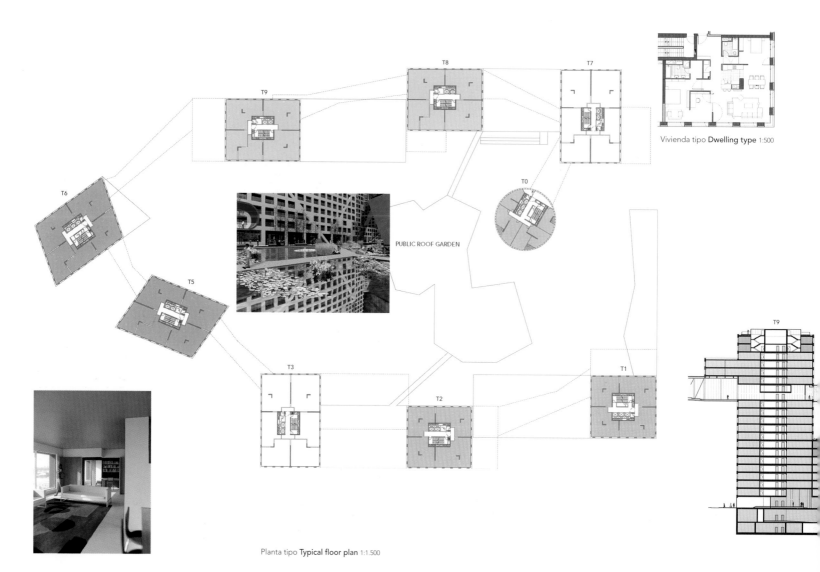

T9

T8

T7

Vivienda tipo **Dwelling type** 1:500

T6

PUBLIC ROOF GARDEN

T0

T5

T3

T2

T1

T9

Planta tipo **Typical floor plan** 1:1.500

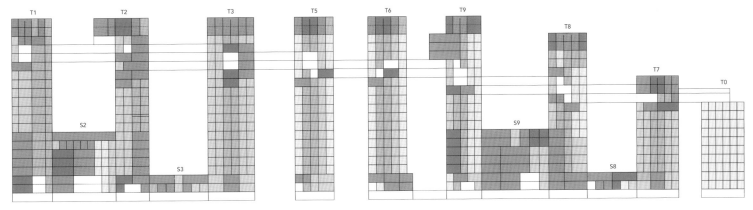

T1 T2 T3 T5 T6 T9 T8 T7 T0

S2 S3 S9 S8

NÚMERO DE HABITACIONES NUMBER OF BEDROOMS	**1** 183 25,4%	**2** 190 26,4%	**3** 183 25,4%	**4** 114 15,8%	**5>** 50 6,9%	720 100%	NÚMERO TOTAL DE UNIDADES OVERALL NUMBER OF UNITS

Tipos de apartamentos
Types of apartments

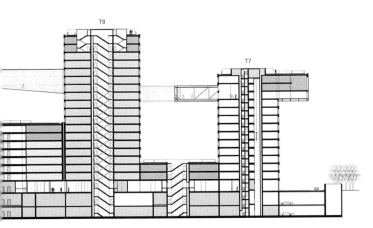

T8

T7

Sección **A** Section

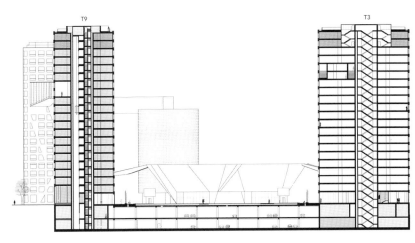

T9

T3

Sección **B** Section 1:1.500

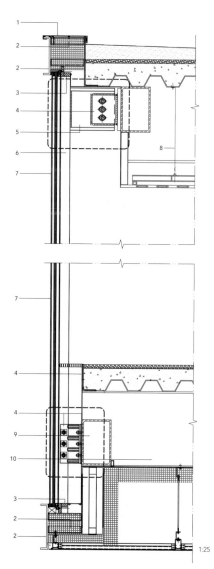

1 PANEL DE ALUMINIO DE
  3 mm DE ESPESOR
2 CANALETA DE ACERO
3 RASTREL HORIZONTAL
  DE ACERO
4 PLANCHA DE ACERO
5 VIGA DE ACERO
6 MONTANTE VERTICAL
  DE ACERO
7 VIDRIO TEMPLADO-
  LAMINADO TEMPLADO
8 TIRANTE
9 SOPORTE DE ACERO
10 VIGA DE ACERO

1 3 mm THICK ALUMINIUM
2 STEEL CHANNEL
3 STEEL TRANSOM
4 STEEL SHEET
5 STEEL BEAM
6 STEEL MULLION
7 LAMINATED TEMPERED GLASS
8 HANGER ROD
9 STEEL BAR
10 STEEL BEAM

Sección transvesal por el puente
Cross section of the bridge

1:25

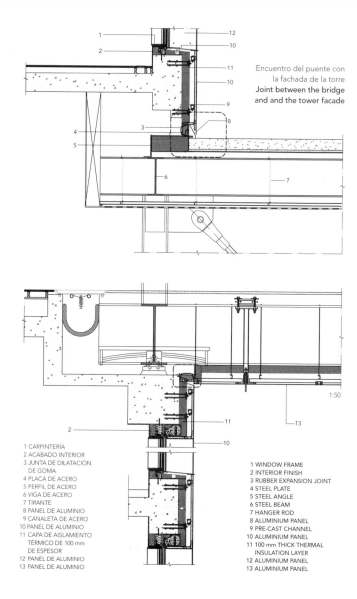

Encuentro del puente con
la fachada de la torre
**Joint between the bridge
and and the tower facade**

1:50

1 CARPINTERÍA
2 ACABADO INTERIOR
3 JUNTA DE DILATACIÓN
  DE GOMA
4 PLACA DE ACERO
5 PERFIL DE ACERO
6 VIGA DE ACERO
7 TIRANTE
8 PANEL DE ALUMINIO
9 CANALETA DE ACERO
10 PANEL DE ALUMINIO
11 CAPA DE AISLAMIENTO
   TÉRMICO DE 100 mm
   DE ESPESOR
12 PANEL DE ALUMINIO
13 PANEL DE ALUMINIO

1 WINDOW FRAME
2 INTERIOR FINISH
3 RUBBER EXPANSION JOINT
4 STEEL PLATE
5 STEEL ANGLE
6 STEEL BEAM
7 HANGER ROD
8 ALUMINIUM PANEL
9 PRE-CAST CHANNEL
10 ALUMINIUM PANEL
11 100 mm THICK THERMAL
   INSULATION LAYER
12 ALUMINIUM PANEL
13 ALUMINIUM PANEL

Detalle de la sección
del puente
**Detail of bridge
section** 1:500

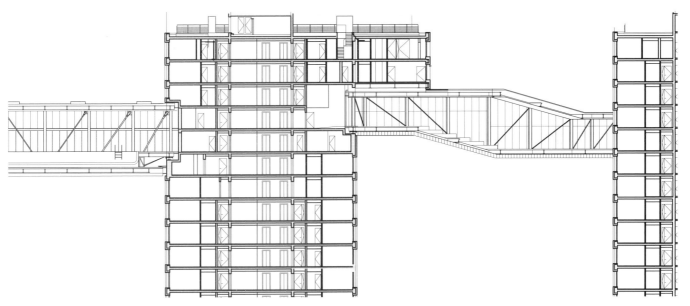

Vestíbulo del hotel
Hotel lobby

Recepción del hotel
Hotel reception

Plaza comercial
Shopping plaza

27,4 % VIVIENDA **LIVING**	17,6 % TRABAJO **WORKING**	16,9 % COMERCIOS/HOTEL **SHOPPING/HOTEL**	10,8 % CENTRO CULTURAL **CULTURAL CENTRE**	27,3 % APARCAMIENTO PÚBLICO **PUBLIC PARKING**

10.900 m² SUPERFICIE DE PARCELA **PLOT AREA**	141.900 m² SUPERFICIE CONSTRUIDA **BUILT UP AREA**	36 % OCUPACIÓN **COVERED AREA**	13,0 EDIFICABILIDAD **FLOOR AREA RATIO**

150 ⌂/ha   389 ☺/ha

indianamap framework data, 2007

1:10.000

REX rex-ny.com

615 West Main Street, Louisville. USA, 2005-2011

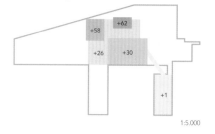

1:5.000

El proyecto Museum Plaza se replantea las estrategias habituales de la promoción inmobiliaria y así el programa cultural es tanto física como espiritualmente el corazón del edificio. La inversión necesaria para un museo de 3.700 m² necesita de otros 140.000 m² de programas asociados. Para no saturar la oferta comercial de Louisvillle, los usos que el proyecto acoge son variados, e incluyen viviendas de lujo, hotel, oficinas y comercios.

La promoción inmobiliaria convencional hubiese colocado el programa público a nivel de la calle y las torres con usos lucrativos encima. En este caso, esta estrategia no era posible, pues los condicionantes del solar hubiesen aislado la planta baja y obligado a aproximar demasiado las torres. Como consecuencia de ello, el zócalo de espacio cultural se eleva 20 alturas por encima de la rasante y las torres se distribuyen por encima y por debajo de esta "isla" de usos públicos.

Dentro de dicha isla de programa público se da una particular sinergia entre comercio y cultura. La proximidad poco habitual entre usos permite que el espacio de arte contemporáneo se imponga sobre el espectro banal de la flexibilidad museística.

Las torres, por el contrario, ven sus superficies y proporciones regidas por criterios estrictamente financieros. Así, con el fin de obtener los mejores beneficios, las viviendas, las oficinas y el hotel se reparten aprovechando al máximo las vistas, las circulaciones y la eficacia estructural.

Museum Plaza rethinks conventional attitudes towards property development. Culture is placed physically and spiritually at the project's center. To support the capital and operational costs of a 3,700 m² museum, a development of over 140,000 m² is required. To avoid over-saturating Louisville's market with any single commercial program, its uses are mixed, including luxury condominiums, hotel, offices, loft apartments, and retail.

Building development convention would typically position the public program at street level and the profit-making towers above. This strategy is not possible at Museum Plaza: the site would isolate any ground-level public program and position the towers implausibly close to each other. To liberate these conditions, the plinth of public program is elevated twenty stories aloft and the towers evenly distributed above and below.

Within the 'Island' of public program, a rare synergy between commerce and culture occurs. Unusual proximities enable the contemporary art space to overcome the banal specter of museum flexibility.

The towers, in contrast, are platonic, and their areas and proportions are dictated by efficiency ratios and financing. To maximize rents and sale prices, the luxury condos and offices above and the hotel and loft apartments below are optimally positioned for views, circulation, and structural efficiency.

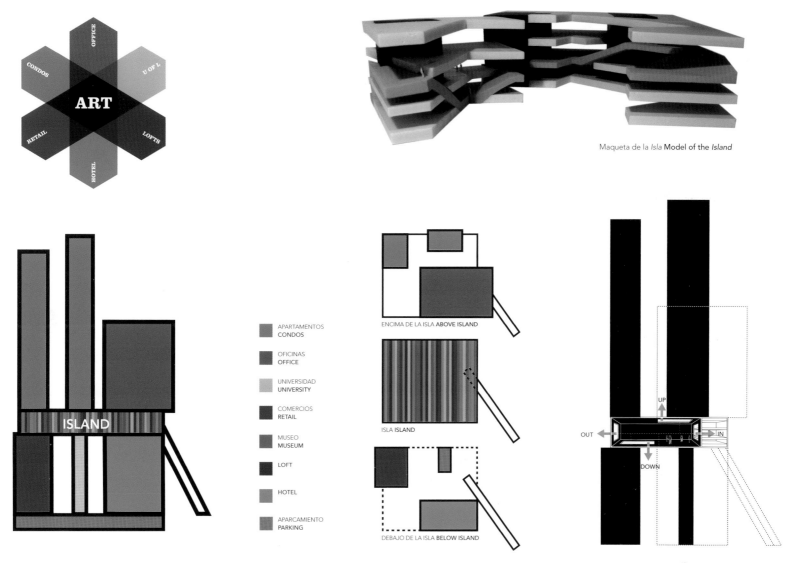

ART

OFFICE
CONDOS
U OF L
RETAIL
LOFTS
HOTEL

Maqueta de la *Isla* **Model of the** *Island*

ISLAND

APARTAMENTOS
CONDOS

OFICINAS
OFFICE

UNIVERSIDAD
UNIVERSITY

COMERCIOS
RETAIL

MUSEO
MUSEUM

LOFT

HOTEL

APARCAMIENTO
PARKING

ENCIMA DE LA ISLA **ABOVE ISLAND**

ISLA **ISLAND**

DEBAJO DE LA ISLA **BELOW ISLAND**

UP

OUT

IN

DOWN

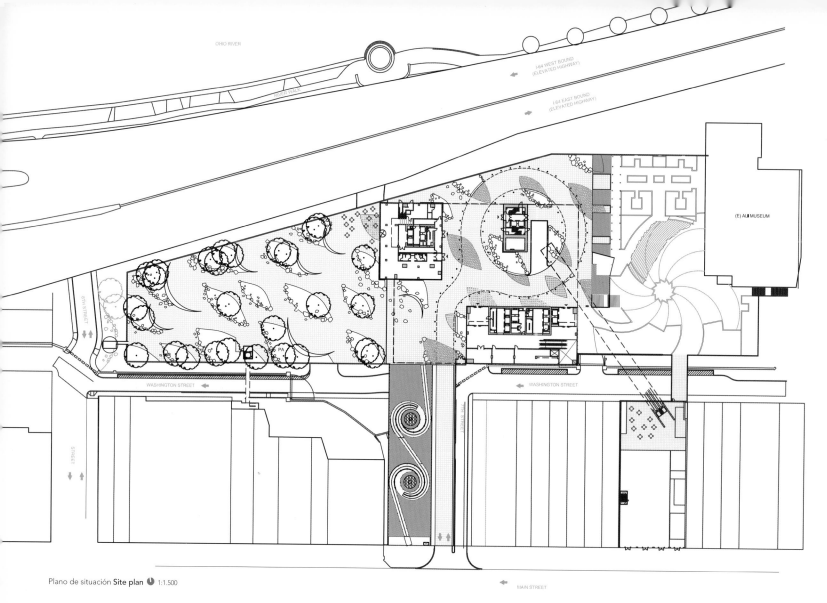

OHIO RIVER

RIVER WALK

I-64 WEST BOUND
(ELEVATED HIGHWAY)

I-64 EAST BOUND
(ELEVATED HIGHWAY)

(E) ALI MUSEUM

8TH STREET

WASHINGTON STREET

WASHINGTON STREET

7TH STREET

STREET

MAIN STREET

Plano de situación **Site plan** 1:1.500

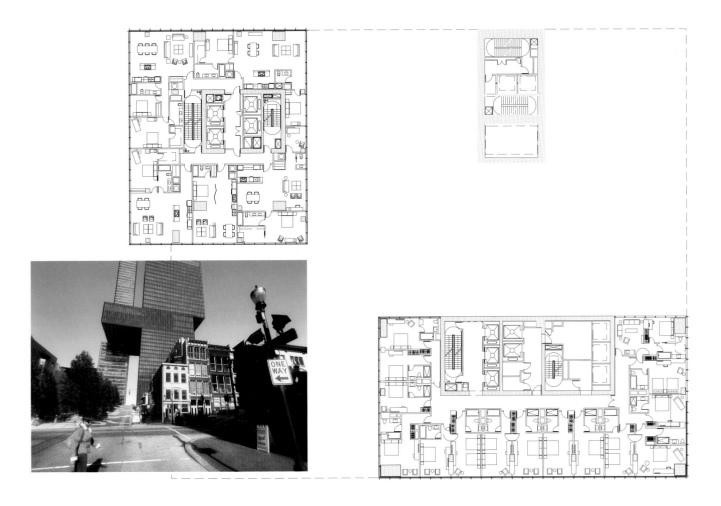

Planta 15: *Loft*, núcleo, hotel **15th floor plan: Loft, core, hotel** 1:500

Suelo-mirador desde la galería
Gallery view down

Vista de la galeria
Gallery view

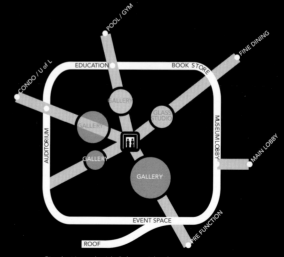

Circulación en la *Isla* **Subway** *Island*

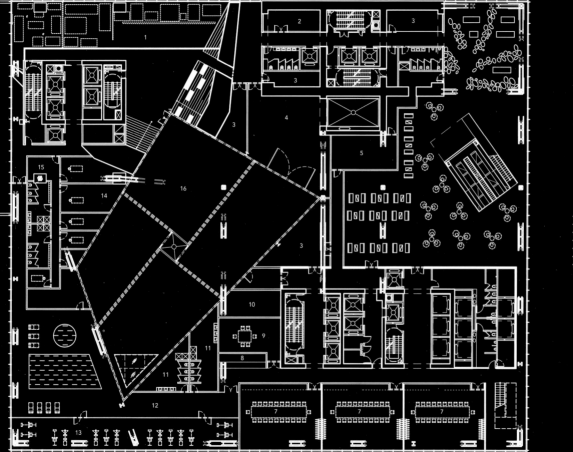

1 INSTALACIONES
2 ALMACÉN
3 ALMACÉN
4 VESTÍBULO DE CARG
5 COCINA
6 VOZ Y DATOS
7 SALA DE REUNIONES
8 DESPENSA
9 SALA DE REUNIONES
10 INSTALACIONES
11 VESTUARIOS
12 RECEPCIÓN
13 GIMNASIO
14 BALNEARIO
15 RECEPCIÓN
16 GALERÍA DE ARTE

1 INSTALATIONS
2 STORAGE
3 STORAGE
4 FREIGHT LOBBY
5 KITCHEN
6 VOICE & DATA
7 MEETING ROOM
8 PANTRY
9 BOARDROOM
10 INSTALATIONS
11 LOOKERS
12 RECEPTION
13 GYM
14 SPA
15 RECEPTION
16 GALLERY

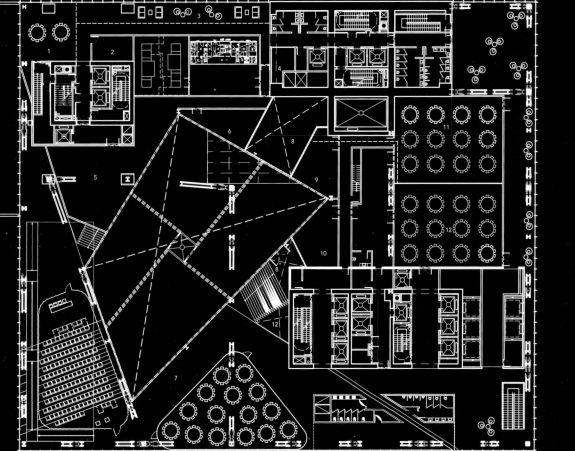

1 COMEDOR COMUNITARIO
DE LOS APARTAMENTOS
2 COCINA DEL CLUB
COMUNITARIO DE LOS
APARTAMENTOS
3 ZONA DE ESTAR COMUNITA
DE LOS APARTAMENTOS
4 BODEGA
5 OFICINAS DE LA
GALERÍA DE ARTE
6 CENTRO EDUCATIVO
7 SALA DE USOS MÚLTIPLES
8 VACÍO
9 ALMACÉN DE LA SALA
DE CONVENCIONES
10 ALMACÉN DE LA SALA
DE USOS MÚLTIPLES
11 SALA DE CONVENCIONES 1
12 SALA DE CONVENCIONES 2

1 CONDO DINING
2 CONDO CLUB KITCHEN
3 CONDO LIVING
4 WINE CELLAR
5 GALLERY ADMIN.
6 EDUCATION CENTER
7 EVENT SPACE
8 OPEN TO BELOW
9 BALL ROOM STORAGE
10 EVENT STORAGE
11 BALLROOM 2
12 BALLROOM 1

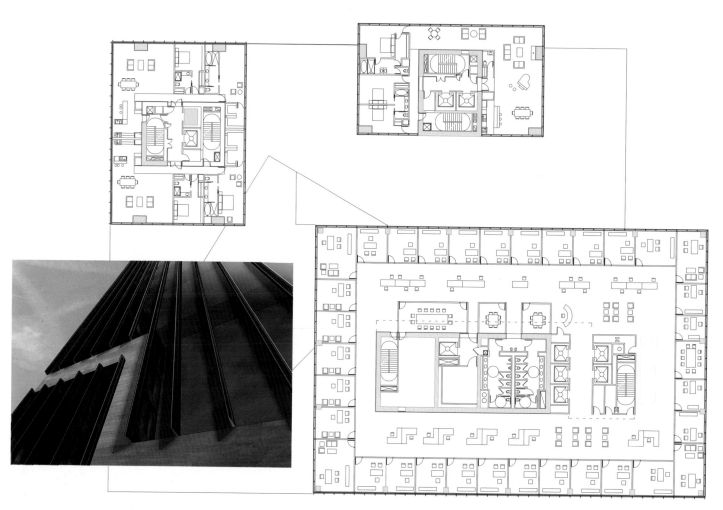

Planta 35: torres de viviendas este y oeste, oficinas
35th floor plan: West condo, East condo, offices 1:500

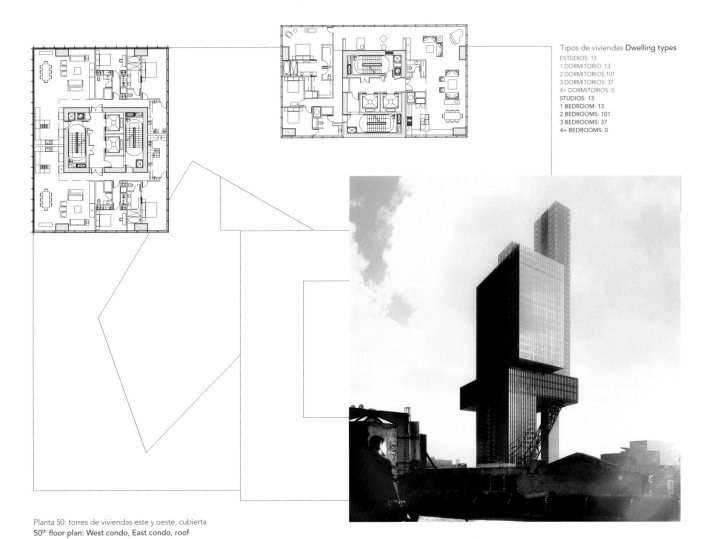

Tipos de viviendas **Dwelling types**
ESTUDIOS: 13
1 DORMITORIO: 13
2 DORMITORIOS:101
3 DORMITORIOS: 37
4+ DORMITORIOS: 0
STUDIOS: 13
1 BEDROOM: 13
2 BEDROOMS: 101
3 BEDROOMS: 37
4+ BEDROOMS: 0

Planta 50: torres de viviendas este y oeste, cubierta
50th floor plan: West condo, East condo, roof

DENSIDADES ● **DENSITIES** ■ VIVIENDAS 58 **DWELLINGS** ■USOS ● **USES** ■

(PHASE 1)

100%
VIVIENDA   22 🚗
LIVING

(PHASE 1)

193 Ω/ha   433 ℮/ha

TRABAJO
WORKING

COMERCIOS
SHOPPING

EQUIPAMIENTOS
CIVIC FACILITIES

OTROS USOS
OTHER USES

2.972 m²(PHASE 1+2)
SUPERFICIE DE PARCELA
PLOT AREA

5.760 m²(PHASE 1)
SUPERFICIE CONSTRUIDA
BUILT UP AREA

58 %(PHASE 1+2)
OCUPACIÓN
COVERED AREA

4 (PHASE 1+2)
EDIFICABILIDAD
FLOOR AREA RATIO

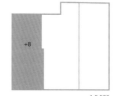

+8

1:2.500

sanborn, 2007

🔘 1:10.000

Peter L. Gluck and Partners gluckpartners.com

89 Grand Avenue, Brooklyn, New York. USA, 2007-

Para esta residencia de estudiantes, el proyecto se centra en la calidad de la vivienda que se proporciona. El tamaño del edificio requiere por normativa de un pasillo doble que condiciona todo el proyecto. A este corredor se le suman unos patios interiores comunicados entre sí. Los patios, además de animar la vida en el interior del edificio, se comportan como sus pulmones: el aire fresco entra desde el jardín por la planta baja y asciende hasta la cubierta, donde es expulsado. Así, todas las habitaciones disponen de ventilación natural cruzada aun teniendo una única exposición.

Por motivos económicos, decidimos emplear un sistema estructural de módulos prefabricados. Dada su mayor resistencia, ya que deben soportar los esfuerzos originados durante su transporte, pudimos volar ciertas partes, abrir huecos en la estructura y patios interiores. Además, el retranqueo que obliga la normativa se obtiene con una composición dinámica de la fachada, que rompe la escala manteniendo la unidad del edificio. El colorido de los patios interiores se refleja también en la fachada, poniendo al edificio en relación con el resto del campus y dirigiendo los recorridos peatonales desde la Grand Avenue.

In this students' dormitory, the focus of our design is the quality of the housing we are providing. Here, the size of the project and the zoning envelope require a double loaded corridor as the primary organizational system. We have animated this sequence with a series of internal courts that are linked together throughout the building. In addition to enlivening the circulation sequence, these spaces become the lungs of the building. Fresh air enters at the ground floor from the rear garden and rises through the entire building section, exhausting at the roof. In this way, all of the units benefit from natural cross ventilation despite having only one exterior exposure.

The pressures of economy prompt us to exploit the structural redundancy of the shop built module. By taking advantage of the added structural capacity needed to transport the modules, we incrementally cantilever the units in and out, thereby animating the overall section and providing space for the interior courts. Moreover, the zoning code setback is achieved dynamically over the façade, breaking down the scale while maintaining the identity of the building. The colour of the interior courts telegraphs through the thickness of the units to the windows, acknowledging the link back to the main campus and addressing the pedestrian approach along Grand Avenue.

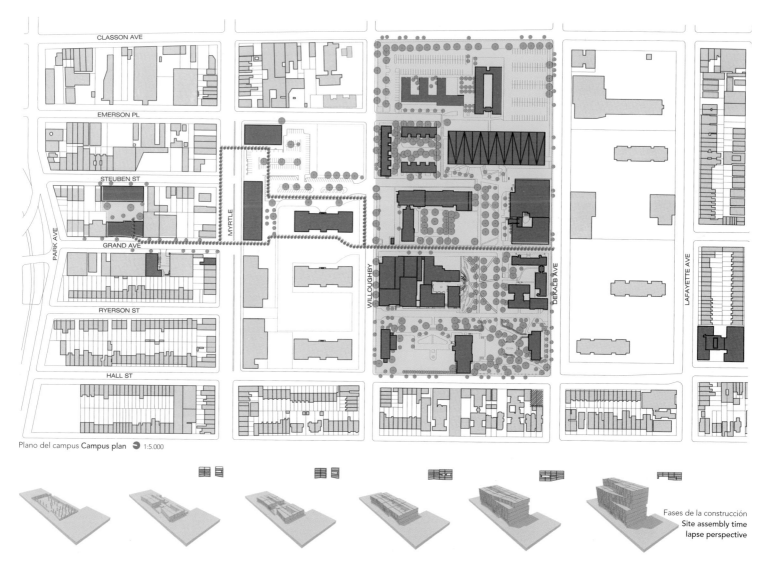

CLASSON AVE

EMERSON PL

STEUBEN ST

PARK AVE

GRAND AVE

MYRTLE

RYERSON ST

WILLOUGHBY

DEKALB AVE

LAFAYETTE AVE

HALL ST

Plano del campus **Campus plan** ➜ 1:5.000

Fases de la construcción
**Site assembly time
lapse perspective**

LA PARCELA Y LOS CONDICIONANTES
DEL PLANEAMIENTO IMPONEN LA
HUELLA DEL EDIFICIO
**SITE AND REAR YARD EQUIVALENT
ZONING GENERATES BUILDING
FOOTPRINT**

VOLUMEN CAPAZ: ALTURA MÁXIMA
DE 24,38 m
**BASIC MASSING – 24,38 m HEIGHT
LIMIT**

ALTURA MÍNIMA DE LA FACHADA
SOBRE LA ALINEACIÓN DE PARCELA
= 12,19 m
**MINIMUM REQUIRED STREETWALL
= 12,19 m**

ALTURA MÁXIMA DE LA FACHADA
SOBRE LA ALINEACIÓN DE PARCELA
= 19,81 m
**MAXIMUM REQUIRED STREETWALL
= 19,81 m**

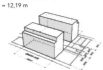

DISEÑO INICIAL DE UN VOLUMEN
SIMPLE SIN RETRANQUEOS
**START DESIGN DEVELOPMENT WITH
SIMPLE VOLUME; NO SETBACKS**

INSERCIÓN DEL NÚCLEO BAJO DE
CIRCULACIONES
**INSERT LOWER CIRCULATION
VOLUME**

EL VOLUMEN SE REDUCE EN TORNO
AL NÚCLEO DE CIRCULACIONES
**BUILDING MASS SHRINKS AROUND
CIRCULATION VOLUME**

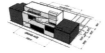

RETRANQUEO CONFORME AL
PLANEAMIENTO
**SETBACK MASSING TO CONFOM TO
ZONING REQUITEMENTS**

LA ALTURA DEL PRIMER RETRANQUEO
DE 12,80 m SE AJUSTA A LA ALTURA
DEL EDIFICIO CONTIGUO
**FIRST SETBACK HEIGHT OF 12,80 m
ALIGNS WITH ADJACENT BUILDING
TO EAST**

INSERCIÓN DEL SEGUNDO NÚCLEO
DE CIRCULACIONES A MEDIA ALTURA
**INSERT MID-LEVEL CIRCULATION
VOLUME**

EL VOLUMEN AUMENTA EN TORNO
AL NÚCLEO DE CIRCULACIONES
**BUILDING MASS EXPANDS AROUND
CIRCULATION VOLUME**

EL SEGUNDO RETRANQUEO DE
18,59 m SE AJUSTA A LA ALTURA DEL
OTRO EDIFICIO ADYACENTE
**SECOND SETBACK HEIGHT OF
18,59 m ALIGNS ADJACENT
BUILDING TO WEST**

INSERCIÓN DEL NÚCLEO SUPERIOR
DE CIRCULACIONES
**INSERT UPPER-LEVEL CIRCULATION
VOLUME**

EL VOLUMEN SE REDUCE EN
TONO AL NÚCLEO SUPERIOR DE
CIRCULACIONES
**BUILDING MASS EXPANDS AROUND
CIRCULATION VOLUME**

SE RECORTA EL VOLUMEN EN
LA ENTRADA AL EDIFICIO: LA
FORMALIZACIÓN QUEDA COMPLETADA
**STREET LEVEL ENTRY CUT ADDED
BUILDING MASSING COMPLETE**

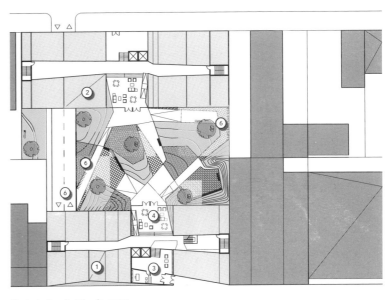

Planta de situación **Site plan** 1:1.000

1 FASE 1 DE LA NUEVA RESIDENCIA DE ESTUDIANTES
2 FASE 2 DE LA NUEVA RESIDENCIA DE ESTUDIANTES
3 VESTÍBULO DE ACCESO
4 SALA COMÚN
5 APARCAMIENTO CUBIERTO PARA BICICLETAS
6 ACCESO DE VEHÍCULOS AL APARCAMIENTO SUBTERRÁNEO

1 PHASE I OF NEW GRADUATE STUDENT DORMITORY
2 PHASE II OF NEW GRADUATE STUDENT DORMITORY
3 ENTRY LOBBY
4 STUDENT LOUNGE
5 COVERED BICYCLE PARKING
6 CAR ENTRY TO BASEMENT PARKING

Estudio urbanístico y volumétrico
Zoning analysis and massing

Alzado este
East elevation

Alzado oeste
West elevation

1:500

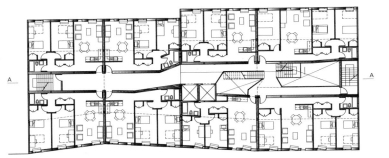

Planta primera **First floor plan**

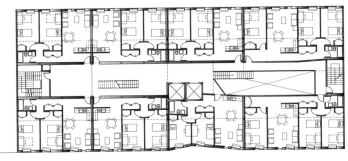

Planta segunda **Second floor plan**

Planta sótano **Basement plan**

Planta baja **Ground floor plan** 1:500

Planta séptima **Seventh floor plan**

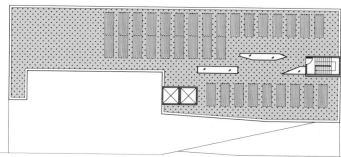

Planta de cubierta **Roof plan**

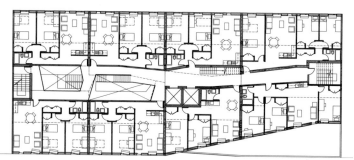

Planta quinta **Fifth floor plan**

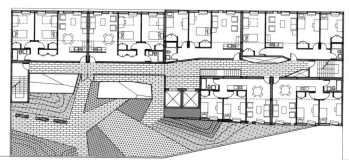

Planta sexta **Sixth floor plan**

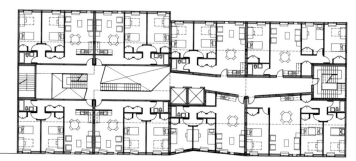

Planta tercera **Third floor plan**

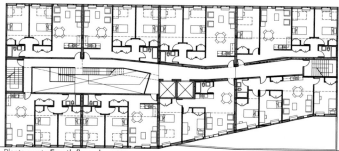

Planta cuarta **Fourth floor plan** 1:500

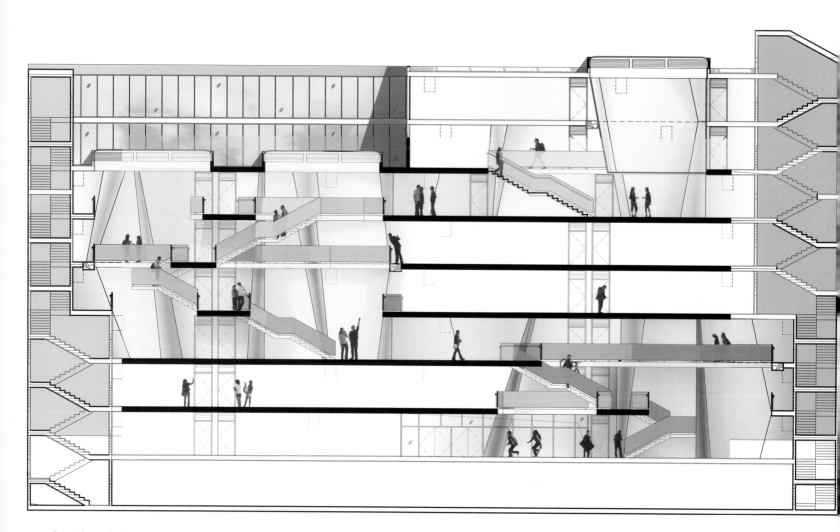

Sección longitudinal **A Section longitudinal** 1:250

Circulación del aire y ganancias térmicas
Air circulation and heat gain

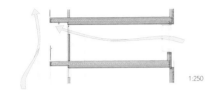

1:250

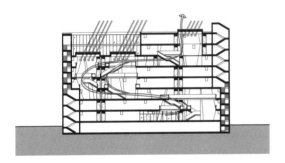

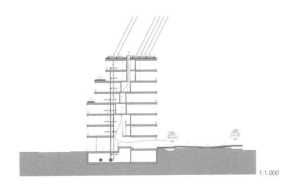

1:1.000

Diagrama del sistema de prefabricación
Off-site construction diagram

Tipos de viviendas **Dwelling types**
ESTUDIOS: 0
1 DORMITORIO: 0
2 DORMITORIOS: 44
3 DORMITORIOS: 14
4+ DORMITORIOS: 0
STUDIOS: 0
1 BEDROOM: 0
2 BEDROOMS: 44
3 BEDROOMS: 14
4+ BEDROOMS: 0

Tipos de viviendas **Dwelling types** 1:500

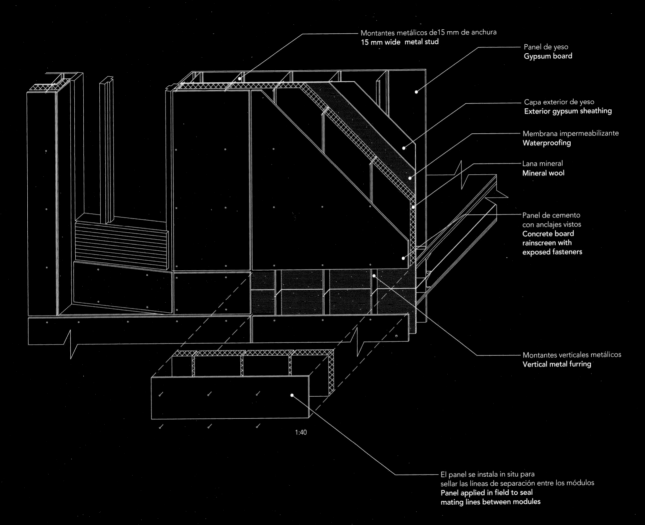

Montantes metálicos de15 mm de anchura
15 mm wide metal stud

Panel de yeso
Gypsum board

Capa exterior de yeso
Exterior gypsum sheathing

Membrana impermeabilizante
Waterproofing

Lana mineral
Mineral wool

Panel de cemento
con anclajes vistos
**Concrete board
rainscreen with
exposed fasteners**

Montantes verticales metálicos
Vertical metal furring

1:40

El panel se instala in situ para
sellar las líneas de separación entre los módulos
**Panel applied in field to seal
mating lines between modules**

Axonométrica de fachada **Facade axonometric**

100 %
VIVIENDA
LIVING

TRABAJO
WORKING

COMERCIO
SHOPPING

EQUIPAMIENTOS
CIVIC FACILITIES

OTROS USOS
OTHER USES

2.403 m²
SUPERFICIE DE PARCELA
PLOT AREA

2.613 m²
SUPERFICIE CONSTRUIDA
BUILT UP AREA

54,9 %
OCUPACIÓN
COVERED AREA

1,1
EDIFICABILIDAD
FLOOR AREA RATIO

129 ⌂/ha   437 ☺/ha

1:2.500

1:10.000

MGM Morales, Giles morales-giles-mariscal.com

Calle de Ariza 5, Úbeda. Spain, 2006-

El proyecto se ubica en un solar con una situación muy singular. Situados frente a un parque público, en el centro de Úbeda, y con un futuro edificio de equipamiento público adosado.

El proyecto propone una edificación fuertemente ligada al espacio público, no sólo por su condición de albergar viviendas colectivas, sino por la necesidad de un patio de manzana que, indiscutiblemente se ve obligado a convertirse en la prolongación del parque público que se anticipa al proyecto. Proponemos así la apertura de un pasaje que incentivará el flujo urbano a través de este espacio verde común de nueva creación.

El acceso a las viviendas se producirá mediante el ingreso en calles de uso privado que desembocan en los patios de acceso. Se ha querido humanizar así los patios de luces, para que sean recorridos y cruzados no sólo por las miradas sino por las personas que acceden a sus viviendas. Es la última prolongación de un espacio libre y continuo que empezó en el parque.

Respecto a la tipología de las viviendas, hemos sido muy sistemáticos y modulares. En vez de desarrollar unas "viviendas tipo" cuya repetición nos produjera una rígida implantación, hemos modulado las habitaciones, y desarrollado unos paquetes-módulo-habitacionales en relación con los patios y fachadas.

This project is located on a plot whose situation is quite unique. They face a public park in the centre of Ubeda, with an adjacent future public service building.

The project proposes a construction that is strongly linked to the public space, not only because it holds collective housing but also because of the need for an inner patio on the block that would have to become an extension of the public park that the project anticipates. We so propose the opening of a passage that will promote urban flow through this newly created common green area.

Entrance to the homes will be by entering private streets that open up to the entrance patios. In this way, we wished to humanise the light patios so that they would be crossed not only visually by those walking by, but also physically, by the people entering their homes. It is the final extension of a free and continuous space that began in the park.

Regarding the typology of the homes, we were very systematic and modular. Instead of developing 'model' homes whose repetition would have caused us rigidity in building, we made modules of the rooms and developed packages-modules-rooms related to the patios and facades.

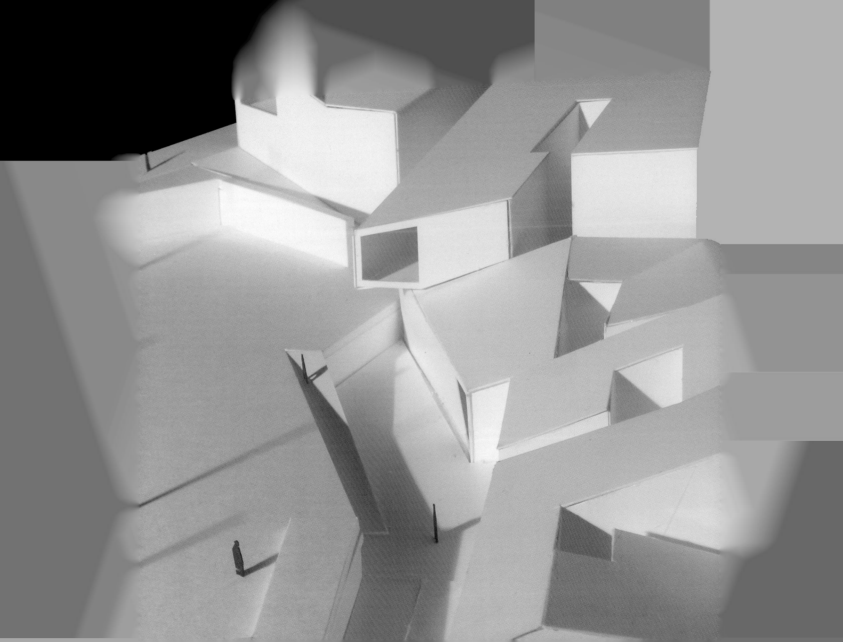

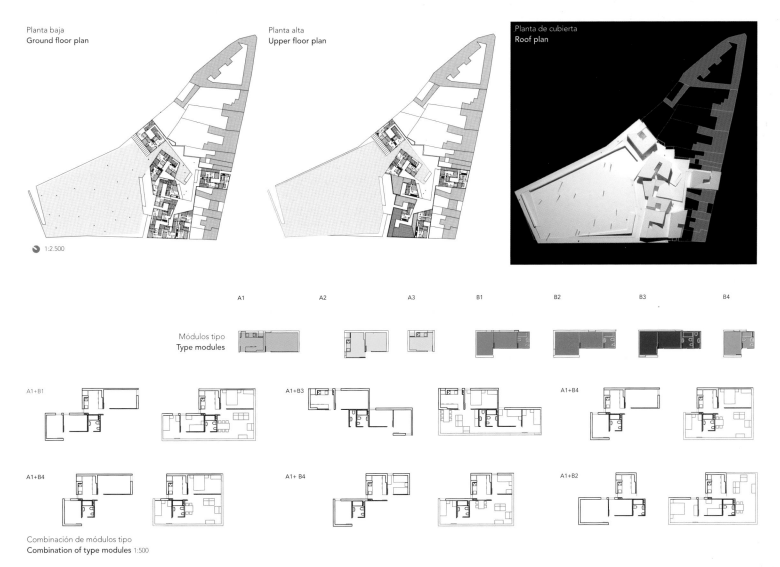

Planta baja
Ground floor plan

Planta alta
Upper floor plan

Planta de cubierta
Roof plan

1:2.500

A1 A2 A3 B1 B2 B3 B4

Módulos tipo
Type modules

A1+B1

A1+B3

A1+B4

A1+B4

A1+ B4

A1+B2

Combinación de módulos tipo
Combination of type modules 1:500

Planta baja **Ground floor plan** 🌑 1:1.000

Planta primera **First plan**

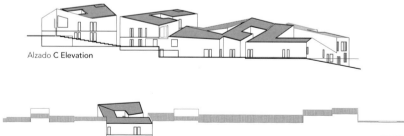

Alzado **C Elevation**

Alzado **A Elevation** 1:1.000

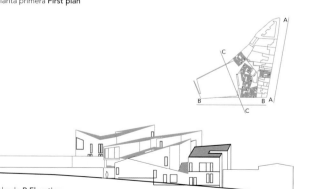

Alzado **B Elevation**

268 Density projects

Seccion A Section

Seccion B Section

Seccion A Section

Seccion B Section

Seccion C Section

Seccion D Section

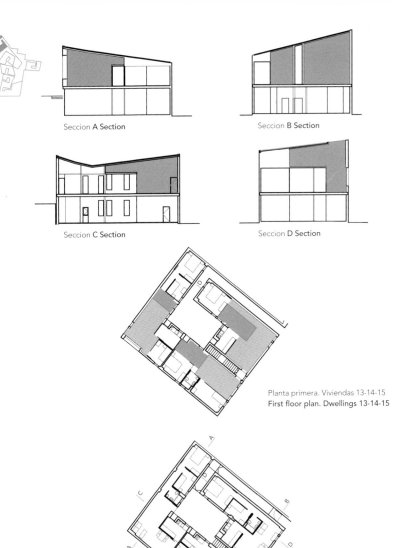

Planta primera. Viviendas 13-14-15
First floor plan. Dwellings 13-14-15

Planta baja. Viviendas 25-26-27
Ground floor plan. Dwellings 25-26-27

Planta Primera. Viviendas 28-29-30
First floor plan. Dwellings 28-29-30

Planta baja. Viviendas 16-17-18
Ground floor plan. Dwellings 16-17-18

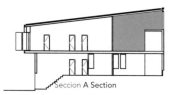

Seccion A Section

Seccion B Section

Planta primera. Viviendas 22-23-24
First floor plan. Dwellings 22-23-24

Planta baja. Viviendas 10-11-12
Ground floor plan. Dwellings 10-11-12

Seccion A Section

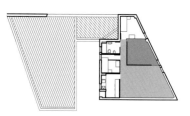

Planta primera. Viviendas 8-9
First floor plan. Dwellings 8-9

Planta baja. Viviendas 8-9
Ground floor plan. Dwellings 8-9

1:500

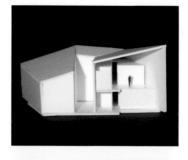

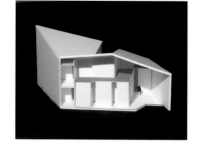

TRASTERO **ESTORAGE**

DOBLE ALTURA SOBRE SALÓN
VOID OVER LIVING ROOM

Sección **A** Section

Sección **B** Section

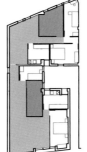

Planta baja. Viviendas 1-2
Ground floor plan. Dwellings 1-2

Tipos de viviendas **Dwelling types**
ESTUDIOS: 0
1 DORMITORIO: 0
2 DORMITORIOS: 12
3 DORMITORIOS: 16
4+ DORMITORIOS: 3
STUDIOS: 0
1 BEDROOM: 0
2 BEDROOMS: 12
3 BEDROOMS: 16
4+ BEDROOMS: 3

Planta primera. Viviendas 19-20
First floor plan. Dwellings 19-20

Sección **A** Section

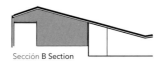

Sección **B** Section

Sección **C** Section

Sección **D** Section 1:500

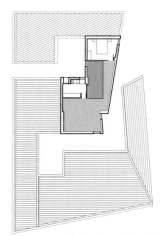

Planta primera. Vivienda 31
First floor plan. Dwelling 31

Planta baja. Viviendas 4-5-6-7
Ground floor plan. Dwellings 4-5-6-7

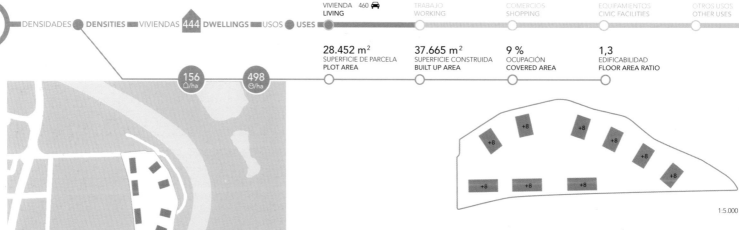

DENSIDADES ● DENSITIES ■ VIVIENDAS 444 DWELLINGS ■ USOS ● USES ■

100 %
VIVIENDA   460 🚗
LIVING

TRABAJO
WORKING

COMERCIOS
SHOPPING

EQUIPAMIENTOS
CIVIC FACILITIES

OTROS USOS
OTHER USES

28.452 m²
SUPERFICIE DE PARCELA
PLOT AREA

37.665 m²
SUPERFICIE CONSTRUIDA
BUILT UP AREA

9 %
OCUPACIÓN
COVERED AREA

1,3
EDIFICABILIDAD
FLOOR AREA RATIO

156
⌂/ha

498
⊙/ha

22

1:5.000

1:10.000

Atelier Thomas Pucher & Bramberger

thomaspucher.com, bramberger-architects.at

Rebase Street, Tartu. Estonia, 2006-2010

El proyecto se desarrolla en dos tipos de edificio diferentes: por un lado, los edificios junto al río se asemejan a las villas suburbanas, mientras que el edificio emplazado del lado de la ciudad es un bloque más urbano. Ambos tipos de edificios se complementan en su concepto funcional, orientación y tipología de vivienda, proporcionando un total de 444 viviendas. Los tipos van desde pequeños apartamentos muy flexibles a grandes viviendas con espacios generosos.

La tipología de villas apiladas se sitúa en el lado del río, mientras que los bloques lineales alojan viviendas pasantes en doble altura. Los edificios junto al río se organizan de forma sencilla y compacta: un atrio central recorrido por una escalera atraviesa el interior del edificio. A su alrededor se disponen las viviendas en cada planta, organizadas alrededor de un anillo interior de servicios que comprende los accesos, armarios, baños, saunas y en ocasiones las cocinas. El anillo externo, que dispone del sol y las vistas, aloja las zonas de día y los dormitorios. Este anillo, al carecer de elementos estructurales, permite distintas configuraciones mediante el uso de tabiques divisorios ligeros, y está rodeado por un balcón de forma irregular.

The project develops two types of buildings: while the one on the river represents the villa type, the other –facing the city– tends to be a more urban type. Building types complement each other in terms of functional concept, orientation and housing typology. Together they provide a great variability of 444 apartments. Types vary from very flexible apartments to maisonettes with very spacious room configurations.

The stacked Villas are placed by the riverside and city-slabs are organized with cross-stacked apartments, running through the width of the building. Buildings are organised in a very simple and compact way. The lobby, with the staircase and its thin, spiral atrium is in the centre of the building. Apartments are organised around this centre like a ring with a clear separation in two zones. The inner part is formed by a continuous service ring with entrances, wardrobes, toilets, bathrooms saunas, and sometimes kitchens. The outer part is embodied by the spacious living ring, oriented to the sun and the view. It provides flexible space without load bearing elements. Thus it is possible to organise it individually with light weight walls. The living ring is surrounded by a continuous balcony with an irregular edge.

THE CITY SLAB

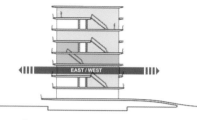

Concepto
Amplio espacio de este a oeste
Concept
Generous space from east to west

Planta de situación **Siteplan** 🌓 1:5.000

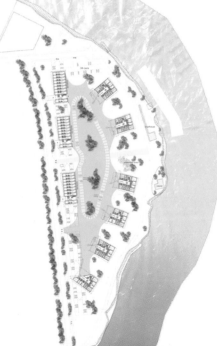

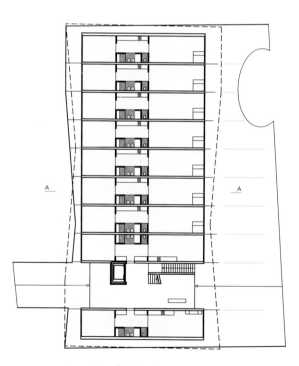

Planta primera **First floor plan**

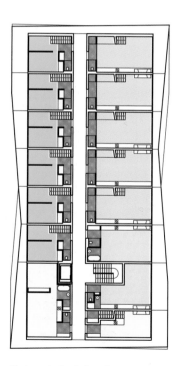

Planta cuarta **Fourth floor plan**

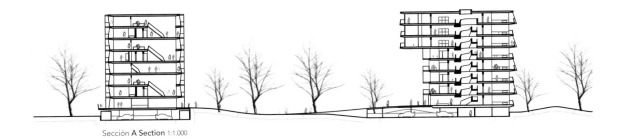

Sección **A Section** 1:1.000

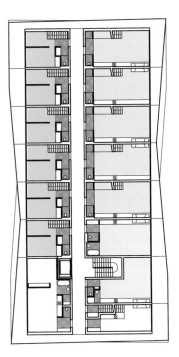

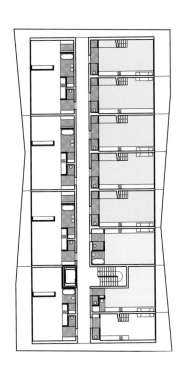

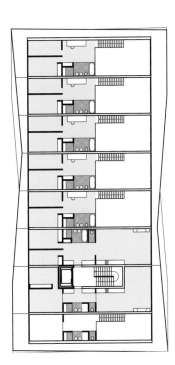

Planta quinta **Fith floor plan**

Planta séptima **Seventh floor plan**

Planta octava **Eighth floor plan** 1:500

THE RIVER TOWER

Concepto
Flexibilidad/ organización de las viviendas
Concept
Flexibility / the organisation of the flats

Planta octava **Eighth floor plan**

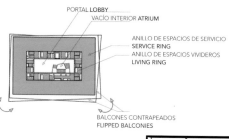

PORTAL **LOBBY**
VACÍO INTERIOR **ATRIUM**

ANILLO DE ESPACIOS DE SERVICIO
SERVICE RING
ANILLO DE ESPACIOS VIVIDEROS
LIVING RING

BALCONES CONTRAPEADOS
FLIPPED BALCONIES

Alzado sur **South elevation** 1:1.000

Planta cuarta **Fourth floor plan**

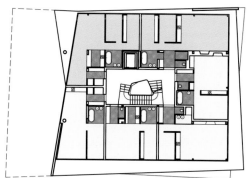

Planta primera **First floor plan** 🕐 1:500

Detalle de las terrazas **Flipping balconies detail**

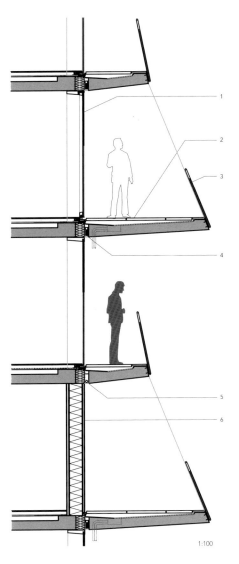

1 FACHADA: HUECOS
FACHADA DE VIDRIO Y
CARPINTERÍA DE MADERA
2 BALCÓN
FORJADO DE HORMIGÓN
RECUBIERTO DE RESINA EPOXY
COMO IMPERMEABILIZANTE.
SUELO: ENTARIMADO
DE MADERA TRATADA
TÉRMICAMENTE APOYADO
SOBRE RASTRELES O
PAVIMENTO DE PIEDRA SOBRE
UNA CAPA DE GRAVA
3 BARANDILLA
MONTANTES DE ACERO
INOXIDABLE Y MALLA
METÁLICA
4 PERSIANAS
SISTEMA INTEGRADO DE
PERSIANAS ENCASTRADO EN
EL FORJADO
5 ILUMINACIÓN
SISTEMA INTEGRADO DE
LUMINARIAS ENCASTRADAS
EN EL FORJADO
6 FACHADAS: PAÑOS OPACOS
PANEL DE MADERA REVESTIDO
DE ALUMINIO

1 FACADE –GLASS
GLASS FACADE WITH
WOODEN FRAMES
2 BALCONY
CONCRETE SLAB WITH
WATERPROOF AND FROST
RESISTING EPOXY RESIN
COATING.
FLOORING: THERMAL
TREATED WOODEN
BOARDING ON SUPPORTING
STANDS OR STONE PLATES
ON GRAVEL BED
3 RAILING
STAINLESS STEEL
CONSTRUCTION WITH
STRAINED METAL MESH
4 SHADING
INTEGRATED SHADING
DEVICE
5 LIGHTING
INTEGRATED LIGHTING
DEVICE
6 FACADE – PANEL
WOODEN PANEL WITH
ALUMINIUM CLADDING

1:100

23

DENSIDADES ● **DENSITIES** ■ VIVIENDAS 84 **DWELLINGS** ■ USOS ● **USES** ■

96,7 %
VIVIENDA 86 🚗
LIVING

TRABAJO
WORKING

3,3 %
COMERCIOS
SHOPPING

EQUIPAMIENTOS
CIVIC FACILITIES

OTORS USOS
OTHER USES

185 ⌂/ha

656 ⊕/ha

4.537 m²
SUPERFICIE DE PARCELA
PLOT AREA

7.441 m²
SUPERFICIE CONSTRUIDA
BUILT UP AREA

33,1 %
OCUPACIÓN
COVERED AREA

1,6
EDIFICABILIDAD
FLOOR AREA RATIO

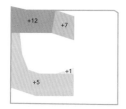

1:2.500

digitalglobe, 2007

🚲 1:10.000

Cino Zucchi Architetti zucchiarchitetti.com

Darsena di Città Lotto 4, Ravenna. Italy, 2007-2009

Este edificio de viviendas responde a la variedad de escalas presente, a la evolución de los modos de habitar y a la relación con el paisaje circundante. En la base del diseño se encuentra la gran ocasión que proporciona la construcción de un nuevo parque urbano y un paseo a lo largo del puerto de Ravenna. El diseño se apoya en una serie de bandas paralelas: el paseo frente al agua, el parque y la nueva calle. La claridad tipológica del proyecto asegura la adaptación de la escala urbana a la escala más íntima de la vida diaria. En él, la disposición de los volúmenes, que sigue los requerimientos del plan urbanístico, permite obtener vistas hacia la ciudad y el mar y crea un patio abierto al nuevo parque.

El volumen más elevado ocupa el lado norte del solar, junto al agua, y optimiza la orientación de las viviendas. El cuerpo bajo, por su parte, abraza el espacio central entre ambos edificios. Un puente habitado conecta los dos edificios, consolida la silueta del edificio en el lado del agua y crea un gran pórtico hacia el puerto.

The residential building relates to various scales, reasoning on the evolution of the ways to live and their relationship with the landscape. The great occasion for the construction of a new city park and a public waterfront along the Dock is at the base of the planning. The design is supported by a series of parallels strips: the new walkway along the water, the park, and the new street. The clarity of the typological system is the best guarantee of this ability to convert the general scale of the city into the intimate one of daily life. The disposition of volumes, which follows the setting of the new city design, responds to the long view towards the city, the sea and constructs a courtyard opened towards the new park. The higher volume is located at the northern side of the site, next to the new waterfront, and maximizes the good exposure of the apartments. The lower body folds to embrace the central space between the two buildings. An 'inhabited bridge' connects the two buildings, unifying the silhouette towards the water and creating one large loggia opened on the new walkway.

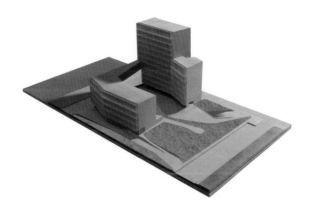

Planta de situación **Site plan** 🌑 1:2.500

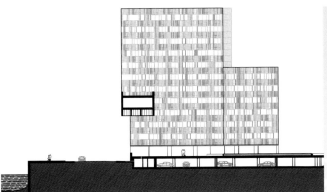

Alzado sur **South elevation** 1:1.000

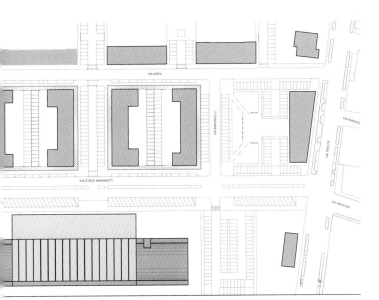

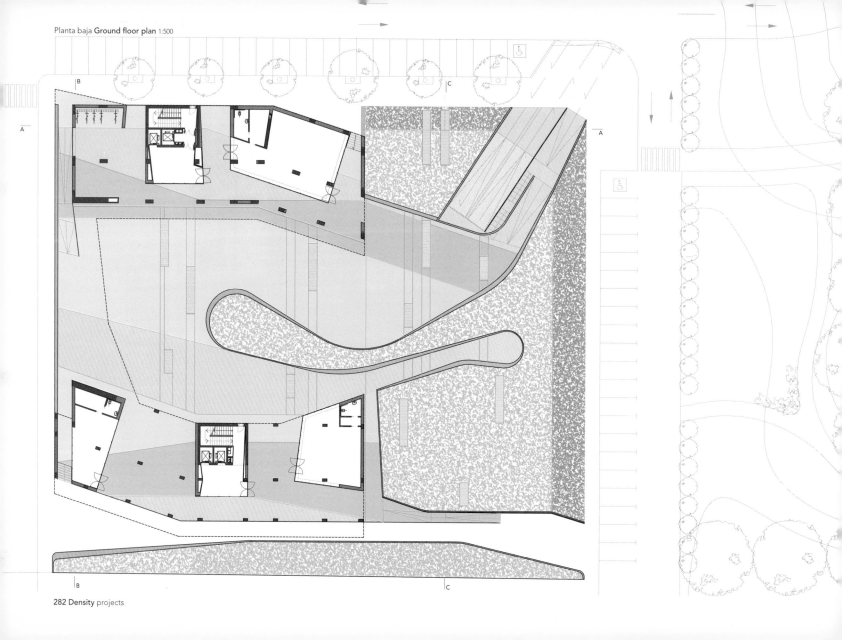

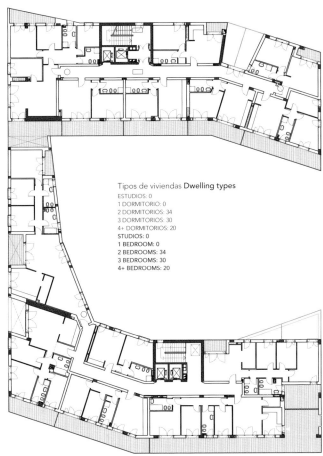

Tipos de viviendas Dwelling types

ESTUDIOS: 0
1 DORMITORIO: 0
2 DORMITORIOS: 34
3 DORMITORIOS: 30
4+ DORMITORIOS: 20
STUDIOS: 0
1 BEDROOM: 0
2 BEDROOMS: 34
3 BEDROOMS: 30
4+ BEDROOMS: 20

Planta cuarta Forth plan 1:500

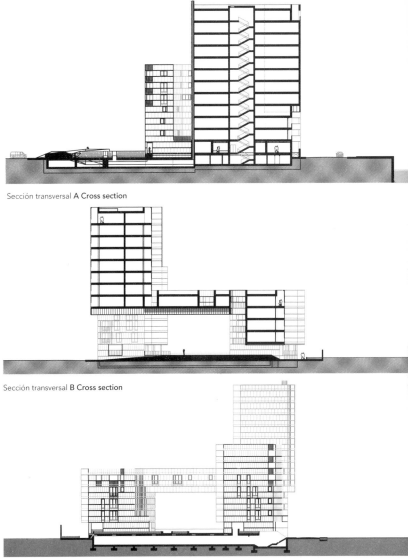

Sección transversal A Cross section

Sección transversal B Cross section

Sección transversal C Cross section 1:1.000

42,8 %
VIVIENDA
LIVING

TRABAJO
WORKING

11 %
COMERCIOS
SHOPPING

46,2 %
RESIDENCIA ANCIANOS/CENTRO MUJERES MALTRATADAS
CENTRE FOR THE ELDERLY/SHELTER FOR ABUSED WOMEN

1.407 m²
SUPERFICIE DE PARCELA
PLOT AREA

7.389 m²
SUPERFICIE CONSTRUIDA
BUILT UP AREA

100 %
OCUPACIÓN
COVERED AREA

5,2
EDIFICABILIDAD
FLOOR AREA RATIO

256 ⌂/ha   672 ⊕/ha

Todos los datos se refiere a la suma de los edificios A y B
All data refer to the addition of both buildings A and B

the geoinformation group/interatlas, 2007

1:10.000

+7
+2+4
EDIFICIO B
BUILDING B

+7
+4
+2
EDIFICIO A
BUILDING A

1:5.000

Brenac & Gonzalez brenac-gonzalez-architectes.com

64, 80 rue de la Convention, Paris. France, 2005-2008

Los edificios proyectados constituyen dos piezas fundamentales del nuevo puzzle urbano que se está levantando en el emplazamiento del antiguo hospital Boucicaut de Paris.

La diversidad programática se materializa en capas superpuestas dentro de cada edificio. Esta disposición de usos exige un gran dominio de su funcionamiento, pues conlleva distribuciones espaciales y técnicas diversas.

Hemos buscado un funcionamiento claro y la legibilidad de los espacios desde la planta de acceso, mediante un núcleo central que contiene todas las circulaciones verticales y vestíbulos en doble altura a modo de calles interiores.

La diversidad programática se expresa al exterior mediante la fragmentación volumétrica de cada edificio en dos volúmenes separados por una cubierta ajardinada y revestidos de diferentes materiales (ladrillo y zinc).

Para poner de relieve las diferencias entre ambos edificios, hemos preferido recalcar sus semejanzas y buscado un efecto de simetría aparente respecto al paisaje urbano en que se insertan. Los dos edificios parecen idénticos a primera vista, por su materiales, forma y composición de fachada, pero se trata en realidad de mellizos y no de gemelos.

These building projects make up two fundamental parts of the new urban puzzle that is being built in the place of the old Boucicaut hospital in Paris.

The programmatic diversity is materialised in two overlapping layers inside each building. This order of uses requires an important command of their function and thus entails diverse spatial and technical distribution.

We have sought a clear function and legibility of the spaces from the main entrance floor. We have done so by means of a central nucleus that contains all of the vertical circulations and foyers at a double height, working as indoor streets.

Programmatic diversity is expressed on the outside through the volumetric fragmentation of each building into two volumes separated by a garden-roof and covered in different materials (brick and zinc).

To highlight the differences between the two buildings, we have chosen to stress their similarities and look for an apparent symmetrical effect according to the urban landscape in which they have been placed. The two buildings seem identical at first glance because of their material, form, and façade composition. However in reality, the buildings are fraternal twins and not identical twins.

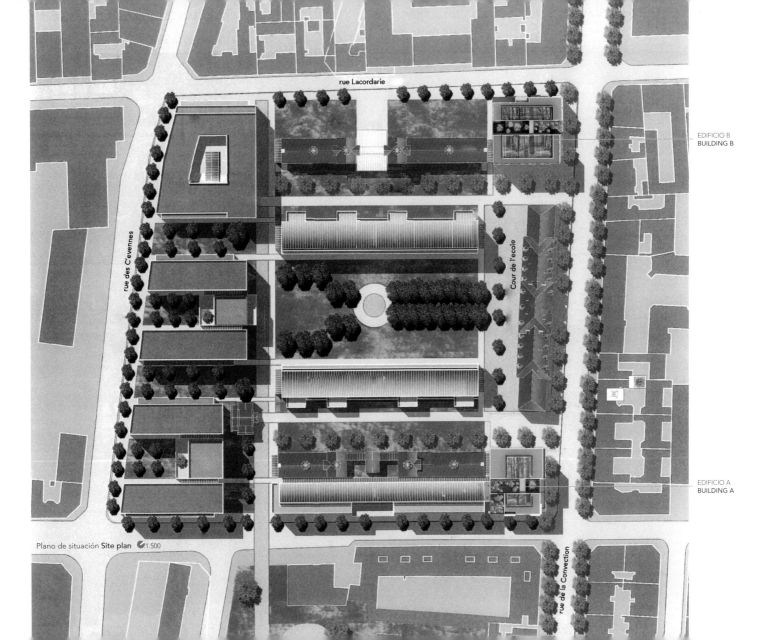

rue Lacordarie

rue des C'evennes

Cour de l'ecole

EDIFICIO B
BUILDING B

EDIFICIO A
BUILDING A

rue de la Convection

Plano de situación **Site plan** 1:500

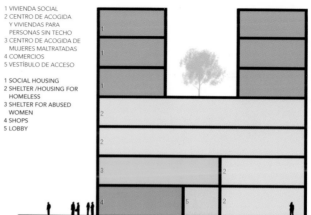

Rue Lourmer

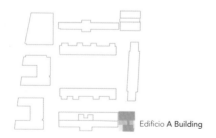

Edificio A Building

Planta baja Ground floor plan 1:500

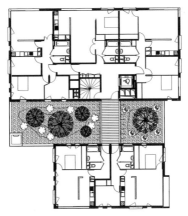

Planta tercera **Third floor plan**

Planta cuarta **Fourth floor plan**

Planta quinta **Fifth floor plan**

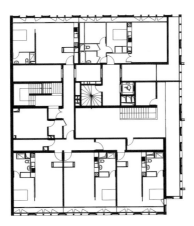

Entresuelo **Mezzanine floor plan**

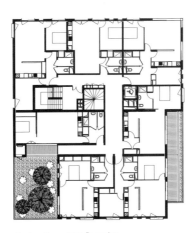

Planta primera **First floor plan**

Planta segunda **Second floor plan**

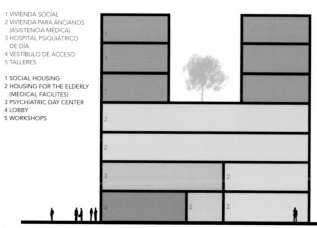

1 VIVIENDA SOCIAL
2 VIVIENDA PARA ANCIANOS
  (ASISTENCIA MÉDICA)
3 HOSPITAL PSIQUIÁTRICO
  DE DÍA
4 VESTÍBULO DE ACCESO
5 TALLERES

1 SOCIAL HOUSING
2 HOUSING FOR THE ELDERLY
  (MEDICAL FACILITES)
3 PSYCHIATRIC DAY CENTER
4 LOBBY
5 WORKSHOPS

Rue Lacordaire

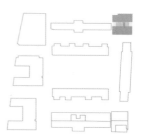

Edificio B Building

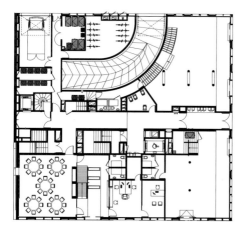

Planta baja **Ground floor plan** 1:500

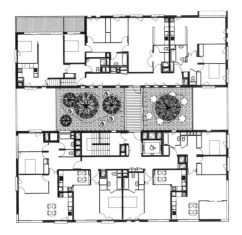

Planta tercera **Third floor plan**

Planta cuarta **Fourth floor plan**

Planta quinta **Fifth floor plan**

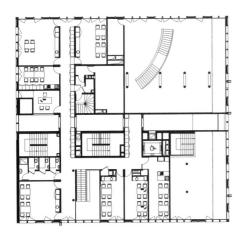

Entresuelo **Mezzanine floor plan**

Planta primera **First floor plan**

Planta segunda **Second floor plan**

86,4 %
VIVIENDA
LIVING

TRABAJO
WORKING

13,6 %
COMERCIOS
SHOPPING

EQUIPAMIENTOS
CIVIC FACILITIES

OTROS USOS
OTHER USES

993 m^2
SUPERFICIE DE PARCELA
PLOT AREA

7.326 m^2
SUPERFICIE CONSTRUIDA
BUILT UP AREA

100 %
OCUPACIÓN
COVERED AREA

6,3
EDIFICABILIDAD
FLOOR AREA RATIO

322 ⌂/ha

692 ◉/ha

sanborn, 2007

1:10.000

+11
+5
+5
+7
1:2.500

Kohn Pedersen Fox kpf.com

122 Greenwich Street, New York. USA, 2005-2009

El barrio de Greenwich Village, nacido tras la Independencia de los Estados Unidos, es uno de los más antiguos de Manhattan y concentra gran cantidad de la arquitectura histórica de la ciudad. Cualquier añadido a la abigarrada trama existente debe por tanto respetar la arquitectura tradicional, el carácter artístico de la vida en el barrio y la inercia histórica que trasmiten sus calles.

El proyecto de vivienda de lujo One Jackson Square, situado en el borde de este barrio histórico, propone una respuesta espectacular al contexto que lo rodea.

Initially developed after the American Revolution, Greenwich Village is one of Manhattan's oldest neighborhoods and home to the highest concentration of early architecture in the city. Any new addition to this intricate and historic urban fabric must, therefore, respect the quality of its existing architecture, the nature of the artistic life within its boundaries, and the feeling of history that permeates its streets.

Located on the western edge of the Village, the new One Jackson Square luxury residential development creates a dramatic architectural response to this celebrated historic district.

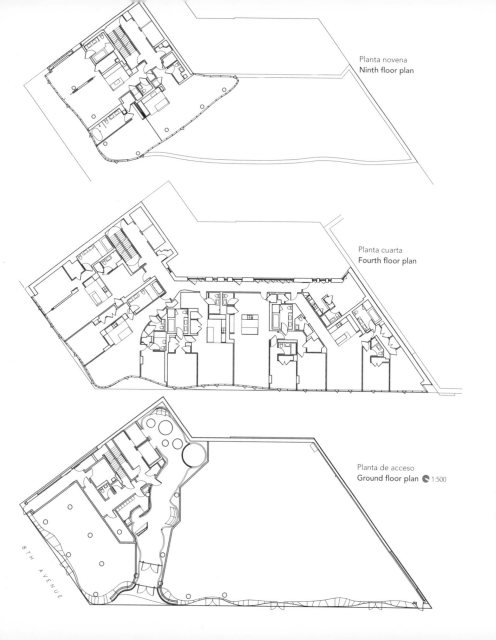

Planta novena
Ninth floor plan

Planta cuarta
Fourth floor plan

Planta de acceso
Ground floor plan 🌀 1:500

8TH AVENUE

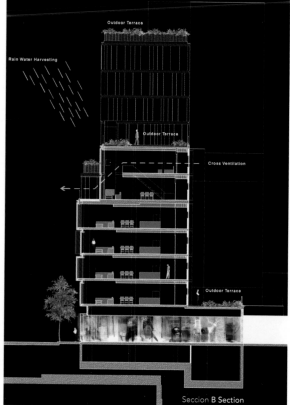

Outdoor Terrace

Rain Water Harvesting

Outdoor Terrace

Cross Ventilation

Outdoor Terrace

Seccion **B Section**

39,9 %
VIVIENDA
LIVING

7,6 %
TRABAJO
WORKING

3,4 %
COMERCIOS
SHOPPING

EQUIPAMIENTOS
CIVIC FACILITIES

49,1 %
APARCAMIENTO PÚBLICO
PUBLIC PARKING

577 △/ha   **741** ⬡/ha

1.957 m²
SUPERFICIE DE PARCELA
PLOT AREA

26.010 m²
SUPERFICIE CONSTRUIDA
BUILT UP AREA

76,2 %
OCUPACIÓN
COVERED AREA

13,3
EDIFICABILIDAD
FLOOR AREA RATIO

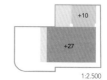

1:2.500

sanborn, 2007

1:10.000

Oppenheim Architecture+Design

oppenoffice.com

3801 N. Miami Avenue, Miami, USA, 2005-2009

El proyecto COR pretende ser el primer edificio híbrido sostenible y representativo de la sinergia entre arquitectura, el cálculo de estructuras y la ecología. Con una altura de 122 m, el edificio extrae de su entorno la energía que consume, empleando los últimos avances en aerogeneradores y placas solares, e integrándolos en su arquitectura. El esqueleto estructural externo, simultáneamente, sustenta el edificio, aísla térmicamente, proporciona sombra, sirve de cerramiento a los balcones y de armazón a los aerogeneradores. La sostenibilidad del proyecto se aborda aplicando múltiples estrategias, integradas en el proceso de diseño, con el fin de optimizar el consumo y la producción de energía.

El proyecto dotará al distrito del Diseño de Miami de espacios flexibles, tanto residenciales como de trabajo. Los módulos son apartamentos dúplex y viviendas en una sóla planta que se pueden convertir en viviendas de gran tamaño.

COR intends to be the first sustainable, mixed-use condominium, representing a dynamic synergy between architecture, structural engineering and ecology. Rising nearly 122 m, this building extracts power from its environment utilizing the latest advancements in wind turbines, photovoltaic cells, and solar hot water generation –while integrating them into its architectural identity. A hyper-efficient exoskeleton shell simultaneously provides building structure, thermal mass for insulation, shading for natural cooling, enclosure for terraces and armatures for turbines. The sustainability concept for COR encompasses multiple strategies, integrated through design, for efficient consumption and production of energy.

Reaching 29 stories over the Design district in Miami –COR will offer expansive residential and professional spaces with versatile and bright interiors. The residential units are composed of duplex units and flats which can be reconfigured for larger residences.

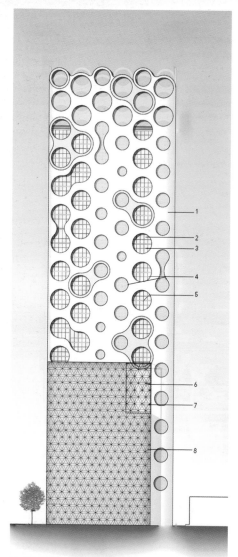

Alzado norte **North elevation**

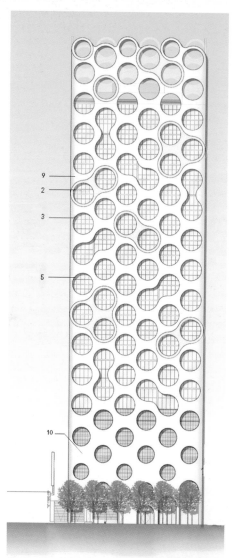

Alzado sur **South elevation**

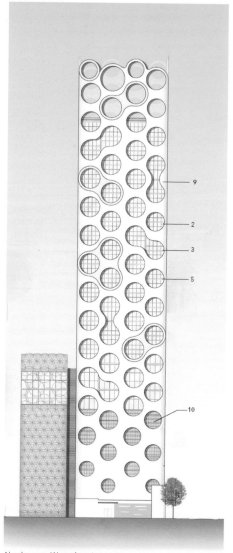

Alzado oeste **West elevation** 1:1.000

1 ACABADO DE ESTUCO
   BLANCO
2 CARPINTERÍA DE ALUMINIO
3 VIDRIO LAMINADO
   RESISTENTE A HURACANES DE
   COLOR AZUL VERDOSO
4 RELLENO DE ESTUCO RAYADO
   EN LAS ZONAS RECORTADAS
   DEL MURO EXTERIOR
5 FORJADO DE HORMIGÓN
   ENLUCIDO CON ESTUCO
6 BASTIDOR METÁLICO PARA LA
   REJA
7 REJA METÁLICA DECORATIVA
8 ACABADO DE ESTUCO
   RAYADO COINCIDENTE CON
   LA PANTALLA METÁLICA
9 ACABADO DE ESTUCO
   BLANCO
10 REJA METÁLICA MUY
   DENSA PARA OCULTAR EL
   APARCAMIENTO

1 WHITE STUCCO FINISH
2 ALUMINUM FRAME WINDOWS
3 HURRICANE RESISTANT,
   LAMINATED, CLEAR, LIGHT
   BLUE-GREEN GRASS
4 SCORED STUCCO FILL
   PATTERN (SURFACE SET BACK
   FROM THICKNESS OF WALL)
5 CONCRETE SLAB WITH WHITE
   STUCCO
6 METAL FRAME SCREEN
   PATTERN
7 METAL DECORATIVE SCREEN
8 STUCCO WITH DECORATIVE
   SCORE PATTERN TO MATCH
   METAL SCREEN
9 WHITE STUCCO FINISH
10 DENSE METAL GRATE TO
   SCREEN PARKING

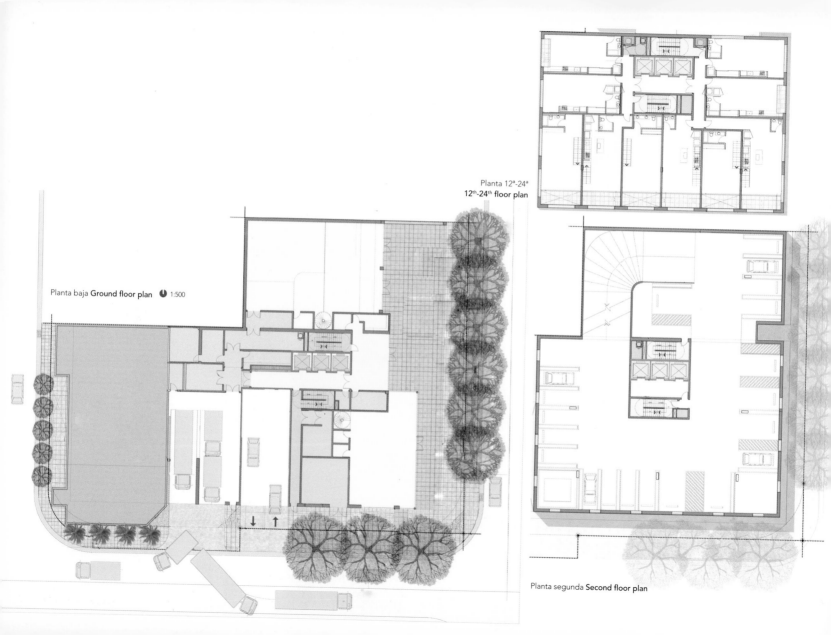

Planta 12ª-24ª
12th-24th floor plan

Planta baja **Ground floor plan** ⊕ 1:500

Planta segunda **Second floor plan**

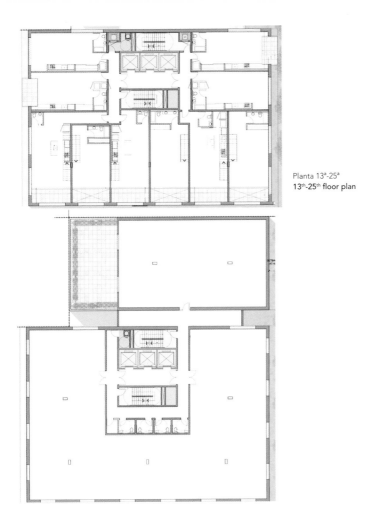

Planta 13ª-25ª
13th-25th floor plan

Planta 9ª **9th floor plan**

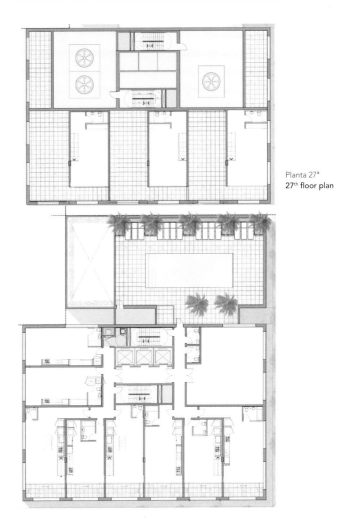

Planta 27ª
27th floor plan

Planta 11ª **11th floor plan**

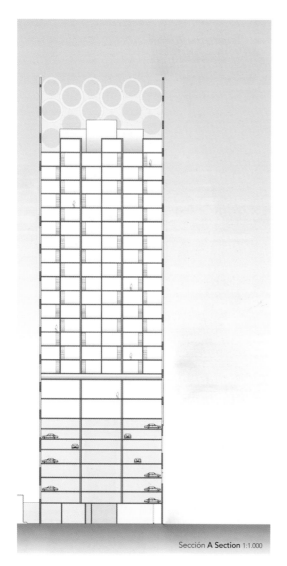

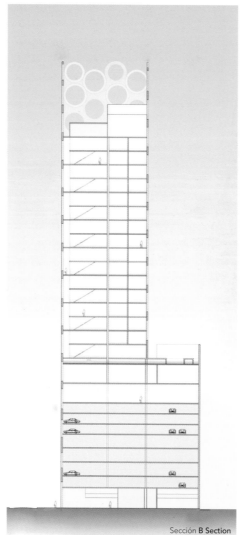

Aerogeneradores en el esqueleto estructural
Wind turbines in the exoskeleton

Sección **A** Section 1:1.000

Sección **B** Section

| 100 %
VIVIENDA
LIVING | TRABAJO
WORKING | COMERCIOS
SHOPPING | EQUIPAMIENTOS
CIVIC FACILITIES | OTROS USOS
OTHER USES |

| 1.845 m²
SUPERFICIE DE PARCELA
PLOT AREA | 3.030 m²
SUPERFICIE CONSTRUIDA
BUILT UP AREA | 65 %
OCUPACIÓN
COVERED AREA | 1,6
EDIFICABILIDAD
FLOOR AREA RATIO |

217 Ò/ha   766 Ø/ha

1:2.500

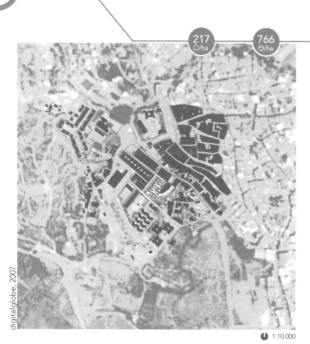

digitalglobe, 2007

1:10.000

Flexo Arquitectura

Calle San José Barranco, Cuevas del Almanzora. Spain, 2006-

Incorporamos criterios de sostenibilidad (ciclo de vida) desde la primera decisión del proyecto. Esto implica la selección de los principales materiales de construcción según su contenido de energía primaria, la selección del sistema constructivo y la consideración de la forma arquitectónica como táctica de control climático.

El patio como generador

La vivienda tipo se configura alrededor de un patio que ofrece las siguientes ventajas: actúa como intercambiador energético en un clima cálido, garantizando la protección solar (toldos) y evaporación (fuentes, vegetación) en verano y las ganancias energéticas en invierno; garantiza control lumínico y protección visual; y se configura como una habitación más externa, propia de climas cálidos.

Implantación. Generación y negociación del sistema

Proponemos un sistema de configuración flexible resultado de la adición de una vivienda-patio-dúplex que negocia las condiciones de adaptación al entorno incorporando un pasaje-plaza que garantiza el acceso a todas las viviendas y ofrece áreas de relación de microclima controlado (vegetación de hoja caduca y láminas de agua).
El sistema ofrece gran flexibilidad en la determinación de las viviendas simplex situadas en planta ático considerando como parámetros de configuración la ubicación de los núcleos húmedos y los accesos a las viviendas o conjunto de viviendas.

We incorporate sustainability criteria (life cycle) from the first project decision. This implies the selection of the main construction materials according to their primary energy content, the selection of the constructive system and the consideration of the form as a climate control tactic.

The patio as a generator

The dwelling type configured around a patio that offers the following advantages: It acts as an energy exchanger in a warm climate, guaranteeing solar protection (awning) and evaporation (fountains, vegetation) in the summer and energy profits in the winter; It guarantees the control of light and visual protection; It is configured as yet another more external room, typical of warm climates.

Introduction, generation and negotiation of the system

We propose a flexible configuration system, the result of the addition of a dwelling-patio-duplex that negotiates the adaptation conditions to its surroundings by incorporating a passage-plaza which provides the entrance to all of the dwellings and offers a meeting place with a controlled microclimate (deciduous plants and sheets of water). The system is highly flexible in the determination of the one-storey dwellings located in the attic. It considers the location of wet nuclei and entry to the dwellings or group of dwellings as parameters of configuration.

5

6

7

8

9

10

11

12

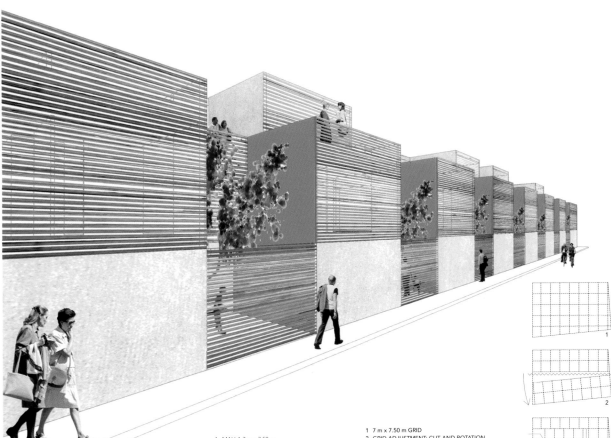

1

2

3

4

Vista desde la calle
View from street

1 MALLA 7 m x 7,50 m
2 ADAPTACIÓN MALLA CORTE + ROTACIÓN
3 ADAPTACIÓN ACCESIBILIDAD PASAJE +
   PLAZAS
4 YUXTAPOSICIÓN VIVIENDAS SIMPLES
5 PRIVADO/COLECTIVO
6 LLENO/VACÍO
7 NÚCLEOS FIJOS
8 EXTERIOR PRIVADO/COLECTIVO
9 ÁRBOLES + FUENTES
10 PAVIMENTACIÓN
11 BRISAS
12 COLECTOR SOLAR/ACUMULADOR AGUA

1 7 m x 7.50 m GRID
2 GRID ADJUSTMENT: CUT AND ROTATION
3 ACCESSIBILITY ADJUSTMENTS:
   PASSAGEWAY AND COURTYARDS
4 JUXTAPOSITION OF ONE-STOREY
   DWELLINGS
5 PRIVATE/COMMUNAL
6 FIGURE/GROUND
7 FIXED CIRCULATION CORES
8 PRIVATE/COMMUNAL OUTDOOR SPACES
9 TREES AND FOUNTAINS
10 PAVING
11 BREEZES
12 SOLAR COLLECTORS/WATER TANKS

27 dúplex
2 simplex

11 simplex

dúplex + simplex

Planta baja **Ground floor plan**

Planta primera **First floor plan**

Planta segunda **Second floor plan** 🔵 1:1.000

Tipo **1** Type

Tipo **2** Type

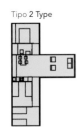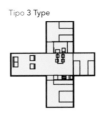

Tipo **3** Type

Tipo **4** Type

Tipo **5** Type 1:500

Tipos de viviendas **Dwelling types**

ESTUDIOS: 0
1 DORMITORIO: 0
2 DORMITORIOS: 7
3 DORMITORIOS: 33
4+ DORMITORIOS: 0
STUDIOS: 0
1 BEDROOM: 0
2 BEDROOMS: 7
3 BEDROOMS: 33
4+ BEDROOMS: 0

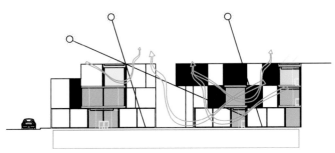

Sección transversal **A Cross section**

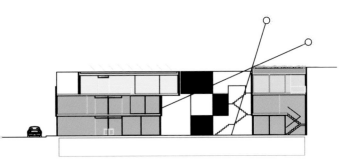

Sección transversal **B Cross section** 1:500

Vista interior **Inside view**

100 %
VIVIENDA 164 🚗
LIVING

TRABAJO
WORKING

COMERCIOS
SHOPPING

EQUIPAMIENTOS
CIVIC FACILITIES

OTROS USOS
OTHER USES

280
△/ha

796
◎/ha

6.000 m²
SUPERFICIE DE PARCELA
PLOT AREA

22.000 m²
SUPERFICIE CONSTRUIDA
BUILT UP AREA

29,3 %
OCUPACIÓN
COVERED AREA

3,6
EDIFICABILIDAD
FLOOR AREA RATIO

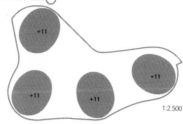

1:2.500

scankort, 2007

🕐 1:10.000

3XN Architects 3xn.dk

Nordhavnen, Copenhagen. Denmark, 2006-2009

El proyecto Norhavnen Residences responde a requerimientos de individualidad e identidad. El posicionamiento libre de los edificios de planta circular en el solar sustituye a la retícula urbana, al tiempo que mantiene e incluso aumenta la densidad. La planta circular sin esquinas proporciona mejores vistas y más luz natural, su comportamiento aerodinámico es mejor y, a igual superficie, requiere menos perímetro de fachada, lo cual redunda en una mayor eficiencia energética.

El proyecto se asemeja a una pila de platos, gracias a la distribución irregular en cada planta de los balcones prefabricados. La distribución de estos balcones permite disfrutar del clima exterior y de la vista hacia el cielo, ya que cada balcón no se sitúa exactamente sobre el que tiene debajo.

A una escala mayor, el proyecto aporta individualidad e identidad al lugar. En cuanto a la relación entre edificios, éstos se levantan situados sobre un plinto que funciona como jardín comunitario para realizar actividades al aire libre. A escala urbana, los edificios circulares carecen de direccionalidad y se integran mejor en el paisaje heterogéneo del antiguo puerto.

The Nordhavnen residences respond to demands of individuality and identity. The circular floor plan buildings in a free site plan have replaced the traditional urban grid, while maintaining, even optimising, density. Circular buildings without corners provide for better views and more daylight; wind turbulence is avoided by the aerodynamic design; and they have an optimum balance between floor area and facade, meaning high energy efficiency.

The image of a 'pile of plates' is achieved by using balcony additions to each floor –with varied positions. The balconies are prefab elements, all alike. One result is the benefits of being able to enjoy outdoor climate. Another is that the view to the sky is unlimited as the upper balcony is not shading the lower.

Individuality and a strong identity are the results on the larger scale. On neighbourhood scale, the circular buildings are placed 'randomly' upon an elevated level. This protective area is softly shaped, has green plants, and provides spaces for outdoor activities like barbecuing and sunbathing, and for children to meet and play.

At an urban scale, circular shaped buildings have no primary direction and therefore integrate more willingly into the rather heterogeneous environment of the former docks.

 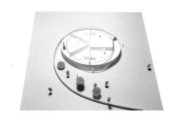  

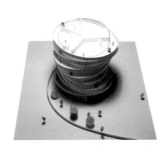   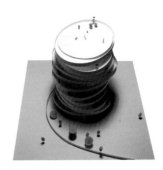

Planta de aparcamientos **Parking floor plan** 1:1.000

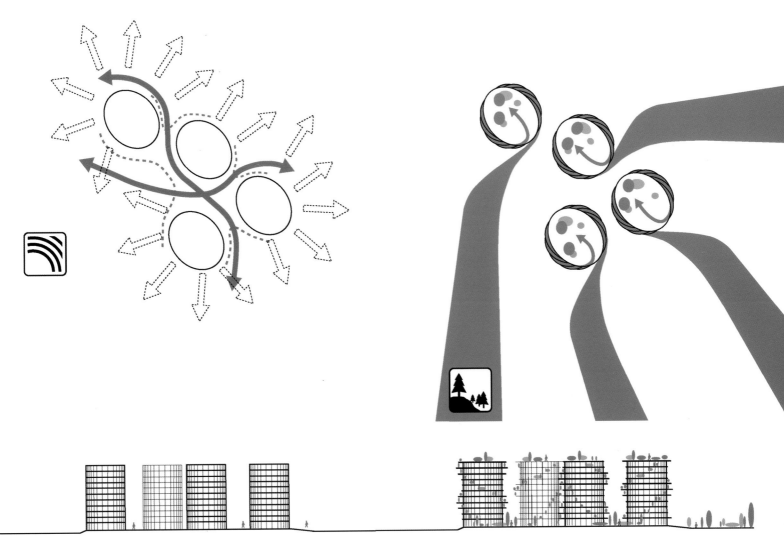

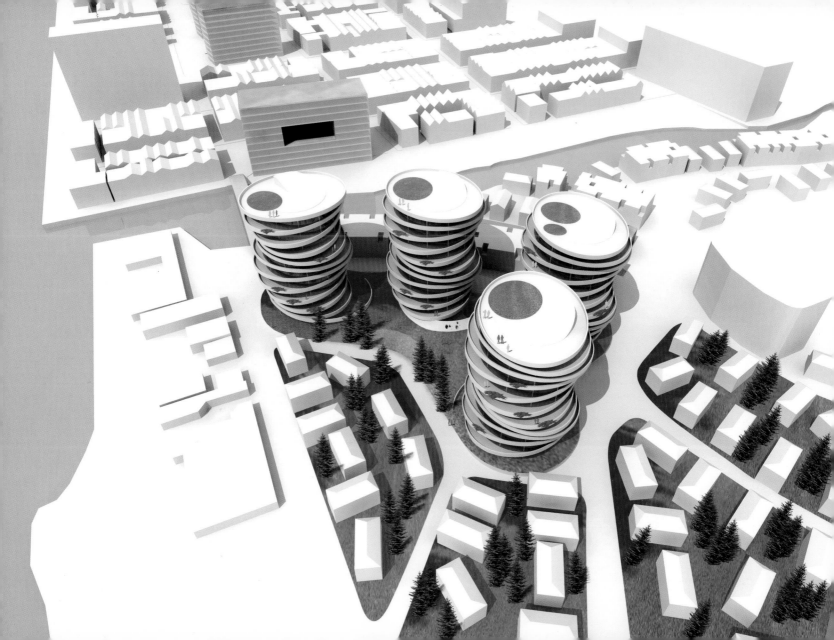

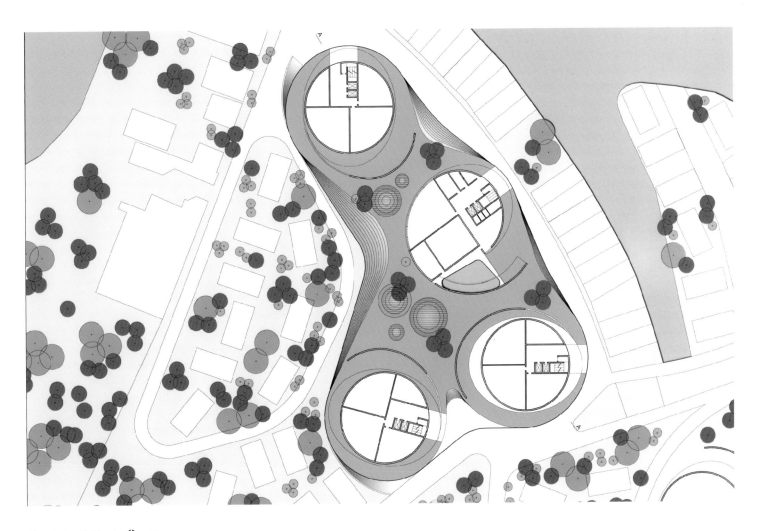

Plano de situación **Site plan** 🌐 1:1.000

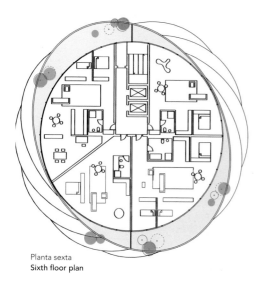

Planta sexta
Sixth floor plan

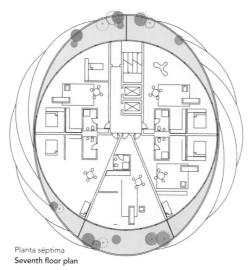

Planta séptima
Seventh floor plan

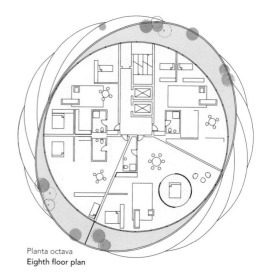

Planta octava
Eighth floor plan

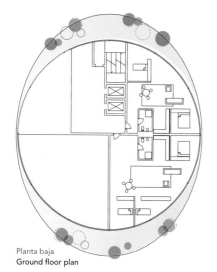

Planta baja
Ground floor plan

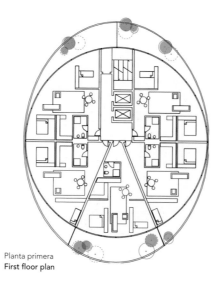

Planta primera
First floor plan

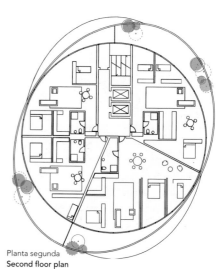

Planta segunda
Second floor plan

314 Density projects

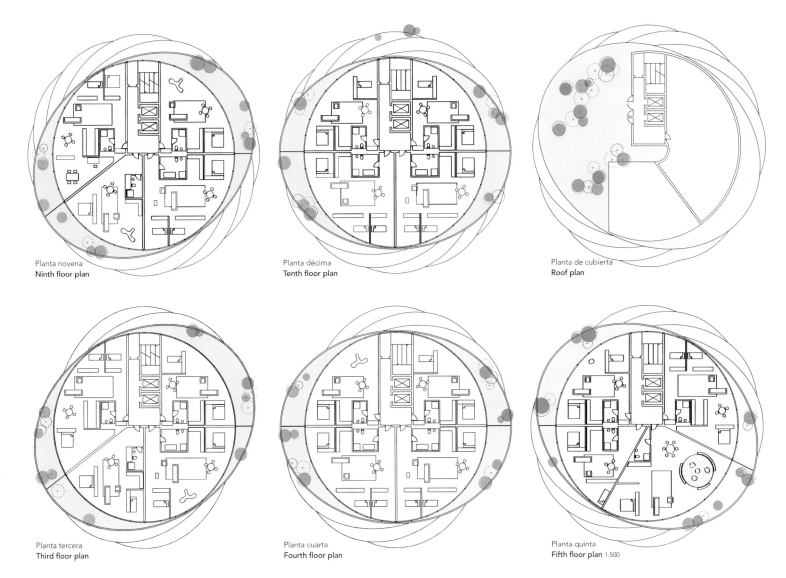

Planta novena
Ninth floor plan

Planta décima
Tenth floor plan

Planta de cubierta
Roof plan

Planta tercera
Third floor plan

Planta cuarta
Fourth floor plan

Planta quinta
Fifth floor plan 1:500

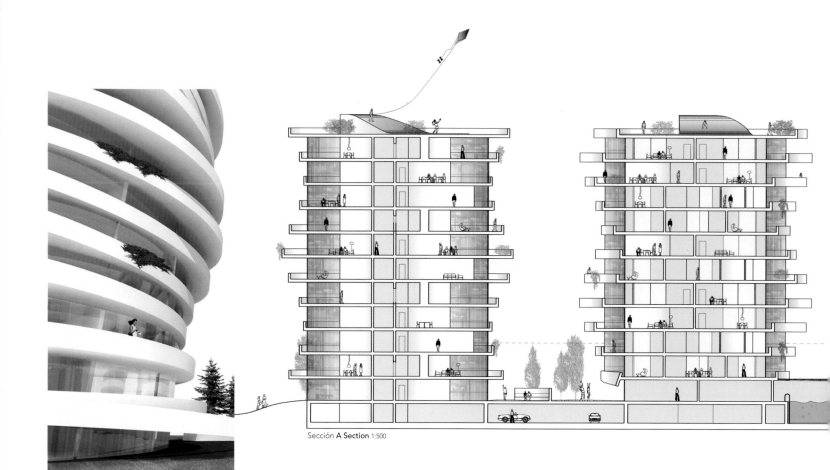

Sección **A Section** 1:500

Tipos de viviendas **Dwelling types**

ESTUDIOS: 0
1 DORMITORIO: 8
2 DORMITORIOS: 106
3 DORMITORIOS: 54
4+ DORMITORIOS: 0

STUDIOS: 0
1 BEDROOM: 8
2 BEDROOMS: 106
3 BEDROOMS: 54
4+ BEDROOMS: 0

29

DENSIDADES ● **DENSITIES** ■ VIVIENDAS 501 **DWELLINGS** ■ USOS ● **USES**

| 83,3%
VIVIENDA
LIVING | 16,7 %
TRABAJO/COMERCIOS
WORKING/SHOPPING | | EQUIPAMIENTOS
CIVIC FACILITIES | OTROS USOS
OTHER USES |

239 ⌂/ha   852 ⊘/ha

| 21.000 m²
SUPERFICIE DE PARCELA
PLOT AREA | 62.844 m²
SUPERFICIE CONSTRUIDA
BUILT UP AREA | 50,7 %
OCUPACIÓN
COVERED AREA | 3
EDIFICABILIDAD
FLOOR AREA RATIO |

scankort, 2007

1:10.000

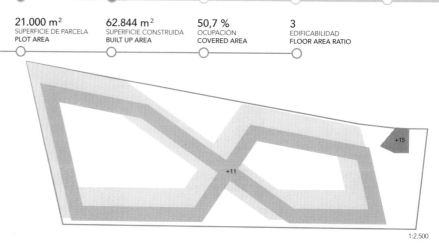

+15

+11

1:2.500

Big big.dk

Richard Mortensens Vej 61-81, Copenhaguen.
Denmark, 2006-2010

El proyecto Big House se sitúa en el extremo sur del nuevo barrio de Orestad, al borde del Copenhaguen Canal y con vistas a lo espacios abiertos de Kalvebod Fælled. El edificio aloja una amplia variedad tipológica para acoger a todo tipo de usuarios: mayores, jóvenes, familias o solteros. La forma de lazo sirve para crear dos espacios bien diferenciados, separados por el nudo del lazo, el cual alberga las áreas comunes de 500 m². En este lugar, el edificio está atravesado por un pasaje de 9 m de ancho que conecta dos áreas de la ciudad: el parque al oeste y la zona del canal al este.

En vez de separar el programa residencial del comercial en dos volúmenes distintos, ambos usos se reparten horizontalmente por el edificio. Las viviendas se sitúan en las últimas plantas, mientras que el comercio se localiza en la base. Como resultado, las diferentes capas horizontales que se obtiene están dotadas de cualidades propias: las viviendas disfrutan de la luz solar y el aire fresco, mientras que el espacio de oficinas se mezcla con la vida de la calle.

Big House is located in Southern Orestad on the edge of the Copenhagen Canal and with a view of the open spaces of Kalvebod Fælled. The building offers homes for people in all of life's stages: the young and the old, nuclear families or singles. The bow-shaped building creates two distinct spaces, separated by the centre of the bow which hosts the communal facilities of 500 m². At the very same spot, the building is penetrated by a 9 m wide passage that connects the two surrounding city spaces: the park area to the west and the channel area to the east.

Instead of dividing the different functions of the building –for both habitation and trades– into separate blocks, the various functions have been spread out horizontally. The apartments are placed at the top while the commercial program unfolds at the base of the building. As a result, the different horizontal layers have achieved a quality of their own: the apartments benefit from the view, sunlight and fresh air, while the office leases merge with life on the street.

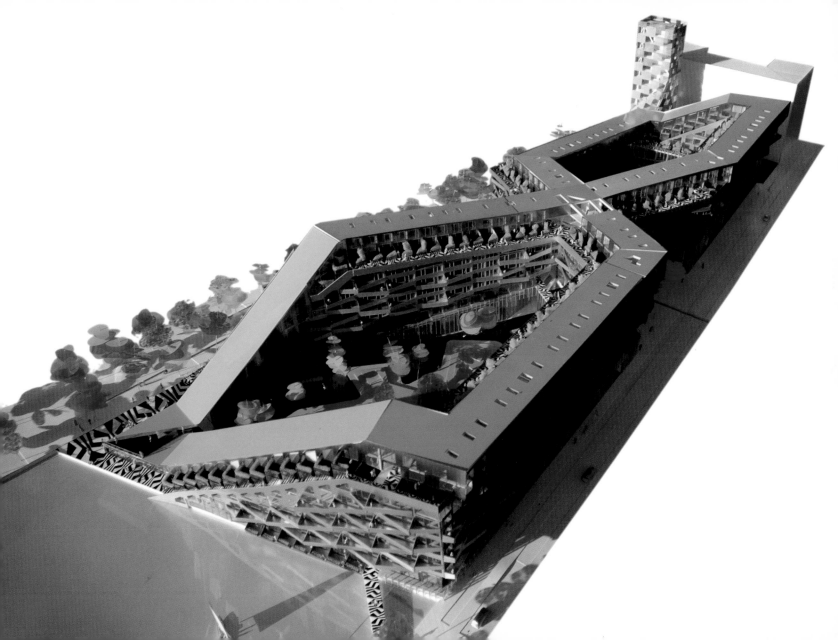

Manzana cerrada y torre
Closed city block and tower

Dos manzanas cerradas, plaza y campanile
Two city blocks, square and campanile

Big House
Big House-Big House

Manzana cerrada subdividida verticalmente
Vertically divided city block

Manzana cerrada subdividida horizontalmente
Horizontally divided city block

Planta comercial
Commercial floor

+ Viviendas unifamiliares adosadas
+ Terrace houses

+ Apartamentos
+ Apartments

+ Áticos
+ Penthouse

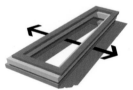

Ruta peatonal
Public route

Torsión
Torsion

Deformación
Deformation

Optimización de la luz natural
Daylight optimization

Planta comercial
Commercial floor

+ Viviendas unifamiliares adosadas
+ Terrace houses

+ Apartamentos
+ Apartments

+ Áticos
+ Penthouse

Ruta
Route

320 Density projects

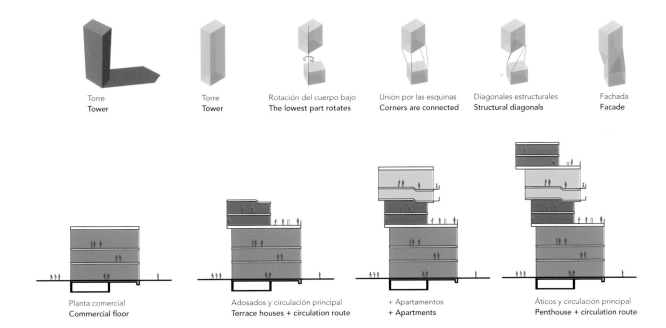

Torre
Tower

Torre
Tower

Rotación del cuerpo bajo
The lowest part rotates

Unión por las esquinas
Corners are connected

Diagonales estructurales
Structural diagonals

Fachada
Facade

Planta comercial
Commercial floor

Adosados y circulación principal
Terrace houses + circulation route

+ Apartamentos
+ Apartments

Áticos y circulación principal
Penthouse + circulation route

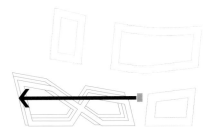

Vista desde las plantas bajas de la torre sobre la manzana
Views from the lower floors beyond the block

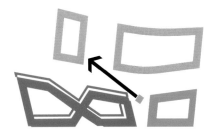

Vista desde las plantas superiores de la torre sobre la manzana
Views from the upper floors over the big block

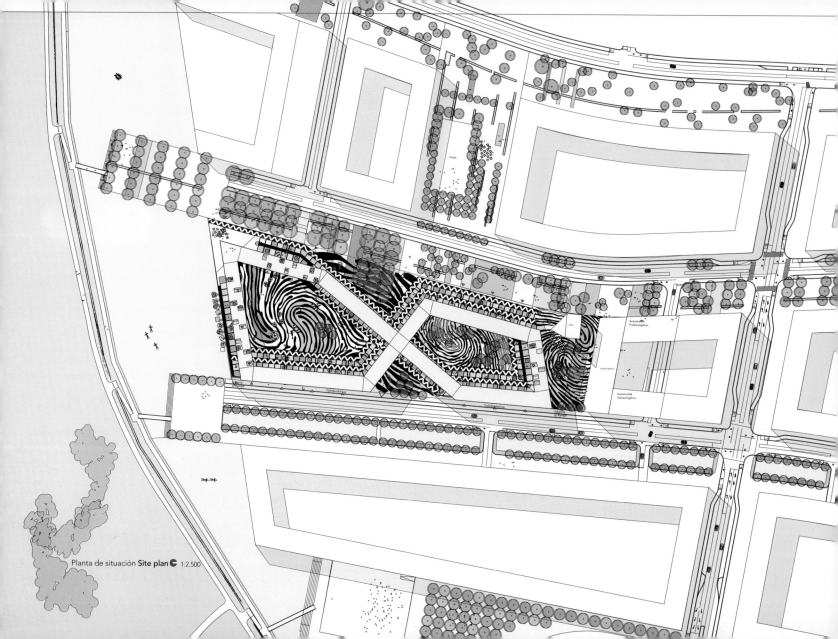

Planta de situación **Site plan** ℂ 1:2.500

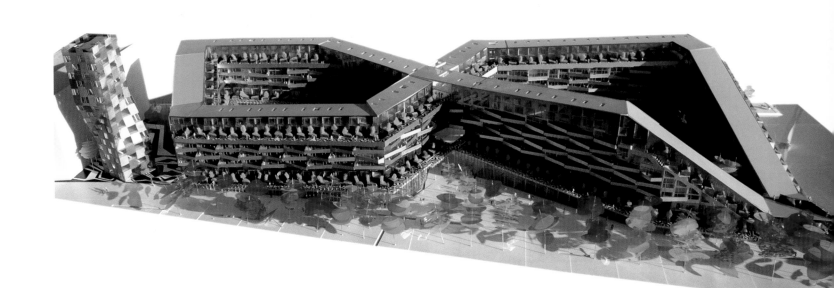

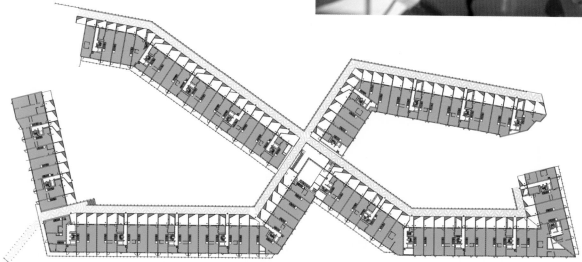

Planta baja **Ground floor plan** ◔ 1:1.500

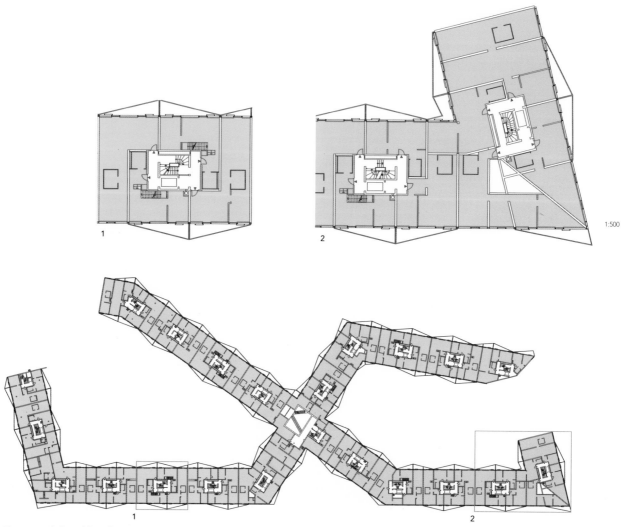

1

2

1:500

1

2

Planta segunda **Second floor plan** 1:1.500

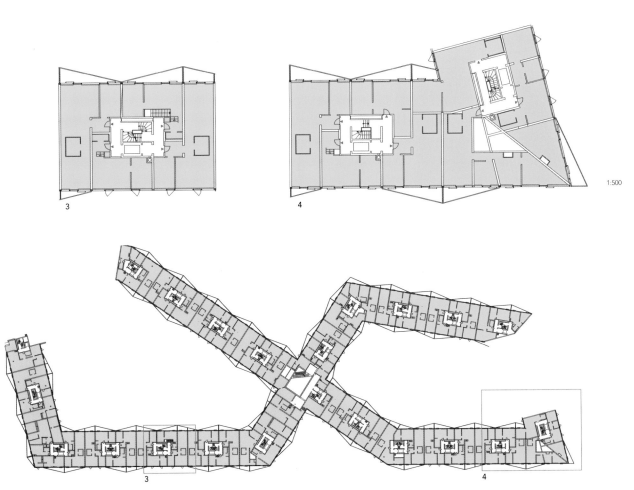

1:500

Planta tercera **Third floor plan** 1:1.500

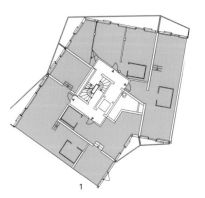

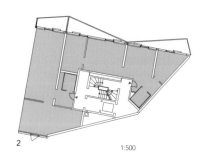

1:500

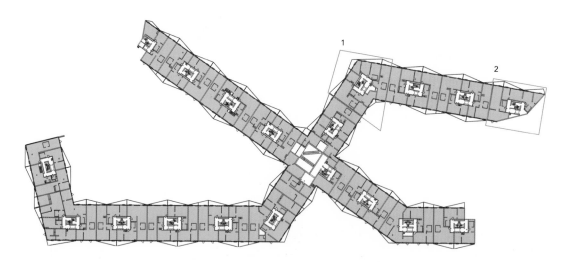

Planta cuarta **Fourth floor plan** 1:1.500

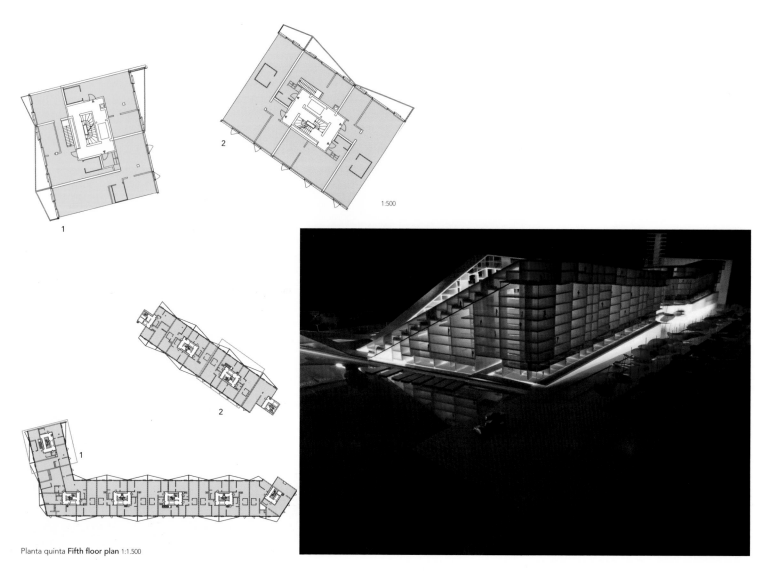

1:500

Planta quinta **Fifth floor plan** 1:1.500

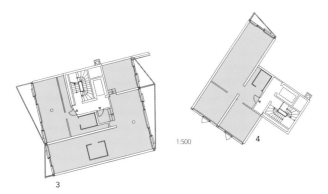

1:500

3

4

4

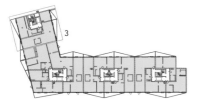

3

Planta sexta **Sixth floor plan** 1:1.500

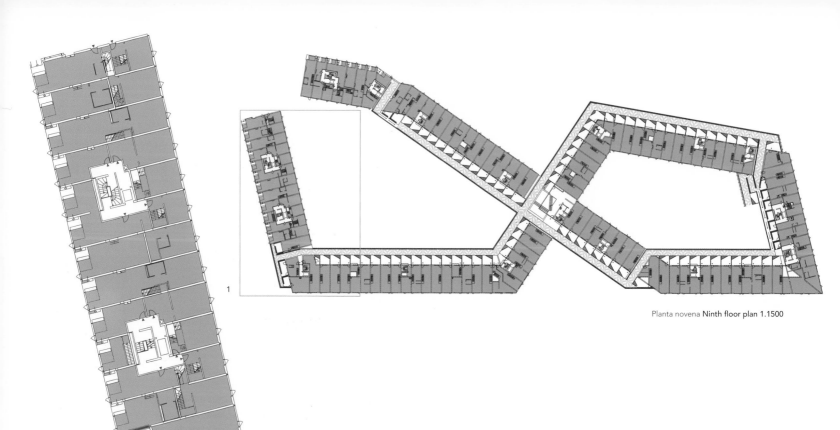

Planta novena **Ninth floor plan** 1.1500

1

1:500

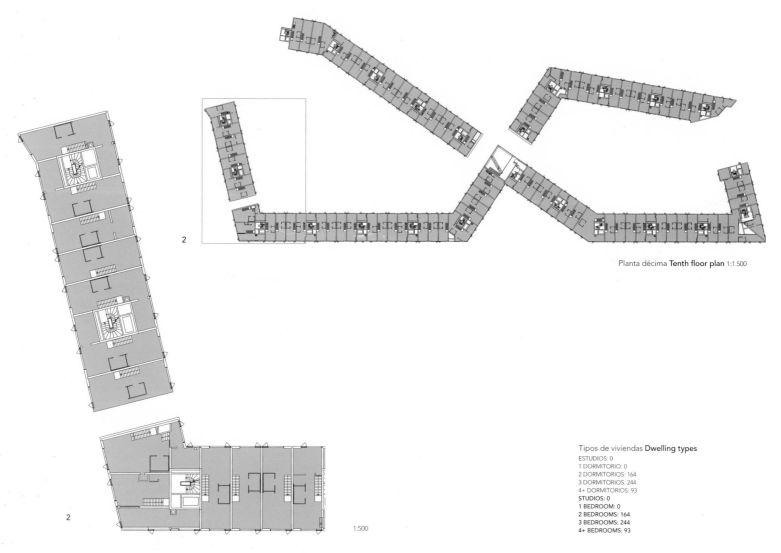

2

Planta décima **Tenth floor plan** 1:1.500

2

1:500

Tipos de viviendas **Dwelling types**
ESTUDIOS: 0
1 DORMITORIO: 0
2 DORMITORIOS: 164
3 DORMITORIOS: 244
4+ DORMITORIOS: 93
STUDIOS: 0
1 BEDROOM: 0
2 BEDROOMS: 164
3 BEDROOMS: 244
4+ BEDROOMS: 93

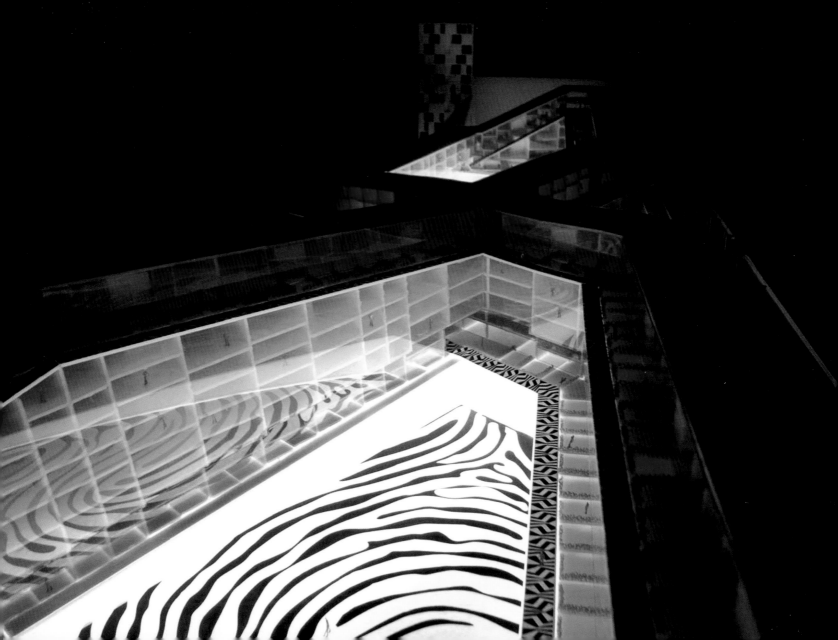

30

DENSIDADES ● **DENSITIES** ■ VIVIENDAS **145 DWELLINGS** ■ USOS ● **USES**

87,4 % VIVIENDA 288 🚗 LIVING	**0,1 %** TRABAJO WORKING

COMERCIO SHOPPING   EQUIPAMIENTOS CIVIC FACILITIES

12,5 % APARCAMIENTO PÚBLICO PUBLIC PARKING

300 Δ/ha   **919** ⊖/ha

4.830 m² SUPERFICIE DE PARCELA PLOT AREA

38.554 m² SUPERFICIE CONSTRUIDA BUILT UP AREA

73,1 % OCUPACIÓN COVERED AREA

7,8 EDIFICABILIDAD FLOOR AREA RATIO

+5

+25

1:2.500

NASA

1:10.000

Studio Gang Architects studiogang.net

1624 E. 56th Street, Chicago. USA, 2006-2010

La sucesión de parques y bulevares de Chicago tiene su origen en la planificación del siglo XIX, que abrió grandes espacios verdes en los barrios de la ciudad, los cuales hubieran admitido un aumento de densidad y escala en sus bordes. Sin embargo, muchas de estas áreas junto a los espacios verdes han permanecido tradicionalmente infrautilizadas. Así, en lugar de edificios en altura que hubiesen podido disfrutar de la luz natural y las zonas verdes, los bulevares están a menudo jalonados por aparcamientos, pequeñas estructuras temporales o estaciones de servicio. El proyecto Solstice on the Park, un edificio de viviendas en altura, se sitúa sobre un antiguo aparcamiento frente al Jackson Park, sede de la Exposición Colombina de 1893.

El proyecto, ubicado junto al histórico edifico Windermere, consta de 25 plantas, y la formalización de su fachada sur responde al azimut solar, que determina la inclinación de los paños de vidrio de las zonas de día para que estos espacios permanezcan en sombra durante el verano. Además, el proyecto consta de estrategias complementarias para mejorar su sostenibilidad, y aloja 145 viviendas, oficinas, jardines exteriores comunes, sala de fiestas, salas de reuniones y aparcamiento.

Chicago's chain of parks and boulevards is part of an infrastructure constructed in the 19th century for creating green open space in neighbourhoods throughout the city. The wide-open spaces set up an opportunity for increased density and scale in the architecture along their edges. However, these edges have remained extremely under-utilized in many neighbourhoods. Instead of tall, handsomely designed dwellings served by natural light and green spaces, boulevards are sometimes bordered by parking lots, small temporary structures and even gas stations. Solstice on the Park, a high-rise residential building, replaces an existing parking lot looking south over the 600-acre Jackson Park, the site of 1893 World's Columbian Exposition.

Solstice on the Park, adjacent to historic Windermere House, stands 25 stories tall with its south facade shaped by solar access. Wedges of the building's living spaces are chiseled to create a 'self-shaded' surface. Additional 'green' strategies contribute to its excellent sustainability balance. Included in its built-up area are 145 dwellings, as well as amenities such as outdoor gardens, a party room, offices, conference spaces and parking.

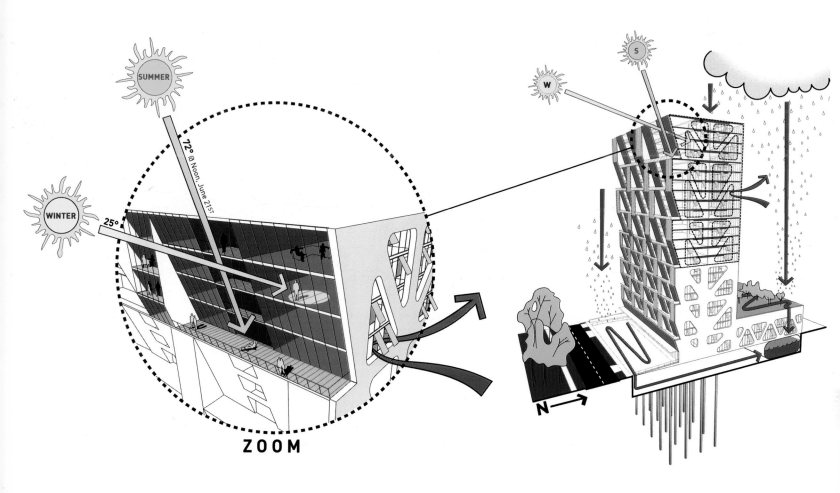

SUMMER

72° @ Noon, June 21ST

WINTER

25°

ZOOM

W

S

N

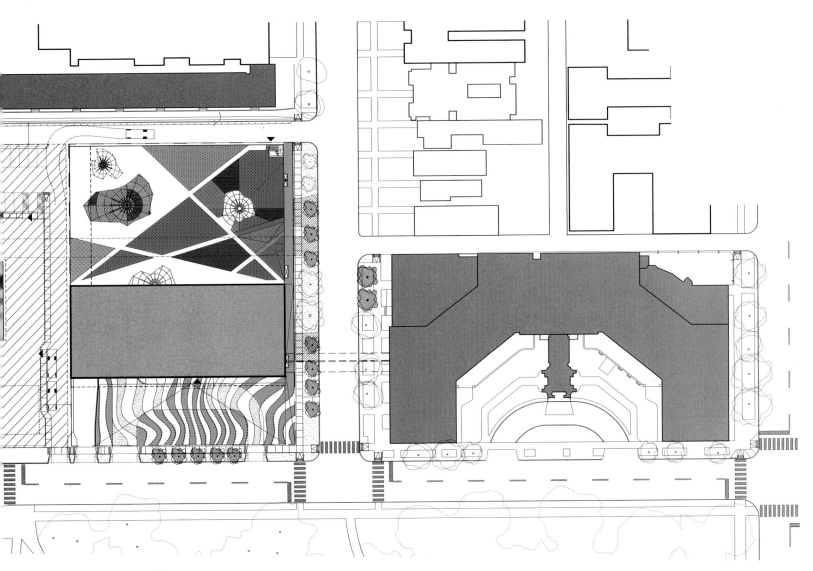

Plano de situación **Site plan** ⊕ 1:1.000

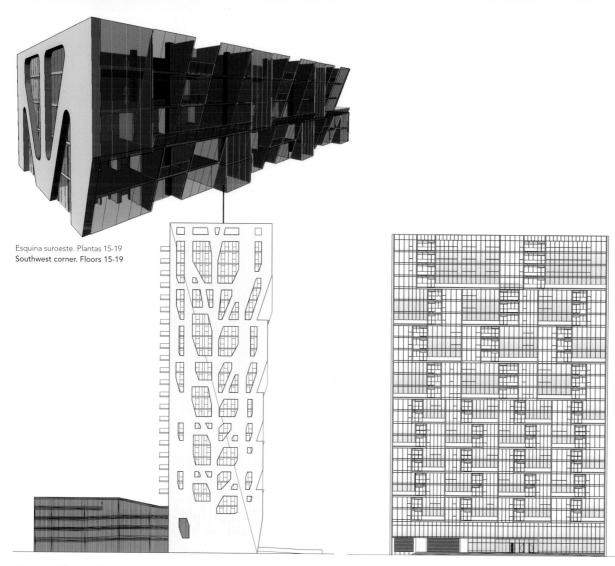

Esquina suroeste. Plantas 15-19
Southwest corner. Floors 15-19

Alzado oeste **West elevation**

Alzado sur **South elevation**

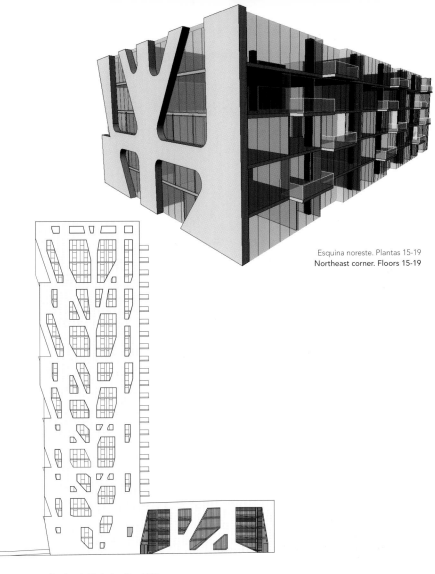

Esquina noreste. Plantas 15-19
Northeast corner. Floors 15-19

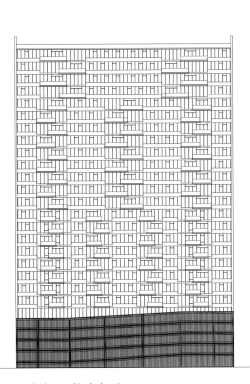

Alzado norte **North elevation**

Alzado este **East elevation** 1:1.000

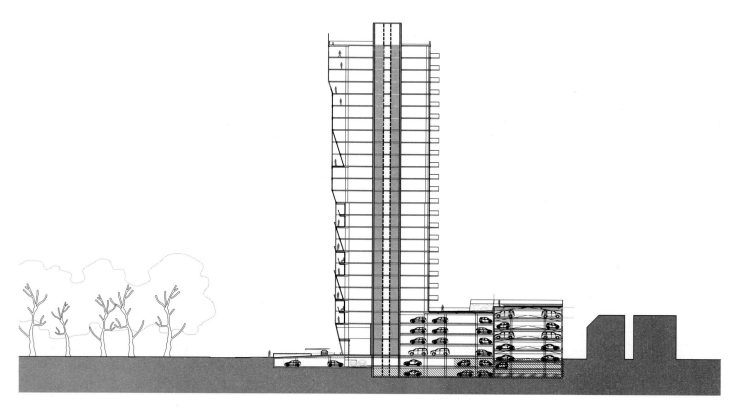

Planta 23ª **23rd floor plan**

Sector 3: plantas 22-25
4 VIVIENDAS POR PLANTA
MURO CORTINA INCLINADO DE 4 ALTURAS
FRENTE VIDRIADO DE 5 MÓDULOS

Tier 3: Floors 22-25
4 UNITS PER FLOOR
4 STORY INCLINED GLASS CURTAINWALL
5 MODULE BAY WINDOW

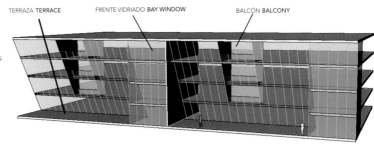

TERRAZA **TERRACE**   FRENTE VIDRIADO **BAY WINDOW**   BALCÓN **BALCONY**

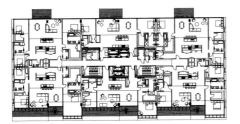

Planta 14ª **14th floor plan**

Sector 2: plantas 13-21
6 VIVIENDAS POR PLANTA
MURO CORTINA INCLINADO DE TRES ALTURAS
FRENTE VIDRIADO DE 4 MÓDULOS

Tier 2: Floors 13-21
6 UNITS PER FLOOR
3 STORY INCLINED GLASS CURTAINWALL
4 MODULE BAY WINDOW

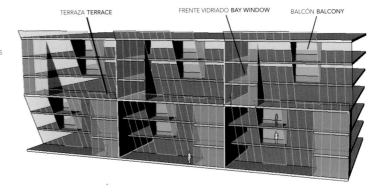

TERRAZA **TERRACE**   FRENTE VIDRIADO **BAY WINDOW**   BALCÓN **BALCONY**

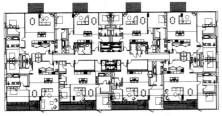

Planta sexta **Sixth floor plan** 1:1.000

Sector 1: plantas 5-12
8 VIVIENDAS POR PLANTA
MURO CORTINA INCLINADO DE DOS ALTURAS
3 FRENTE VIDRIADO DE 3 MÓDULOS

Tier 1: Floors 5-12
8 UNITS PER FLOOR
2- STORY INCLINED GLASS CURTAINWALL
3 MODULE BAY WINDOW

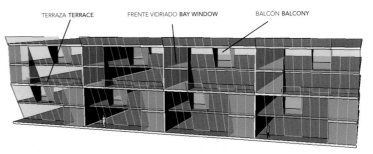

TERRAZA **TERRACE**   FRENTE VIDRIADO **BAY WINDOW**   BALCÓN **BALCONY**

66,7 %
VIVIENDA 400
LIVING

TRABAJO
WORKING

33,3 %
COMERCIOS
SHOPPING

EQUIPAMIENTOS
CIVIC FACILITIES

OTROS USOS
OTHER USES

20.000 m²
SUPERFICIE DE PARCELA
PLOT AREA

60.000 m²
SUPERFICIE CONSTRUIDA
BUILT UP AREA

31 %
OCUPACIÓN
COVERED AREA

3
EDIFICABILIDAD
FLOOR AREA RATIO

203 Ⓓ/ha   **936** Ⓔ/ha

scankort, 2007

① 1:10.000

1:2.500

3XN Architects 3xn.dk **/UNStudio** unstudio.com
in cooperation with Gehl Architects gehlarchitects.dk

Pier 4, Aarhus Harbour, Aarhus. Denmark, 2007-2010

EL proyecto *Lighthouse* es el primero enmarcado dentro de la gran transformación del sector norte del puerto de Aarhus. Sobre una península rodeada de agua se reúnen un hotel/balneario, edificios de apartamentos, una torre de viviendas y un paseo marítimo orientado a Poniente. El acceso al último piso de la torre es público, permitiendo a todos disfrutar de vistas únicas sobre la Bahía de Aarhus.

Los edificios cuentan con cafés y restaurantes, además de plazas abiertas de uso público. La mayor parte de los automóviles estarán aparcados bajo rasante, liberando pues el paso a peatones y ciclistas.

Un aspecto muy especial de la actuación es la mezcla de vivienda en régimen de venta y alquiler. En efecto, es la primera vez que un ayuntamiento danés exige una proporción tan grande de vivienda protegida en alquiler en una promoción de este tipo.

The Lighthouse project is the first project in the large transformation of the Aarhus north harbour. It offers a hotel/wellness centre, apartment buildings and an apartment tower, all on a peninsula surrounded by water, plus a new harbour promenade with evening sun and public access to the tower's top-floor skybar with unique views of the Aarhus Bay.

The residences vary with cafes, restaurants and open squares which enable common free-time activities. Most cars will be parked underground, giving optimum conditions for pedestrians and cyclists.

A very special feature will be the mix of owner-occupied and rental houses. This is the first time a Danish municipality requires such a high portion of non-profit rental houses in this kind of urban seaside projects.

NORD

VEST

ØST

SYD

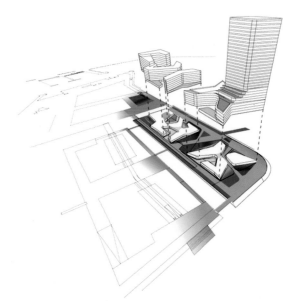

ZONAS DE
DEPORTES Y
JUEGOS
**SPORTS
GAMES AREAS**

PASEOS
PÚBLICOS
**PUBLIC
PROMENADES**

VIVIENDAS
HOUSING

OFICINAS
OFFICES

CAFETERÍA-
RESTAURANTE
**RESTAURANT-
CAFÉ**

HOTEL
HOTEL

DEPORTE
SPORT

CULTURA
CULTURE

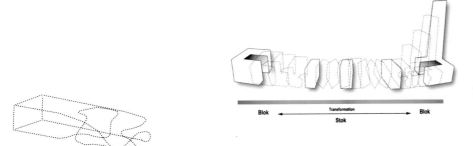

Blok ← Transformation → Blok
Stok

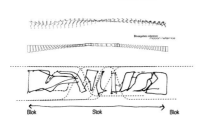

Transformations reference

Bruagsytes referior
mororion reference

Blok ← Stok → Blok

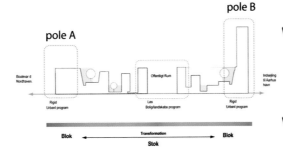

pole A pole B

Boulevard
Nordhaven

Offentligt Rum

Indsejling
til Aarhus
havn

Rigid
Urbant program

Los
Boligiandskabs program

Rigid
Urbant program

Blok ← Transformation → Blok
Stok

MANZANA CERRADA:
+ patios interiores
- delante y detrás; sin vistas al mar para todos
BLOCK:
+ inner courtyards
- front and back, not views for all

BLOQUE LINEAL:
+ luz y aire entre los bloques
- sin vistas al mar para todos
- los bloques están demasiado cercanos
BAR:
+ light and air between volumes
- no views to sea for all
- volumes too close

COMBINACIÓN:
+ optimización de las vistas
+ los patios dan al mar y al canal
- un único volumen se adentra en el mar
- no hay diferenciación de escalas
ALTERNATING:
+ optimized views
+ courtyards to sea and canal
- one long volume towards the sea
- no scale differentiating

X:
+ estructura abierta con vistas para todos
+ adaptación a la normativa de planeamiento
- carece de vistas transversales
X:
+ open structure, views for all
+ relating to masterplan rules
- no visual cross connections

DINÁMICO:
+ abierto a la ciudad y al mar
+ se ajusta a la normativa del plan
+ las aberturas permiten vistas la mar
+ establece una jerarquía de espacios públicos y privados
DYNAMIC:
+ opens to sea and city
+ maintain masterplan corners
+ openings ensure views to sea
+ establish hierarchy of private & public spaces

LIGHTHOUSE:
+ patios de distinto carácter
+ plazas urbanas junto al mar
+ jardines junto al canal
+ vistas desde todos lo edificios
+ volúmenes bajos sobre las plazas: diferentes escalas
+ cubiertas practicables y miradores hacia el mar
LIGHTHOUSE:
+ courtyards with variating characters
+ urbane plazas by sea
+ green spaces by canal
+ low volumes to plazas, scale differentiation
+ optimum views from all buildings
+ roof terraces and platforms with views to sea

Light House/áreas flexibles entre el espacio público y el privado
Light House/soft zones between private and public space

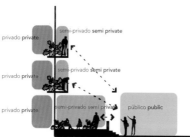

privado **private**   semi-privado **semi private**

privado **private**   semi-privado **semi private**

semi-privado semi **private**   público **public**

Los jardines delanteros se utilizan 2 o 3 veces más que los balcones y terrazas
Front gardens are used 2-3 times more than balconies and terraces

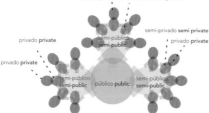

privado **private**   semi-privado **semi private**

privado **private**   semi-privado semi-**public**   semi-privado **semi private**

privado **private**   semi-público semi-**public**   público **public**   semi-público semi-**public**   privado **private**

privado **private**

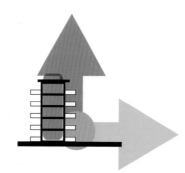

Espacio privado:
Espacio exterior privado que no está en contacto con el espacio público o semipúblico.
Terrazas:
Balcones en los pisos superiores
El ámbito doméstico
Jardines en planta baja sin contacto visual con el espacio público

Private space:
Private outdoor areas that are not directly in contact with the public or semi public space
Terraces:
Balconies on the upper floors
The private home
Front gardens without visual contact with the public space

Espacio semi-privado:
Zonas de espacio exterior que están directamente en contacto con el espacio público o semipúblico
Balcones (en los pisos más bajos)
Jardines delanteros y traseros en planta baja
Terrazas
Espacios alrededor de los accesos

Semi private space
Private outdoor areas that are directly in contact with the public or semi public space
Balconies (Lower floors)
Front and back gardens
Terraces
Spaces around private entrances

Espacio semi-público
Áreas y funciones accesibles al mismo grupo de usuarios, por ejemplo, a los residentes
Patios de los edificios de vivienda
Zonas de juegos y otras actividades en el espacio semipúblico

Semi public space
Areas and functions accessible to the same group of users, e.g. the residents
Residential court yards
Areas for playing and other activities in the semi public space

Espacio público:
Áreas y funciones accesibles a todos
Calles
Accesos
Plazas
Paseo marítimo y canal
Zonas de juegos y deportes en el espacio público

Public space:
Areas and functions accessible to everyone
Streets
Access streets
Squares
Esplanade and canals
Areas for playing and sport activities in the public space

Área de vivienda **Residential zone**
Área residencial semi-privada **Semi private residential zone**

 Del lado de la plaza pública
Área residencial soleada (sol desde la mañana al mediodía o del mediodía a la noche) frente a la plaza pública
Jardines semi-privados en planta baja y accesos comunes, clara separación entre público y privado, zona con protección frente al clima

Facing public square
Sunny residential zone (noon and evening sun or noon and morning sun) facing the public space
Semi private, urban front gardens and common entrances, clear cut between private and public, zone with local protection against the climate

 Frente al paseo marítimo
Área residencial soleada (sol de tarde) frente al espacio público
Jardines semi-privados en planta baja y accesos comunes, zona con protección frente al clima

Facing public canal street
Sunny residential zone (noon and evening sun) facing public space
Semi private, urban front gardens and common entrances, zone with local protection against the climate

 Frente a la calle
Área residencial frente a la calle
Accesos semi-privados y zonas comunes

Facing public street
Residential zone facing the street
Semi-private entrance areas and common areas

1D Frente a los patios semi-públicos
Área residencial soleada (sol de mañana o de tarde) frente al patio semi-público

Facing semi public court yards
Residential zone with sun (morning, noon or evening sun) facing semi public court yard

Tipos de viviendas **Dwelling types**
ESTUDIOS: 0
1 DORMITORIO: 0
2 DORMITORIOS: 0
3 DORMITORIOS: 122
4+ DORMITORIOS: 283
STUDIOS: 0
1 BEDROOM: 0
2 BEDROOMS: 0
3 BEDROOMS: 112
4+ BEDROOMS: 283

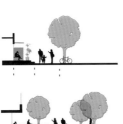

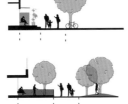

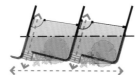

√ Protección frente al clima: cubierta sobre el acceso, pantallas contra el viento y ajardinamiento
Protection against climate, roof over entrance, wind shields, planting

√ Separación rotunda entre público y privado mediante la diferencia de nivel, la barandilla y los escalones
Clear definition of difference between public area throughout level difference, balustrade and stairs

√ Definición de las zonas públicas que deberán ser mantenidas por el municipio: zonas ajardinadas, barandillas
Definition of public area that is maintained by the municipalities: planting zone, balustrade

√ Posibilidad de construir trasteros
Posibility of storage

√ Conexión visual y física con el espacio público: accesos, ejes visuales, escalones
Visual and physical link to the public space: entrances, visual link, stairs

√ Buen contacto entre el espacio privado y el semi-privado
Good contact between the private and the semi private

√ Áreas con multitud de posibilidades
Zones with many possibilities

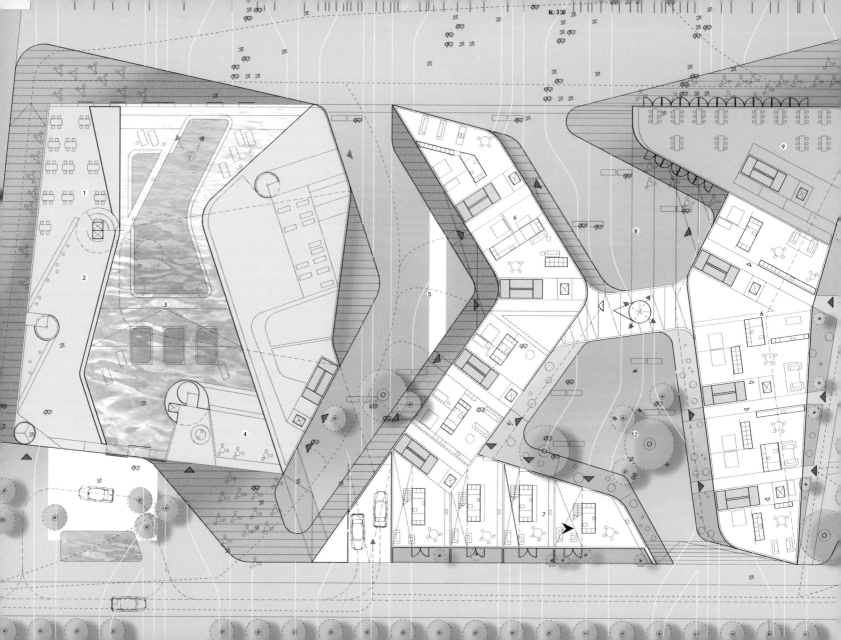

kt.: 3:00

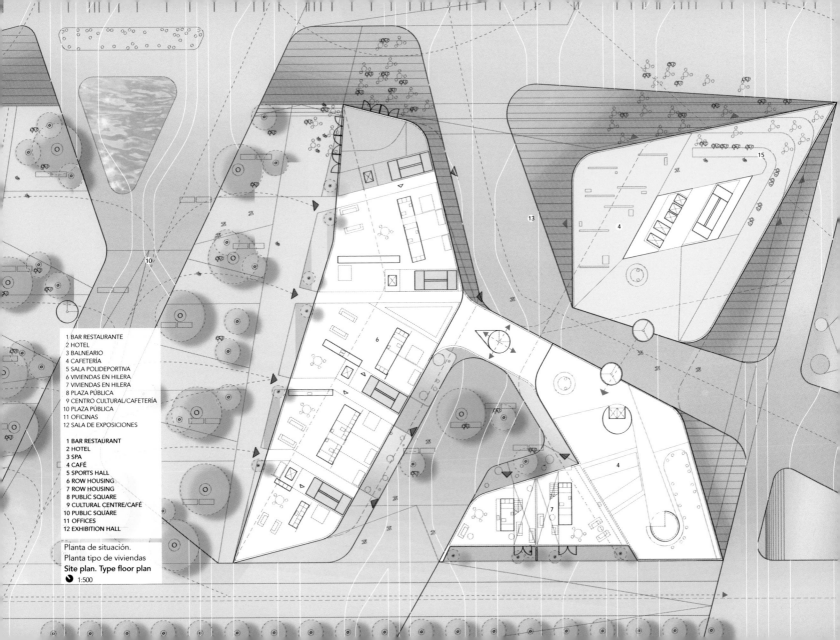

1 BAR RESTAURANTE
2 HOTEL
3 BALNEARIO
4 CAFETERÍA
5 SALA POLIDEPORTIVA
6 VIVIENDAS EN HILERA
7 VIVIENDAS EN HILERA
8 PLAZA PÚBLICA
9 CENTRO CULTURAL/CAFETERÍA
10 PLAZA PÚBLICA
11 OFICINAS
12 SALA DE EXPOSICIONES

1 BAR RESTAURANT
2 HOTEL
3 SPA
4 CAFÉ
5 SPORTS HALL
6 ROW HOUSING
7 ROW HOUSING
8 PUBLIC SQUARE
9 CULTURAL CENTRE/CAFÉ
10 PUBLIC SQUARE
11 OFFICES
12 EXHIBITION HALL

Planta de situación.
Planta tipo de viviendas
Site plan. Type floor plan
1:500

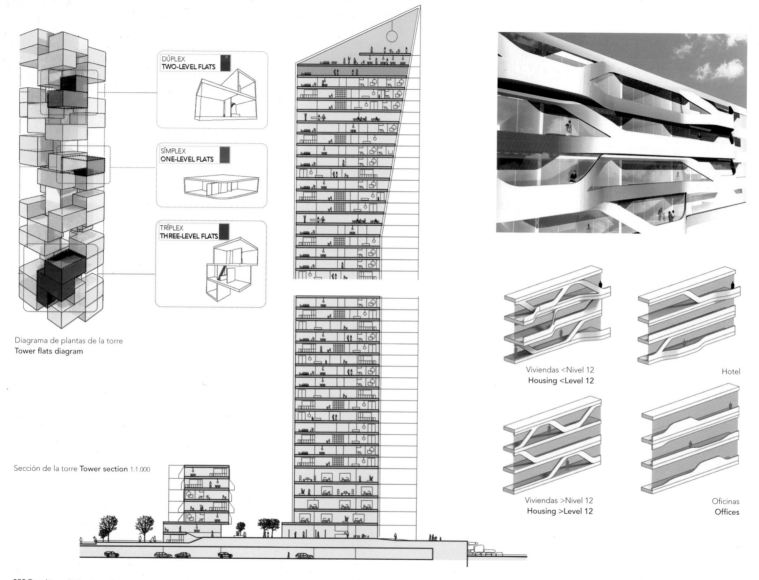

DÚPLEX
TWO-LEVEL FLATS

SÍMPLEX
ONE-LEVEL FLATS

TRÍPLEX
THREE-LEVEL FLATS

Diagrama de plantas de la torre
Tower flats diagram

Sección de la torre **Tower section** 1:1.000

Viviendas <Nivel 12
Housing <Level 12

Hotel

Viviendas >Nivel 12
Housing >Level 12

Oficinas
Offices